P9-CAT-303

PEYOTE HUNT

The Sacred Journey of the Huichol Indians

SYMBOL, MYTH, AND RITUAL SERIES

General Editor: Victor Turner

Shlomo Deshen and Moshe Shokeid, *The Predicament of Homecoming: Cultural and Social Life of North African Immigrants in Israel*

Mircea Eliade, *Australian Religions: An Introduction*

Frederick Karl Errington, *Karavar: Masks and Power in a Melanesian Ritual*

Raymond Firth, *Symbols: Public and Private**

Alf Hiltebeitel, *The Ritual of Battle: Krishna in the* Mahābhārata

Bennetta Jules-Rosette, *African Apostles: Ritual and Conversion in the Church of John Maranke*

Frank E. Manning, *Black Clubs in Bermuda: Ethnography of a Play World*

Sally Falk Moore and Barbara G. Myerhoff, eds., *Symbol and Politics in Communal Ideology: Cases and Questions**

Nancy D. Munn, *Walbiri Iconography: Graphic Representation and Cultural Symbolism in a Central Australian Society*

Barbara G. Myerhoff, *Peyote Hunt: The Sacred Journey of the Huichol Indians**

Victor Turner, *Dramas, Fields, and Metaphors: Symbolic Action in Human Society**

Victor Turner, *Revelation and Divination in Ndembu Ritual**

* Also available as a Cornell Paperback.

PEYOTE HUNT

The Sacred Journey of the Huichol Indians

BARBARA G. MYERHOFF

Cornell University Press

ITHACA AND LONDON

Copyright © 1974 by Cornell University

All rights reserved. Except for brief quotations in a review, this book, or parts thereof, must not be reproduced in any form without permission in writing from the publisher. For information address Cornell University Press, 124 Roberts Place, Ithaca, New York 14850.

First published 1974 by Cornell University Press.
Published in the United Kingdom by Cornell University Press Ltd.,
2–4 Brook Street, London W1Y 1AA.

First printing, Cornell Paperbacks, 1976

International Standard Book Number (cloth) 0-8014-0817-2
International Standard Book Number (paper) 0-8014-9137-1
Library of Congress Catalog Card Number 73-16923
Printed in the United States of America by Vail-Ballou Press, Inc.

This work is dedicated to the memory of my parents: Florence Siegel, who taught me that dreams are real, and Norman Siegel, who taught me that greatness can occur in unexpected forms and places.

Foreword

Recently both the research and theoretical concerns of many anthropologists have once again been directed toward the role of symbols—religious, mythic, aesthetic, political, and even economic—in social and cultural processes. Whether this revival is a belated response to developments in other disciplines (psychology, ethology, philosophy, linguistics, to name only a few), or whether it reflects a return to a central concern after a period of neglect, is difficult to say. In recent field studies, anthropologists have been collecting myths and rituals in the context of social action, and improvements in anthropological field technique have produced data that are richer and more refined than heretofore; these new data have probably challenged theoreticians to provide more adequate explanatory frames. Whatever may have been the causes, there is no denying a renewed curiosity about the nature of the connections between culture, cognition, and perception, as these connections are revealed in symbolic forms.

Although excellent individual monographs and articles in symbolic anthropology or comparative symbology have recently appeared, a common focus or forum that can be provided by a topically organized series of books has not been available. The present series is intended to fill this lacuna. It is designed to include not only field monographs and theoretical and comparative studies by anthropologists, but also work by scholars in other disciplines, both scientific and humanistic. The appearance of studies in such a forum encourages emulation, and emulation can produce fruitful new theories. It is therefore our hope that the series will serve as a house of many mansions, providing hospitality for the practitioners of any discipline that has a serious and creative concern with comparative symbology. Too often, disciplines are sealed off, in sterile pedantry, from significant intellectual influences. Nevertheless, our primary aim is to bring to public attention works on ritual and myth written by anthropologists, and our readers will find a variety of strictly anthropological approaches ranging from formal analyses of systems of symbols to empathetic accounts of divinatory and initiatory rituals.

Peyote Hunt contributes to our proliferating knowledge of Man the Pilgrim. The hunt, the voyage, the search, the quest are genres of cultural action as well as literary themes. They must be distinguished from nomadism under economic pressure, travel for the sake of curiosity, and migration for the sake of employment. The quest, particularly the pilgrim quest, always implies a return from a far to a familiar place; it also implies a dichotomy between sacred and profane symbolized by that between Far and Near, and the paradox that the spatially distant (the Far) is veritably the spiritually Near. In going away one seeks to return from exile, in returning "home" one is leaving Home.

What is often implicit in the pilgrimage beliefs of major historical religions is explicit among the Huichol Indians. Barbara Myerhoff made the "peyote pilgrimage" with them. In her book she shows how they travel in small, irregularly collected parties to Wirikuta, a high desert several hundred miles from their habitat in the Sierra Madre Occidental. The Huichols believe that Wirikuta is their original homeland, the place once inhabited by the First People, both deities and ancestors, with animal and cosmic traits. In Wirikuta, according to Huichol mythology, divisions dissolve between sexes and ages, leaders and led, men and animals, plants and animals, men and demigods. Myerhoff shows in detail how three complexes of symbols, focused respectively on the dominant symbols, deer, maize, and peyote, become functionally interdependent, and, for the Huichols, even seem to fuse, at Wirikuta. The deer designates the Huichols' past as nomadic hunters, the maize their present as sedentary cultivators, and the peyote the incommunicable "idioverse" of each individual. Identified by name as the First People, the pilgrims "hunt" the peyote in Wirikuta in the form of "deer prints," shoot the plant's "button" (identified with the budding antlers of the deer demigod who gave them the sacred hallucinogen "in the beginning"), consume peyote together, and quickly return home with sufficient supplies for use in the coming year's ceremonies.

Many books have recently been published on the effects of hallucinogenic agents on personality and culture. Myerhoff's book differs significantly from most in that it treats peyote among the Huichols as only one constituent, though a most vital one, in their ritual complex. Its power is regarded as a divine gift, a sacred trust; the visions it gives are not to be spoken of. They are of and for the inmost self. Though the plant may be consumed in common, there is no communion; each has his own vision. In this way, home is symbolically sealed off from Wirikuta, the familiar real from the far Real, even when peyote is eaten "for kicks" in secular settings. It is not made to invade the pragmatic world of work—it is part of the "work of the gods," as Christian Communion wine is part of the "divine work" of the liturgy.

Dr. Myerhoff demonstrates that systems of ritual symbols have more than one level. Some are concerned with the maintenance of the natural and cultural orders. But others—notably those associated with Wirikuta—represent inversions of those orders. This process of inversion (or "reversal," as Norbeck has called it) itself stands for a process of creative de-differentiation, a seminal undoing, which in implicit Huichol thought endows the pilgrims with power to renew their social and personal lives. They become, transiently, gods, founders, initiators, unencumbered by the cultural baggage they normally rely upon and prize. This is the moment of peril which cannot last but without which their culture would have no dynamism.

Paradoxically, the Huichol pilgrims, transformed into gods, become essentially more human in their relationships with one another on the pilgrim way and during their brief stay in the inverse world of Wirikuta. This relationship is *communitas*, which I have called "a direct, immediate, and total confrontation of human identities" (Turner 1969b: 132). By inverting the verbal and nonverbal symbols which accomplish the segmentation of concrete, historical, idiosyncratic individuals into roles and statuses in the secular world, the pilgrims are liberated from the normative constraints of that world and attain not only intimacy but also a degree of personal vision into the "meaning of things" on the way and at the world's end. Social structure separates men from gods, heaven from earth; social anti-structure transiently but potently reunites them.

Victor Turner

University of Chicago

Contents

Illustrations

Preface

> This is the story of our roots, the roots that go down deep. It is a story that we venerate, that which we hold sacred. It is our life. The maize of five colors, the deer, the peyote. These are our symbols. One cannot be without the other, each is the heart of the other, the essence. They are a unity, they are one, they are ourselves. That is why we must know it well. So I tell it to you.
>
> Ramón Medina Silva
> San Sebastián, 1966

Ramón Medina Silva, a Huichol Indian shaman-priest or *mara'akame*, instructed me in many of his culture's myths, rituals, and symbols, particularly those pertaining to the sacred unity of deer, maize, and peyote.[1] The significance of this constellation of symbols was revealed to me most vividly when I accompanied Ramón on the Huichols' annual ritual return to hunt the peyote in the sacred land of Wirikuta, in myth and probably in history the place from which the Ancient Ones (ancestors and deities of the present-day Indians) came before settling in their present home in the mountains of the Sierra Madre Occidental in north-central Mexico. My work with Ramón preceded and followed our journey, but it was this peyote hunt that held the key to, and constituted the climax of, his teachings.

I have interpreted the journey to Wirikuta as a prototypical ritual—a return to Paradise, a journey back to human origins, a retrieval of man's beginnings, before Creation, when all was oneness. The desire to recover this original condition is found

[1] Peyote, *Lophorora williamsii*, is a small, gray-green hallucinogenic cactus which contains, among other alkaloids, mescalin.

in many cultures, sometimes stated in mythical, sometimes in religious, and sometimes in psychological terms. The peyote hunt provides one version of the fulfillment of a panhuman quest—the desire for total unity among all creatures and all people—and accordingly we find in it significance beyond the specificity of Huichol religion and world view.

Throughout, I have been most concerned with the questions: How do the deer-maize-peyote symbols and the peyote hunt rituals give meaning to Huichol life? I have not attempted to describe all of the Huichols' religion or cosmology. The deer-maize-peyote symbol complex at the heart of this interpretation by no means exhausts Huichol religious symbolism, and even this symbol set is not considered in its entirety. No doubt, many of its meanings are untouched here. And Huichol ritual life extends much beyond the peyote hunt. Also I have not attempted to write a comprehensive ethnographic portrait of Huichol culture. In many ways this book is personal and subjective; it is my interpretation of Ramón's interpretation of the symbols, myths, and rituals that make Huichol life unique and beautiful—the unification of the deer, the maize, and the peyote found in Wirikuta when the *mara'-akame* leads his people to hunt the peyote.

The circumstances leading to my meeting with Ramón and his wife and the manner in which we conducted our work together are given in detail later. Here I would like to indicate some of the limits resulting from my choosing to work so closely and nearly exclusively with him. I soon realized that I could not maintain significant and lasting relationships with other Huichols without jeopardizing my ties to Ramón. I worked with other Huichols, but these bonds were always mediated through Ramón, with whom I was considered to have established a primary relationship. Although these other Huichols offered information, most of my investigation was limited to a single informant, and this informant was a specialist and a religious leader, by no means to be regarded as a typical Huichol citizen. Since most of our communications concerned specialized materials about religion and symbolism, my access to information concerning affairs of social life was sharply curtailed. I did not obtain detailed knowledge concerning the important matters of kinship, economics, politics, and technology, although such knowledge would have enhanced my understanding of religion and symbolism. Ramón's dedication, intelligence, and erudition, and the sharing of our parallel interests contributed to greater depth and specialization in my own study, although breadth and scope were sacrificed by my decision to work with him. The ethnographic background material given here is drawn from secondary sources and intended only to provide a context for interpreting the questions that are the heart of the work. For personal and professional reasons I was not able to live among the Huichols in the Sierra; this fact is responsible for the most conspicuous lacunae in this study.

Ramón's specialized status as *mara'akame* created advantages and disadvantages in my work with him. His understanding of his religion was not typical of the Huichols' any more than an ordained priest's views typify those of his congregation. Under some circumstances the layman's point of view is most significant, but sometimes the opinion of the specialist is more valuable. In this case, working with a typical Huichol would have resulted in a very different interpretation from that given here, and working with another *mara'akame* would also have made a difference. The verbatim texts reproduced in this work were dictated by Ramón, and systematic cross-validation with other informants was not possible for the reasons mentioned; I have tried, however, to indicate where material given to me coincides with or departs from other ethnographic sources or where I have reason to suspect biases and distortions on Ramón's part. Most of his biases are attributable to his role as *mara'akame*. The shaman-priest has a skewed view of the Huichol pantheon, favoring certain deities over others. He prefers certain hallucinogenic plants to others and he is more deeply involved than most with the deer-maize-peyote complex. There is reason to suppose that different religious views would be generated by those Huichols considered sorcerers, by those who set out to achieve the status of *mara'akame* but fail, and by those who are out of favor with their community.

Texts and Translations

The texts dictated by Ramón were an essential source of information for this study. The process of recording and translating them was exceedingly difficult and was carried on in collaboration with two fellow anthropologists, Peter T. Furst and Joseph E. Grimes. Furst and I gathered the tapes and then worked with Grimes and his wife Barbara on the translations from Huichol into English. The Grimeses, in conjunction with their work for the Summer Institute of Linguistics, had spent nearly fifteen years with the Huichols conducting linguistic and ethnographic studies; they are among the handful of non-Huichols fluent in that language, which belongs to the Uto-Aztecan family. In working on the texts, we were all concerned with retaining characteristic Huichol prose style as much as possible, but many concessions to clarity were inevitable. If translated literally, much of the material would have been incomprehensible to an outsider.

Grimes provides a concrete illustration of a literal translation of a sequence in a typical Huichol myth:

Méríkütsü níu xéwítű müpáü tiyűkűhüawétü 'aniuyéikakái tűní,
(Well, it is said, one thus saying to himself was,)
Káműtsű . . .
(Say there . . .)

A satisfactory idiomatic translation of the statement is: "Well, it is said, once there lived someone who thought to himself, 'Say there.' "

Grimes is certainly the most reliable authority on Huichol oral tradition. He has offered the following statement concerning Huichol myth and narrative styles:

> The ordinary style for telling Huichol myths presupposes a good deal of background information on the part of the audience. For example, in one story the characters are not named until about halfway through. Furthermore it is not considered necessary to go into detail about all of the actions involved in the story. Many of the myths, when translated into English, sound as if they consist of nothing but, "They went there. Having gone there they said that. Having said it, they lifted it up. They went to where he comes up, one comes up. When they arrived there he said to himself, 'I wonder if this is the way it is. If that is how he is, my heart is not that way. My arrows do not tell me this.' " In other words, unless one knows the basic theme of the story well one is absolutely lost in what seems like a maze of gibberish.[2]

The sensitivity of the Huichol narrator to the understanding of his audience is clearly one criterion of his artistry and success. This sensitivity is exemplified by the marked difference in styles of myths designed to be told to children, who do

[2] Personal communication, Mexico City, 1967.

not command the lore and symbolism familiar to their parents. The straightforward style and linear chronology of the story in Chapter 4, "When the Mara'akame Plays the Drum and Flies the Children to the Land of the Peyote," illustrates a narrative designed to reach an untutored audience.

In the taping sessions, Ramón presented much information in many different forms, and our texts consisted of formal myths, chants, exegetical comments, and interviews, as well as informal conversations, reflections, and philosophical speculations. At first Ramón dictated texts only in Spanish, but after a time, he gave them first in Huichol, followed by a Spanish version. The former were always longer, more intense, involving gestures, weeping, rejoicing, jumping about, whipping out objects for illustration, often using violin or song. When recording the Huichol texts he would don full ceremonial attire and dictate only in the semidarkness of the windowless hut or in the empty countryside. After giving the Huichol texts, he would pause and then offer the simpler, flatter, shorter, less urgent, and obviously less sacred Spanish rendition.

Ramón wanted his texts to be completely clear, but would not let us err in the direction of assuming incorrect or facile equivalences of his cultural and linguistic categories with ours; he was always diligent in correcting us and insisted repeatedly on his points when he felt we had lost an important nuance of phrase or form. His aesthetic concern with his productions was no less profound than his interest in accuracy in matters of content, as is apparent in reading the transcriptions. As Furst and I became familiar with Huichol literary style, we were able to rely more and more on Ramón rather than the Grimeses to translate texts from Huichol to Spanish. Ramón was remarkably fluent and articulate in both languages, and this method reduced textual ambiguities considerably.

Orientation and Organization

Throughout this work I have attempted to consider Huichol religion and symbolism primarily in their own terms, on the assumption that one of the most important responsibilities of an anthropologist is to devote great care to the "native model," giving it as much attention and credence as the "analyst's model." In this case, the meaning of Huichol religion had to be sought in the continually reiterated statements to the effect that the purpose of the peyote hunt was "to give unity, . . . [because] we are doing this [ritual] so that we might have a bond between us, so that everything may become one." Similarly, when Ramón explained that the peyote pilgrims, the *peyoteros*, were the Ancient Ones going back to their home during the peyote hunt, it became clear to me that his statement had to be taken as literal, not symbolic. The *peyoteros* were not "acting like" the deities or impersonating them. There was no place for "as if's" in the ritual; the participants had been transformed, and for them the experience was immediate and direct, not symbolic. My interpretation of this ritual return and the role of the three major symbols of the peyote hunt—the deer, the maize, and the peyote—draws heavily on some of the theories of three anthropologists, Victor Turner, Claude Lévi-Strauss, and Clifford Geertz. The writings of Mircea Eliade, Max Gluckman, Arnold van Gennep, Mary Douglas, Alan Watts, and C. G. Jung have also proved to be very helpful.

My main goal is to help fulfill Ramón's most cherished wish—that of presenting and preserving something of the power and beauty of his customs, his symbols, his stories, so that one can see why, despite all the physical hardships and privations of his people, he maintained the conviction that "it is not a bad thing being a Huichol."

This work combines many kinds of information, verbatim texts dictated by Ramón, ethnographic data and analysis, and speculative and personal material. Chapter 1 concerns Ramón and Lupe, their backgrounds, personal characteristics, roles, self-perceptions, and aspirations, and describes some of my experiences with them and the methods we employed in working together. The second chapter is devoted to a general ethnographic and historical description. Chapter 3 concerns Huichol religious institutions and beliefs. The fourth chapter provides a description of a single complex ritual within the religion, the peyote hunt, and presents two versions of the event—my own account as participant-observer and a mythical idealized version of the event as given by Ramón. Chapter 5 reviews the primary theoretical sources used in this interpretation and analyzes the significance of the deer, the maize, and the peyote as a set of key religious symbols. The function of these symbols in the peyote hunt ritual in particular and Huichol religion in general is examined in the final chapter.

Guide to Pronunciation

The phonetic system used in this book is basically Spanish. In both Spanish and Huichol pronunciation, the accent falls on the penultimate syllable unless otherwise indicated. Regional differences in the pronunciation of Huichol words are common and often extreme. Differences between pronunciation of Huichol terms used here and those given by other writers are indicated in the text. I have used Grimes's pronunciation as authoritative. Apostrophe indicates glottal stop. *W* is pronounced as *v* in English, and, following Nahuatl usage, *x* is pronounced as *sh* in English.[3]

Acknowledgments

I am indebted to many people. Peter T. Furst and I collaborated long and well on much of this material, and his expertise on many matters in which I had little training was invaluable. I have already mentioned the Grimeses and their generous assistance in the translation of texts. Johannes Wilbert, director of the University of California at Los Angeles Latin American Center, was both mentor and stalwart friend. With his help I obtained a Ford Foundation International Comparative Studies Grant which financed part of this research. Hilda Kuper, with her love of anthropology, her imagination and profundity, was a splendid teacher and model. My friend and colleague Sally Falk Moore consistently offered encouragement and criticism in a finely balanced mixture. Victor Turner is responsible not only for much of the theoretical substance of this work but for its existence in the present form as well. Though I have never studied with him formally, I consider myself his student.

My students and friends Craig J. Calhoun and Riv-Ellen Prell-Foldes shared the joys and pains of producing this volume, the tedious mechanics as well as the delights of discovery. They, along with Nicola Moore, Gregory Dimmitt, and Terry Tombs who typed and helped to edit the manuscript, were underpaid, overworked, and always good-humored.

[3] Spelling and translations used here were suggested by Joseph E. Grimes, and conform most closely to the usages of the Huichols in San Sebastián, Guadalupe Ocotán, and San Andrés Cohamiata.

Gavin Courtney, Robert J. Wunsch, and Ruth Adams gave the work thorough and critical readings. Carlos Castaneda and I often talked about shamans and sorcerers, and his deep understanding of these matters contributed greatly to my own thinking. Deena Metzger helped to make this work a part of my everyday life because it became a part of hers. As a poet, she was alive to the beauty of the texts and symbols and always kept me aware of the aesthetic dimensions of Huichol thought and culture. Lee, Nicolas, and Matthew Myerhoff were usually patient and always devoted. They cared about this work because I did and let me go even when they wanted to be with me. To all these people I am grateful.

In June 1971, five days after I had visited Ramón and Lupe in Tepíc, Lupe telephoned to tell me that Ramón was dead. On June 23 there had been a celebration at his *rancho* in the Sierra—drinking, a quarrel, a shooting. Lupe had tried to get Ramón out of the mountains for medical help, but he had died on the way down, and she had brought his body to Tepíc. After that I lost touch with Lupe for several months. When I heard from her again, she had returned to the mountains, where she was working intensively on yarn paintings and studying Huichol religion. Perhaps she would become a *mara'akame*. This seemed, she said, something Ramón would have approved of. In this way, she could preserve a part of him and her life with him. But Ramón, ultimately, would be irreplaceable. The man was an artist, an ambassador for his people, a metaphysician, and a splendid human being. His world and ours are diminished by his absence.

It is difficult to speak of my debt to Ramón and to Lupe. This is their work as much as mine. My part of it is conveying something of a way of life that is beautiful, as they say, because it is right. I have tried to tell it as they told it to me, so that it shall not be forgotten.

B. G. M.

Los Angeles, California

PEYOTE HUNT

The Sacred Journey
of the Huichol Indians

CHAPTER 1

Ramón and Lupe

This comes to us from Ancient Times, so that we could unite all there is in our lives, so that we could sustain ourselves. I do not know how many years it has been like that or how many years it will remain so. But I do not think that there can be life for us without these things.

Ramón Medina Silva

The Huichols are among the lesser-known Indians in Mexico. There are perhaps nine thousand of them in the more inaccessible reaches of the Sierra Madre Occidental and spread about in the states of Durango, Jalisco, Nayarít, and Zacatecas. Their way of life is old and distinctive, and outside influences—from Aztec, through Spanish-Catholic, to modern western industrial—have changed them remarkably little. Recently the Huichols have received attention from North American "hippies" intent upon discovering the "mysteries" of their religious use of peyote and from tourists fascinated with their superb paintings made of colored wool yarn.

More and more often in recent years, Huichol Indians can be seen in the cities—Tepíc, Guadalajara, Mexico City—in twos and threes, quietly padding through bus depots, public markets, and on the road in single file. Their splayed, brown feet in one-strap thong sandals tell of long walking out of the mountains. They are clearly set apart from the urban world around them. They never speak to outsiders unnecessarily. They are grandly aloof except with one another, when upon occasion their gravity gives way to short outbursts of cavorting and laughter. These people, unlike most other Mexican Indians, reveal no evidence of feeling oppressed or conquered, however poor and dirty they may be. Occasionally one is startled to see them in full ceremonial attire, standing on an ordinary street corner. In loose, white *manta* calf-length pants and skirts, blouses and capes bordered with vibrant stars, butterflies, flowers, squirrels, mice, deer, and many nameless whimsical birds and animals, they are alive with color. Beads in thick twined ropes of gold and white and blue adorn the women's necks and ears, and are woven into bands on fingers, ankles, and wrists. The men's waists are wrapped in flat, tiny bands of woven bags, and larger embroidered bags are slung over their shoulders.

These are topped by sombrero-like hats, decorated with red felt crosses, the brims hung with deer hooves, chrysalis, and bead or felt "danglers" that jump with every movement. Plumed arrows, feathers, or squirrel tails are stuck into the hat band. On their backs the Indians carry more bags and baskets and often water gourds hang off them. Occasionally a tiny, homemade violin or ukelele juts out of a bag or protrudes from beneath a cape. Yet from all this color and diversity a harmony and grace emerges.

Ramón and Lupe were in this resplendent attire when I first beheld them glowing in the semidarkness of the Basilica of Zapopan of Guadalajara in the summer of 1965. They had brought some yarn paintings to show a sympathetic Franciscan Father, Ernesto Loera Ochoa, who had helped the Huichols for many years and who had become an admirer and ardent promoter of their arts. Ramón was then about thirty-eight years old, three or four years older than Lupe. He was slightly built, clean-shaven, lively and lithe, responsive but self-contained, and interested in the world around him. He had a quick intelligence and spoke fluent, even eloquent Spanish. Lupe was more stalwart, a solid, statuesque woman with a comforting air of certainty and strength. Ramón Medina Silva and Guadalupe Rios de la Cruz were their official, "public" Catholic-Spanish names; in addition they had several Huichol names which bespoke other, deeper aspects of their identity. In the public world where I met them, they were known as Ramón and Lupe.

Ramón was from San Sebastián, a community in the Sierra, where his family remained. He had a deeply religious heritage; his paternal grandfather in his day had been one of the most important shaman-priests or *mara'akate* (plural, *mara'akate;* singular, *mara'akame*). When we met, Ramón was an aspiring mara'akame himself, having made three out of the necessary five annual peyote pilgrimages to Wirikuta, the Huichol sacred land. He had preserved his grandfather's frayed headband and wore it on his hat or tied around his box of sacred implements. Ramón's mother was also a learned and religious woman and had made many trips to Wirikuta. And Ramón's younger sister, Concha, was the only practicing woman mara'akame in the Sierra at that time. One of Ramón's texts tells of his family and early life. It begins:

More or less my age is forty, as I am speaking to you here. Perhaps, I am close to forty. When my mother brought me into this world, I came, I don't know from where. But once I started growing up—I must have been five or six years old—my father left us alone. Alone he left us, to make do for ourselves. My mother brought us up according to how one must do such things, as Tayaupá, as Tatewarí gave her the ability, the will, the love.[1]

[1] Tayaupá, also known as Our Father Sun, and Tatewarí, known as Our Grandfather Fire, are two of the major deities in the Huichol pantheon. The latter is especially important in the shamanic complex.

Ramón Medina Silva, Huichol mara'akame, as Tatewarí, the Fire deity, in Wirikuta, 1967. He has led the pilgrims to Wirikuta, to hunt the peyote. He pauses, machete in hand, and rests from his task of cutting brush to feed the campfire.

Because of the father's departure, the family suffered great hardship, and even among other Huichols they were exceptionally poor. While still very young, Ramón became aware that his life would not be an ordinary one:

I began to have those dreams. Sometimes it would happen when I was asleep, sometimes awake, when it was day. It happened one night that Tayaupá spoke to me. He said, "Look, son, do not worry. You must grow a little more so you can go out and become wise, so that you can support yourself." He said, "Do not worry, son. It will be good with you one day." I heard everything. I saw my life. And then I was very happy. I was still a small boy, five, six, seven years old. I would wake up happy because Tayaupá would say to me, "You are going to do this and that and the other. You will make fine things, things of color. You will understand this and that. It is for this that you were born." At first, I was frightened. I did not know. I began to reflect. I began to listen to them, to those old men when they told our stories, that which is our history.

When Ramón was around eight years old, he was bitten on the foot by a poisonous snake and nearly died. His grandfather the mara'akame was summoned and revealed that the snakebite was sent as punishment because Ramón's father had failed to fulfill a promise he had made to the deities to journey to Wirikuta. The grandfather sucked out the poison, cleansed Ramón with his sacred feathers, and chanted all that night and the following day. Then he revealed to the boy that Tatewarí had chosen him to become a mara'akame. If he lived, his grandfather said, it would be a sign that this was Ramón's destiny.

The boy was in terrible pain and completely paralyzed for over six months. But he didn't die and little by little began to be able to drag himself about and finally to walk. During this period of his life he spent much time alone and began to reflect on what his grandfather had revealed. He grew more serious and began to accept the idea of becoming a mara'akame. His mother was very supportive, and when his courage failed she sustained and consoled him. This was clearly a turning point in his life.

From this time on, Ramón was set apart.

I started to think, to understand: "Oh, this is what they told me, that I was to become a mara'akame." And then some people said, "Ah, what is that boy going to be good for? He will never be able to help us in anything. Always he goes alone, always he is reflecting." I would be embarrassed, but what is one to do? And I would think to myself, "Whatever those great ones say, whatever Tatewarí and Tayaupá says, that is the correct thing. If one does it that way one will do it well." That is how I did it, learning this way and that, how one cures, how one goes to Wirikuta, how one learns all those stories of ours which are our history. How one makes the sacred things, the offerings. All that. It takes many years, much thought, to do such things. Much work, much sacrifice. Now I see that I grew up well.

And indeed, the work of a mara'akame is extraordinarily demanding, intellectually, physically, and spiritually. It requires great religious knowledge, social skill, dramatic and aesthetic gifts, for the mara'akame must undertake the sacred, ecstatic journey to other worlds, to command the spirits, communicate with the deities, defend his patients, and interpret the supernatural to his people. It is a role that very few can hope to fill, as will be seen.

Ramón continually struggled to earn a living in the Sierra but was forced to leave his family and work on mestizo haciendas far from his home to support them. While still in his teens, lonely and far from home, he met Lupe, who had con-

Lupe, Ramón's wife, in Wirikuta, 1967. Lupe, as the mara'akame's wife, has many duties and responsibilities during the pilgrimage, even though on this trip she is a *primero.* Here she holds the tortillas she has made for all the pilgrims.

tracted to work in the same plantation as Ramón in Nayarít, and after a time they married.

The young couple tried to support themselves by working the scant arable land near the homes of their families in the Sierra but again and again they found it necessary to leave and find work in distant places. Unencumbered by children, they finally decided to attempt earning a living by selling handiwork in Guadalajara, which they had done on previous occasions. Settling on a bit of vacant land on the outskirts of the city in 1966, they erected a tiny hut, a thatched ramada for shade, and cultivated a half acre of maize and beans. The little household was on the Zacatecas road, the road which many Huichols use when walking into the city from the mountains, and inevitably Ramón's home became a meeting and resting place for visitors from the Sierra. Here, Ramón began regular work as a folk artist for a government institute promoting indigenous arts and crafts.

Lupe's position as mara'akame's wife was a precise and demanding one which she took with the greatest seriousness; she "completed" the mara'akame, as she put it. She was required to be exemplary in Huichol morals and well trained in custom and lore, but in addition she assisted Ramón in his frequent supernatural activities. At times of vulnerability, when the mara'akame's special animal helpers were off guard, for example, she would "stand at his back and protect him from sorcerers." When I first met Lupe she had never been to Wirikuta and Ramón was actively preparing her for this experience. He considered her a student of Huichol religion and took special pains with her training in anticipation of the momentous and dangerous experience of her first peyote hunt.

Working with Ramón and Lupe

I had accompanied Peter T. Furst and his wife Dee to the Basilica, where Father Ernesto introduced us to Ramón and Lupe. The Fursts were living in Guadalajara, where Furst was director of the Regional Center of the Latin American Center at the University of California at Los Angeles. At this time I was a graduate student in anthropology at UCLA and while traveling in Mexico had stopped by to visit the Fursts in Guadalajara. They had not been in the city long but had already heard of Father Ernesto's work with the Huichols and had planned to make Ramón's acquaintance.

Ramón's willingness to discuss his yarn paintings that first day was encouraging and we made arrangements to talk with him again. Soon we were drawn deeply into the complex and difficult subjects concerning the mythology depicted in the art work, and it became apparent to him and to ourselves that a systematic and sustained effort was necessary for us to develop anything beyond a superficial understanding of the symbols used in the paintings. Daily sessions with a tape recorder began in Ramón's little hut. At first, Ramón was uncomfortable with the tape recorder but in a very short time treated it with as much concern as we did, pausing when a tape ran out, addressing it affectionately as "our assistant," listening to playbacks of his songs and chants with delight, of his stories with great attention, erasing a passage here, adding a comment there, until he was entirely satisfied with the finished product. He developed a formal introduction and closing statement for each sequence, a sign-off which identified himself in terms of his authentic, indigenous race and culture, his home, the time and place of the recording.

As Ramón's trust in us deepened, the recording sessions

grew longer and richer and he became committed to the idea of producing a book which would preserve his people's customs and beliefs. He felt that these were in jeopardy and might be lost eventually. So strong was Ramón's desire to preserve the knowledge of his culture that he set aside the Huichols' tradition which enjoins them against conveying religious matters to outsiders. Although, or perhaps because, he was illiterate, he appreciated the need to create an accurate written record for he was sensitive to the encroachments of outside cultures which increasingly threatened his indigenous way of life. Wanting this record to be correct and complete, he took great care with our work. Frequently he would ask to hear a song or story days after it had been recorded, or postpone answering a question until he could check it out with someone else, giving us the reply long after we had forgotten asking for it.

The transformative power of the tales was impressive. In the darkness in the tarpaper hut, the corrugated metal walls and hard earth floor faded away as creatures like those embroidered on Ramón's capes and shawls filled the stillness—the ancient "people," Deer Person and Ant Person, the little black She-Dog who helped recreate the world after the Great Flood, the Dove Mother who gave the First People maize, the evil sorcerers and the exploits of the "half-bad" culture hero-trickster, Kauyumari. Then it was mythical time, with Ramón as psychopomp, leading us carefully and faithfully into uncharted and unimagined realms. When we emerged from these sessions into the shock of the bright sun, we were exhausted. Gratefully accepting the shade of the ramada, we would sit about for the rest of the day, watching the afternoon breeze ruffle through the little green and golden maize field.

The summer drew to a close and we had accumulated a great many tapes. It was evident that we had barely begun an enormous and complex task. Huichol religion was turning out to be very intricate and subtle and not at all similar to religions of nearby related Indians. Furthermore, it was impressively free of nonindigenous elements, lacking the blend or overlay of Aztec or Catholic influence which might have been expected. I returned to school and to Los Angeles, a bit overwhelmed, eager to go back to Mexico but pleased at the prospect of having some time to go through the ethnographic literature on the Huichols and mull over the transcriptions of the tapes we had made. The Fursts maintained their contact with Ramón and Lupe and continued to amass material about which we corresponded throughout the year. My exploration of anthropological literature on the Huichols was not rewarding; at that time only two lengthy studies existed, one by Carl Lumholtz in 1902 and the other by Robert M. Zingg in 1938.[2]

Encountering Híkuri

I returned to Guadalajara and continued working with Ramón and Lupe the following summer. We took up where we had left off, with daily taping sessions and holding lengthy planned interviews and unplanned conversations and observation.

At the end of a formal session one afternoon, I attempted to resume a conversation begun earlier inside the hut about *ti peyote*, "Our peyote," or *híkuri*, as Ramón called it affectionately, the hallucinogenic plant which plays such a central role

[2] Carl Lumholtz, *Unknown Mexico* (New York: Scribner, 1902), vol. II; Robert M. Zingg, *The Huichols: Primitive Artists* (New York: Stechert, 1938).

in the religion. "Ramón," I asked, "What would I see if I were to eat peyote?" "Do you want to?" he replied unexpectedly. "Yes, very much." "Then come tomorrow, very early and eat nothing tonight or tomorrow. Only drink a little warm water when you get up in the morning." The Huichols, unlike the neighboring Cora and Tarahumara Indians, have no fear of peyote. Ordinary men, women, and children take it frequently with no sickness or frightening visions, as long as the peyote they use has been gathered properly during an authentic peyote hunt. Ramón assured me that the experience in store for me would be beautiful and important and I trusted him and his knowledge completely by this time.

The next morning he led me into the little hut and began feeding me the small green "buttons" or segments, one after another, perhaps a dozen or more in all. He cut each segment away from the large piece he held and prepared it in no way that I could see, for the small pieces I was given retained all their skin, dirt, and root. The tiny fuzzy white-gray hairs that top each segment were intact and only the small bottommost portion of the root had been pared off. The buttons were very chewy and tough, and unspeakably bitter-sour. My mouth flooded with saliva and shriveled from the revolting flavor, but no nausea came. "Chew well," Ramón urged me. "It is good, like a tortilla, isn't it?" But I was no longer able to answer.

After giving me what he felt was the proper dosage, Ramón indicated that he was going to wait outside and directed me to lie down quietly and close my eyes. For a long time I heard him singing and playing his little violin and then there were new sounds of comings and goings and soft laughter. "They've all come to stare at me and laugh," I thought. "Come on," I imagined them saying to each other.

"Peek inside, we've got a *gringa* [3] in there and we've given her a weed. You can get those anthropologists to eat anything if you tell them it's sacred. She thinks she's going to have a vision!"

But these thoughts were more amusing than ominous, for I really did not believe that Ramón would deceive me. After an inestimable period of time I began to be aware of a growing euphoria; I was flooded with feelings of goodwill. With great delight I began to notice sounds, especially the noises of the trucks passing on the highway outside. Although I discovered that I couldn't move, I was able to remain calm when it occurred to me that this was of no consequence because there was no other place that I wanted to be. My body assumed the rhythm of the passing trucks, gently wafting up and down like a scarf in a breeze. Time and space evaporated as I floated about in the darkness and vague images began to develop. I realized that I could keep track of what was happening to me and remember it if I thought of it not as a movielike flow of time but as a discrete series of events like beads on a string. I could go from one to the next and though the first was perhaps out of sight, it had not disappeared as do events in ordinary chronology. It was like a carnival with booths spread about to which I could always return to regain an experience, a Steppenwolf-like magical theater. The problem of retaining my experience was thus solved. There remained only the hazard of getting lost. But Ramón had prepared me for this; though he was outside the hut, I felt that as my guide and craftsman, he had left me a thread by means of which I could trace and retrace my peregrinations through the labyrinth and thus return safely from any far-flung destination. Assured by this notion, I started out.

[3] Pejorative term for a North American woman.

The first "booth" found me impaled on an enormous tree with its roots buried far below the earth and its branches rising beyond sight, toward the sky. This was the Tree of Life, the *axis mundi* or world pole which penetrates the layers of the cosmos, connecting earth with underworld and heaven, on which shamans ascend in their magical flights. The image was exactly the same as a Mayan glyph which I was to come across for the first time several years after this vision occurred.

In the next sequence, I beheld a tiny speck of brilliant red flitting about a forest darkness. The speck grew as it neared. It was a vibrant bird who, with an insouciant flicker, landed on a rock. It was Ramón as psychopomp, as Papageno—half-man, magic bird, bubbling with excitement. He led me to the next episode which presented an oracular, gnomelike creature of macabre viscosity. I asked it *the question*, the one that had not been out of my mind for months. "What do the myths *mean?*" He offered his reply in mucid tones, melting with a deadly portentousness that mocked my seriousness. "The myths signify—nothing. They mean *themselves.*" Of course! They *were* themselves, nothing equivalent, nothing translated, nothing taken from another more familiar place to distort them. They had to be accepted in their own terms. I was embarrassed that as an aspirant anthropologist I had to be told this basic axiom of the discipline, but I was amused and relieved for in a vague way I had known it all along.

My journey ended many booths later, as I sat concentrating on a mythical little animal, aware that the entire experience was drawing to a close. The little fellow and I had entered a yarn painting and he sat precisely in the middle of the composition. I watched him fade and finally disappear into a hole and I made an extra effort to concentrate on him, convinced that a final lesson—a grand conclusion—was about to occur. Just as he vanished, an image flicked into the corner of my vision. In the upper righthand quadrant of the painting, another being had just jumped out of sight. I had missed him and *he* was the message. There it was! I had lost my lesson by looking for it too directly, with dead-center tight focus, with will and impatience. It was a practice which I knew was fatal to understanding anything truly unique. It was my Western rationality, honed by formal study, eager to simplify, clarify, dissect, define, categorize, and analyze. These techniques, exercised prematurely, are antithetical to good ethnographic work and this I was to learn and learn and forget and relearn. The message could emerge anywhere on the canvas; one had to be alert, patient, receptive to whatever might occur, at any moment, in whatever ambiguous, unpredictable form it assumed, reserving interpretation for a later time. In the years to come, the vision was to serve as my mnemonic for this principle and help me keep it in the foreground of my consciousness for all that was ahead.

I opened my eyes to the sight of Ramón engaging in mysterious actions, leaping about the hut, holding his plumed arrows aloft and waving them vigorously into the corners, as though sweeping something back. He shouted and danced, and when he noticed that I was watching him, he gestured that I should be silent while he sang many songs. At last he looked at me and allowed me to speak. "How do you feel?" he asked. "Oh, Ramón, it was marvelous . . ." and the highlights of the experience began to spill forth. He appeared unwilling to hear these, and kept checking me by repeating, "You feel well?" and, "It was beautiful, eh, many colors, many animals?" "Yes," I persisted, "but what was the meaning?" I was bursting to hear his interpretation and reaction to all that had occurred, already forgetting what I had just "learned," and his refusal baffled me. It was a long time before I knew that it is not proper to tell others one's peyote visions unless one is a mara'akame. Only the latter's visions are intended to convey religious information. Only the mara'akame may transmit communications to the people from the deities; his visions are didactic and rhetorical, containing "messages" and providing guides for men's actions and understandings. The ordinary Huichol's visions are for beauty's sake alone, intensely private and spiritual but less sacred than those of the mara'akame, whose privilege and duty it is to share his messages in great detail. He may even convey them visually, and peyote visions were the source of inspiration for many of Ramón's yarn paintings. Many years later I told Ramón that there in his hut that day my vision was more than beautiful. It had brought me an important message. With obvious ambivalence, he asked me to describe some of the content. During my discourse, he and Lupe exchanged significant glances and laughed uproariously when I described Ramón's appearance as a bird. "That was the bird of a thousand colors," he said, but would not explain who this was or what it meant. He agreed that I had had a true message in my vision and that this was extraordinary. "It was your great gift and you are very lucky. Guard it well," he said solemnly and spoke of it no further.

Ramón's Equilibrium

The taping sessions were pleasantly interrupted from time to time by excursions to the country. Our party usually included a half dozen or so additional Huichol adults and children who would become much more animated and comfortable with us when out of the city. One afternoon Ramón led

Ramón displaying his balance by leaping on the rocks. He is about to spring across the high barranca through which the waterfall courses.

us to a steep barranca, cut by a rapid waterfall cascading perhaps a thousand feet over jagged, slippery rocks. At the edge of the fall Ramón removed his sandals and told us that this was a special place for shamans. We watched in astonishment as he proceeded to leap across the waterfall, from rock to rock, pausing frequently, his body bent forward, his arms spread out, his head thrown back, entirely birdlike, poised motionlessly on one foot. He disappeared, reemerged, leaped about, and finally achieved the other side. We outsiders were terrified and puzzled but none of the Huichols seemed at all worried. The wife of one of the older Huichol men indicated that her husband had started to become a mara'akame but had failed because he lacked balance. I assumed she referred to his social and personal unsteadiness, for he was alcoholic and something of a deviant. I knew I had witnessed a virtuostic display of balance, but it was not until the next day when discussing the event with Ramón that I began to understand more clearly what had indeed occurred. "The mara'akame must have superb equilibrium," he said, and demonstrated the point by using his fingers to march up his violin bow. "Otherwise he will not reach his destination, and will fall this way or that," and his fingers plunged into an imaginary abyss. "One crosses over; it is very narrow and without balance, one is eaten by those animals waiting below."

I could not be sure whether Ramón was rehearsing his equilibrium or giving it public, ceremonial expression that day. In societies without writing, official statements about a person's status and skill are often given in dramatic, ceremonial form. Whether seen as a practice session or as a ritual, the events of the afternoon provided a most demonstrative assertion that Ramón was a true mara'akame, like all authentic shamans, a man of immense courage, poise, and balance.[4]

Ramón's crossings into another world were always conducted fearlessly and deftly. It might be said that in addition to the everyday world and to the supernatural world typically bridged by shamans, Ramón also had access to the third realm—that of official mestizo society, a complex, urban,

[4] In his work with Mexican Indian shamans, Carlos Castaneda also encountered virtuostic displays of balance. An episode strikingly similar to the one described here is recounted in his *A Separate Reality: Further Conversations with Don Juan* (New York: Simon & Schuster, 1971).

industrial nation-state. And here too he moved easily between this threatening intricate domain and his own people, providing an invaluable bridge. He understood the mechanisms of the modern world very well—how to coax an official out of his rigidity, how to manage money and records, how time was kept and what scheduling meant, what contracts required and promised—and all without the aid of literacy. Ramón regarded these machinations somewhat loftily, as necessary but intrinsically foolish and wasteful. He was quick to point out the superiority and priority of indigenous Huichol culture. The mestizos, too, recognized Huichol superiority, he felt, else why would they adorn their government buildings with the double-headed eagle, an ancient indigenous American motif? This clearly indicated that the Mexicans knew that the country really belonged to the Huichols. And when a mestizo crossed himself he was not only reproducing a Catholic symbol, he was also acknowledging the importance of the four cardinal directions, a significant concern in Huichol religion. If one who crossed himself was not fully aware of these implications, that changed nothing.

Ramón felt it was natural that as an intermediary between his people and the deities he should also intervene for them with public officials, and he won them favors, concessions, and aid on many occasions. Regarded by many mestizos in the city as a kind of Indian ambassador, Ramón was called upon to describe his culture to strangers and to demonstrate publicly his arts and skills with ever-increasing frequency. His integrity in all these dealings was impressive.

Ramón was not entirely unique in his poise and dignity. Huichols in general behave as if they believe what they are fond of saying: "Our way of life is beautiful, beautiful because it is right." It is unusual for the Indians of Mexico to appear comfortable in the presence of outsiders. At the turn of the century, Lumholtz had noted that the Huichols were an exception when he observed, "Their self-esteem is equal to anyone. Never for a moment will a Huichol allow that any other race may be superior to his. Even when far away from home, among the whites, the Huichols bear themselves as if they had never known a master" (Lumholtz 1902:24). In Ramón, this self-esteem occasionally bordered on chauvinism, as when he would close his narratives with the announcement that his texts had been related by "an authentic indigenous Mexican, a Huichol of San Sebastián with pure black blood."

Those with a cynical turn of mind on encountering a man like Ramón are immediately suspicious of his "authenticity" as a spiritual specialist and as spokesman for his people, assuming, perhaps, that any man who can be at home outside his milieu cannot possibly be at one with his own world, or perhaps that a spiritual individual can never function well in mundane matters. There is no justification for this view, either in the abstract or in regard to Ramón. It must be affirmed that there are a few men of faith and experience whose worldliness deepens rather than disturbs their identity. Ramón must surely be considered such a man.

Our study of Huichol religion benefited enormously from Ramón's philosophical and speculative turn of mind. Continually searching for underlying ideas and meaning, he was a true metaphysician. In his narratives on maize especially, he revealed himself as a man who was deeply religious but did not take his religious dogma for granted. For Ramón, answers were not self-evident or automatically provided by revered ritual, tales, and ceremonies.

Though identified with his culture most profoundly, Ramón was far from completely absorbed by it. And he was not less questioning and independent in his thinking about Mexican national culture, despite the great power and prestige it commanded in his life. Consider the following excerpt from a spontaneous speech he made on the plight of the Huichols and their future:

> In San Andrés Cohamiata, what is it they say to us? When the Fathers come to those Huichols who are the pure indigenous Mexicans, what is it they tell them? Instead of telling them to follow their history, to follow their stories, to live pure lives as Huichols, to be in unity with all, they say, "Be like the Spaniards." [5] The Father wants all of us to be the same. No, I believe that it is not right. On the contrary, he should help them. He should do these things as they should be, so that the Huichol can go on being an authentic Huichol.
>
> Nowadays, there are Huichols who know a little how to write, who know how to read. Why all these things if not to defend our customs, our history, our land, our people?

The Peyote Hunt

Not all our taping sessions were enlightening and satisfying, however. Often a critical matter would seem to become more obscure with further questioning and at these times Ramón was as distressed as I was. I would never fully understand these matters, he felt, until I had participated in a peyote hunt myself. By this time I fully trusted his judgment concerning my comprehension of his religion and so before leaving Guadalajara, Ramón, Furst, and I made plans to undertake a trip to Wirikuta which Ramón would lead the coming winter.

As far as I can tell, Furst and I were the first anthropolo-

[5] Ramón consistently referred to non-Indian Mexicans or mestizos as "Spaniards."

gists to have had this experience.[6] For reasons not entirely clear, neither Lumholtz, Zingg, nor Grimes participated in the peyote hunt though all spent considerable time with the Huichols, appreciated the significance of the event, and recorded descriptions of it on the basis of secondary accounts. It is possible that they never went to Wirikuta because there is no real provision for witnesses to the ceremony.

Ramón did not exaggerate the importance of participating in the journey, for without it I am certain that I would not have been able to penetrate beyond the surface of the Huichol religion. The peyote hunt is at the very heart of Huichol beliefs. Three interrelated purposes are accomplished during that event: the separate symbols, deer, maize, and peyote, are fused into a single entity; the pilgrims retrieve their spiritual and historical beginnings; and sufficient peyote is gathered to be used in ceremonies at home throughout the year. I had to hear about the ceremony at great length beforehand, to witness it, to participate in it, to talk about it with Ramón afterward, then to ponder my notes for months in order to arrive at the interpretation presented here. Some time after I returned to Los Angeles the pattern of the peyote hunt began to emerge, and ultimately it was the sense of this pattern with its internal consistency and its "fit" with other aspects of Huichol culture which convinced me that my interpretation of the meaning and purpose of the ceremony was valid.

Nevertheless, the interpretation given here is not complete.

[6] The following year Furst filmed a peyote hunt, "To Find Our Life: The Peyote Hunt of the Huichols of Mexico," 1969. Though not an anthropologist by formal training, the Mexican journalist Fernando Benítez has witnessed and written about the peyote pilgrimage with sensitivity and artistry; his works are valuable to general reader and ethnographer alike (Benítez 1968a, 1968b, 1970).

With each passing year since I first encountered the Huichols' return to Wirikuta I have found in this ritual new dimensions, meanings, and beauty that I barely apprehended in the beginning. Genuine sacred symbols and the rituals that contain them are boundlessly rich and ultimately unfathomable and inexhaustible, except for a moment at a time. They are alive and full of power and present new possibilities when beheld at different times and by different people. Ramón understood and communicated the sustaining power of his people's sacred symbols.

CHAPTER 2

Ethnographic and Historical Background

> The Huichol lives freely. He lives there freely in the Sierra. Out in the wind, everywhere. We work as we wish, we go as we please. And the Spaniard? He cannot do this. The Huichol is different because he is free to come and go as he wishes. But the Spaniard must do as the government says. The government has him in this way. The Huichol has government too, but it is not the same. It does not tell us that we cannot do this and that and the other thing.
>
> Ramón Medina Silva

A definitive history of the Huichol people has not yet been written, and because relevant materials are widely scattered, often conflicting and subject to interpretation, and because I do not possess the necessary archeological expertise, I have not attempted to provide such a history. The material given here is confined to matters which bear on the discussion of religion and symbolism that follows. The reconstruction of pre- and postcontact Huichol history suggested below is based on several kinds of evidence—oral traditional, direct historical, and circumstantial. Ultimately, it is the coincidence of these diverse materials on which the validity of this reading must rest.

The first European contact with the Indians of Jalisco and Nayarít occurred in 1524 during the expedition of Francisco Cortés de San Buenaventura (a relative of Hernán Cortés), who came to the area in search of the legendary Amazons. But the area was not deeply affected by the Conquest until 1530–1531, when Nuño de Guzmán penetrated a large part of the western regions of the Sierra Madre Occidental, although not the most rugged and remote segments. The conquered territory subsequently became the Spanish province of Nueva Galícia.

Although some items of Spanish language and culture may have been adopted by the Indians of the Sierra in the early decades following the Conquest, systematic intercourse with Spaniards began only in 1722, when Spanish troops actually penetrated the Sierra. Before long, the Jesuits began concentrating the Cora Indians in large settlements in their present locale, and the Franciscans attempted to establish missions among the Huichols, a project which met with little success. In the early and middle nineteenth century the Coras and the Huichols made occasional forays against the insurgent Mexican nationalists. After the Mexican Revolution, some Coras and Huichols scattered to the coast for a time to escape military action. These dispersions accelerated the Huichol tendency toward residence in ranchos [1] removed from the centralized communities, a preference which has remained a marked characteristic of their present settlement pattern.

"Huichol" appears to be a corruption of an indigenous tribal name adapted during Spanish colonial times and now widely used. The people, however, generally refer to themselves as "Wixárika," a term whose origins are not clear. Neither "Huichol" nor "Wixárika" is found in early His-

[1] *Rancho* is a Spanish term used by the Huichols to refer to one or more huts, the adjoining fields of maize and pasturage, possibly other structures such as oratories for religious objects, and maize storage bins. Roughly, the Huichol rancho consists of members of an extended family and may be thought of as an extended family compound. As in all such arrangements, fission occurs regularly, thus the size of the rancho depends on the phase of the family cycle at a particular time. The minimal rancho, for example, may consist of a man, his wife, and their children.

panic records. The cultural geographer Carl Sauer (1934) cites some suggestive missionary accounts of the sixteenth and seventeenth centuries which bear on the question of early Huichol history. These records describe "wild tribes" in and about the present Huichol homeland with such names as Guisól, Usilíque, Uzare, Guisare, and Vitzúrita, all of which he believes to refer to the people now popularly known as *los Huicholes* (Spanish) (Sauer 1934:14). The Guachichíl, another "wild" or Chichimeca tribe reported in Zacatecas and Jalisco, is also mentioned by Sauer, as well as by Jiménez Moreno (1943) as possible forebears or prototypes of the present-day Huichols. Loosely translatable as "lineage of the dog" (a term whose precise significance is unclear, except that it does not seem to have been pejorative), the Chichimec Indians were regarded by the Aztecs as "northern barbarians." However, differentiations were made by the Aztecs among the various Chichimec peoples, some of whom had mastered certain of the skills and customs of sedentary cultivators. On the bottom of the heap, in the view of the Aztecs and early Spaniards, were the so-called Teochichimeca, or true Chichimeca (known to archeologists as the "Old Desert Culture"). These people evidently subsisted as nomadic hunters and collectors, living in caves or beehive-shaped brush shelters, wearing only crude skins or no clothing at all, and speaking "barbarous tongues."

Of particular interest here is the fact that some Teochichimec tribes evidently had a peyote ceremony which resembles that of the modern Huichol in several important respects. Such a ceremony is described in Book Ten of Father Bernardino de Sahagún's *General History of the Things of New Spain* (1950–1963, first published in 1831). While the name of the tribe is not mentioned in this account, its location appears to be close to the peyote country sacred to the Huichols in the vicinity of San Luis Potosí. It is to this sacred region that Huichols still travel in their annual quest for peyote.

Despite some speculations that the Huichols migrated into the Sierra from the coast, according to Huichol tradition they came from the east or northeast into their present territory, after settling for a time in the region of present-day Guadalajara. Archeological evidence suggests a prehispanic occupation of the valleys and mesas of the Sierra de los Huicholes and the Mesa del Nayar to the north, although it is likely that the Huichols themselves arrived later, perhaps in retreat from the Conquest.[2] (It should be noted that the Indians in the vicinity of Guadalajara who staged an unsuccessful uprising—the Mixton War, 1541—against Spanish rule were forced to flee for refuge into the less accessible regions in the Sierra. There they remained, relatively immune from Spanish pressure until colonial troops occupied the region in the early 1700's.)

But the most interesting evidence of a Huichol migration from the area northeast of their present locale is provided by the Huichols directly in their religious and mythological traditions. Their account of themselves as having originated from the desert region in the east is corroborated by the route taken on the annual peyote hunt, during which they journey out of the mountains through Jalisco, Zacatecas, and finally, to the Chihuahuan deserts of San Luis Potosí. If this historical reconstruction is correct, then in actuality and in

[2] Evidence of prehispanic occupation in this area has been noted independently by Grimes and Furst during field work (personal communication, Mexico City, 1967). Furst describes some of this evidence in Furst and Myerhoff, 1966 and 1971.

myth they do retrace the route of the Ancient Ones. These First People are said to have left their homeland under duress, to have suffered and languished in the mountains until they were led back to Wirikuta by the First Mara'akame, following the original path of their ancestors. Whether or not this reading of history is correct, it is clear that at present when they journey to Wirikuta on their peyote pilgrimages, they cover a terrain in which the most minute geographical features are known, given Huichol names, and completely incorporated into the religion. Mountains, caves, groves of trees, water holes, springs, rivers, and rocks, are among the "sacred places" visited by the Ancient Ones during their exodus according to Huichol oral literature, and revisited by the present-day Huichols during the peyote hunt. It seems inconceivable that such precise familiarity could occur from short, sporadic visits to the area, and unlikely that they could know it and love it so well and weave it so tightly into their religion unless they once actually lived there. Without at least provisional acceptance of this folk explanation of Wirikuta as the land of their origins, it is not possible to account for the Huichols' trek to San Luis Potosí to gather peyote. Peyote grows in more accessible places and of course can be purchased in any large western Mexican market.[3]

It is suggested here, then, that the ancestors of the modern Huichols migrated into the arid inner plateau of north-central Mexico to their present homeland as Chichimec hunters, trav-

[3] "Lophophora [peyote] has a latitudinal distribution of about 1200 km from 20°54′ to 29°47′ North Latitude. It is found along the Rio Grande drainage basin and southward into the high central plateau of northern Mexico lying between the Sierra Madre Oriental and Sierra Madre Occidental. . . . Ecologists describe this large desert area of Texas and northern Mexico as the Chihuahuan Desert" (Anderson 1969:301).

eling from a northern homeland, perhaps the southwest region of what is now the United States.[4]

Using a paleolithic tool kit, these Indians would have hunted small game, gathered wild fruits, cacti, berries, and the like and lived in brush and rock shelters.

The "ancient, ancient Huichol" desert dwellers would have had to come into contact with planters of maize during the social upheaval in this region following the collapse of the great classic civilizations of Mesoamerica in the ninth and tenth centuries A.D. In the course of the subsequent population displacements, the Chichimec bands swept southward into the regions previously inhabited by the sedentary cultivators. These hunters probably remained in contact with the southerners long enough to learn and adopt the agricultural techniques presently practiced in the Sierra.

Equally plausible is that the Chichimeca acquired maize when the southern planters pushed up into the northern plateaus, for there is growing archeological evidence that at various times the entire frontier of prehispanic civilization shifted and extended farther north than once supposed, farther in fact than it did at the time of the Conquest. In the opinion of several authorities (Furst, Coe, Grimes, and Weigand)[5] there is reason to consider the possibility that areas formerly thought to have been either uninhabited or purely Chichimec country actually supported sedentary agricultural communities with well-developed ceramic art and technology. In any event, all the evidence points in the same direction, suggesting that the ancestral Huichols became cultivators relatively

[4] Furst is convinced that contact between the Huichols and cultures of the North American Indians of the Southwest was once very great and he finds many similarities between these two (1972a).

[5] Personal communications, Mexico City, 1965, 1970.

recently and perhaps prior to settling in their present locations in northwest and central Mexico.

Although there is no doubt that the subsistence base of the society shifted from hunting to farming several centuries ago, on the behavioral and ideological level the transition remains incomplete even now. Numerous elements in the culture clearly indicate an extensive residue of a hunting way of life in Huichol world view, myth, and ceremony. Some of these elements are the following: the ubiquitous theme in Huichol mythology of a First Time, when men and animals were one; the emphasis on the deer as the sacred animal, companion of the deities and the mara'akame; the necessity of employing deer blood in numerous ceremonies; the existence of ceremonial deer hunts in which the deer is run down and caught in sacred nets and noose traps; the propitiation of the slain animal by the hunter, who explains to "his brother" why he had to die; the many uses of deer horns by the mara'akame in curing and in ceremony; and the regard for bones as a source of life. All these features are associated with religions organized around hunting.

An interpretation of the Huichols as still in transition in their religion and world view—from high desert nomadic hunter-gatherers to sedentary mountain maize cultivators—also helps to account for the sacredness of all bodies of water, but in particular for the significance of the permanent and rare water holes and springs located in Zacatecas and San Luis Potosí, far from their present homeland. The importance of such sources of water to desert people is self-evident. Similarly, the enormous importance of salt to desert people is readily apparent, and it will be seen that salt figures significantly in Huichol ritual and ceremony.

Several features of social organization likewise suggest a recent nomadic life organized at the band level of sociocultural complexity: lack of political centralization; dispersion of households; absence of any provision for corporate action above the household level; religious autonomy of rancho elders who can and often do take the role of family shamans; bilateral kinship organization resulting in diffuse kindreds and consequent absence of corporate unilineal kinship groups; absence of pantribal sodalities; fragile attachment to the land; loose inheritance patterns; bilocal or neolocal residence. All these characteristics are more likely to be associated with nomadic bands than sedentary agricultural societies.

Thus, the evidence for an incomplete transition by the Huichols to their present way of life is indicated by several kinds of data, direct and indirect: traditions and interpretations by the Huichols themselves, and a combination of social, religious, economic, and ecological factors. And it is in terms of this "incomplete transition" hypothesis that so much of Huichol ideology in general, and the deer-maize-peyote complex in particular, become comprehensible and can be seen to fulfill an essential function.

Present Population, Locale, and Social Organization

The people calling themselves the Wixárika can be found in the mountain ranges in the Mexican states of Jalisco and Nayarít in the Sierra Madre Occidental. Their nearest indigenous neighbors are the Coras, whom they resemble more closely than any other known Mexican group. The population figures for the Huichols are not generally regarded as reliable and indeed they have varied from 3,000 to 4,000 minimum to 10,000 maximum (Vogt 1955:251; *Operación Huicot*, Plan Lerma, 1966). Problems of census-taking in these inaccessible mountain reaches among people whose settlement pattern is dispersed are enormous. Fabila (1959) has estimated that there are around 7,000 Huichols; a more recent estimate is 9,000, of whom 4,000 to 5,000 live within the five Huichol mountain communities in the Sierra Madre (Weigand 1970). The remaining 5,000 are scattered among mixed Huichol-mestizo settlements in the Cora country to the west and north, and in ranchos outside of the Sierra proper, and increasingly in the cities.[6] Together the five Huichol communities cover 4,107.5 square kilometers, with an average population density of slightly over one inhabitant per square kilometer.

The Huichols' isolation is pronounced, owing partly to choice but largely to inaccessibility. There are no roads into the Sierra and the only airplane service available is dependent on such variable factors as weather, condition of airstrips, height of the surrounding maize, and so forth. The country is extremely rugged, with mountains rising to over 9,840 feet and with a mean altitude of 6,560 feet. Steep-walled canyons and deep barrancas inhibit communication of all kinds, and most Huichol movement consists of inter-rancho and inter-community visiting, with long stays in between and the use of the most feasible mode of transportation in this difficult terrain—walking.

Four sociopolitical units are relevant in Huichol life today, community, ranchería, rancho, and nuclear family. The Huichols are citizens within other, larger political units of the Mexican government, such as *município*, state, and, of course,

[6] No attempt is made here to account for the lives and customs of these displaced persons. Very little is known of them, though Weigand's present study of Huichol life in urban settings may fill this conspicuous gap in our knowledge of contemporary Huichol life.

nation, but these divisions are virtually inconsequential to the actions and identity of the people living in the Sierra. In large part sociopolitical units are important to the Huichols in proportion to their correspondence to indigenous arrangements, and their significance decreases at each ascending level as the groups are progressively larger, more inclusive of mestizos, less kin-based, and more removed from rancho religious practices.

There are five communities (Spanish, *comunidades*) in the Huichol region of the Sierra. It appears that no indigenous equivalent unit existed, and as might be expected, one finds participation in and concern with community affairs more limited than in the three other groups. The community, sometimes referred to as a pueblo or town, is basically a foreign institution, legally operating as the official Mexican administration.[7] Yearly elections of officials must be held. There is no provision for formal interaction above the community level, nor do the community officers function as a unified body, judicially or administratively. Thus, intracommunity affairs are ad hoc, and intercommunity affairs less predictable and formal than might be assumed on the basis of the impressive slate of officers. Officers usually are concerned only with their own special areas of responsibility.

It is difficult to classify the level of sociopolitical development of the present-day Huichols. Grimes (1959) and Grimes and Hinton (1961) call the group a tribe. Manning Nash refers to it as a "quasi-tribal system" (1966:61–63). It seems inappropriate to use the term "tribe" in regard to the Huichols except in the loosest sense. No organization embraces,

[7] With few exceptions, this is not a "town" in the sense of a relatively dense, permanent settlement; the exceptions that do exist include large numbers of mestizos.

relates, or integrates the five communities. They cannot be considered either ranked or balanced segments of a larger system because of this lack of articulation among units. Rather the communities may be thought of as a cluster of culturally similar entities, actually societies, with replicated institutions and a sense of commonality. The communities are self-sufficient, self-regulating, autonomous, and in view of the minor role played by secular officials in indigenous affairs, these units may be considered acephalous. The communities resemble a cluster of bands more than a true tribal organization.

Nor can one casually apply the term "peasant" to them. They are agriculturalists but are not related to urban society in the symbiotic pattern which Redfield (1955) suggests is definitive of peasant society. They do not have pronounced attachment—physical or emotional—to the land, nor are they deeply involved in the market economy or cash nexus of nearby urban areas.

The community is made up of one or more rancherías which in turn contain smaller ranchos or compounds. These rancherías often are built around a core of loosely related individuals. At present rancherías are rather ad hoc, often widely dispersed, sometimes unnamed territorial categories. Part of each ranchería is the *kalihué* or religious compound, consisting of several small oratories (Huichol, *xíriki*) grouped around a central dancing plaza.[8] These oratories are fre-

[8] Weigand (1970) notes that these religious structures are not always used and are even permitted occasionally to fall into ruin. He feels that the practice of religion at the ranchería level has broken down since the dislocation of populations at the time of the 1910 revolution. The ranchería, he suggests, was once a tightly knit kinship-based entity that now functions primarily as a territorial category; this decline in kinship orientation has caused the ranchería to become less effective, he feels. But, he goes on to observe, religious life oper-

quently storage sites for the metamorphized ancestors in the form of rock crystals, a fact which lends support to Weigand's (1970) suggestion that kinship considerations were at one time a more dominant factor in the formation of rancherías.

The ranchos may be widely dispersed—a few hours' or even days' walk apart. Ranchos are comprised of an extended family, that is, made up of several nuclear families. The rancho performs many social functions: production, distribution, and consumption of goods; socialization; ritual and ceremony; and curing of the sick. It also provides external as well as internal social regulation, since it has political significance outside the local sphere by virtue of the rancho elder's participation in the town, or community, council. Very often the larger ranchos have a mara'akame in residence or someone who can serve as religious leader, often the rancho elder. The rancho is usually named after the current elder male.

On the rancho, the individual households or nuclear families are comprised of a man, his wife or wives, and their unmarried children. Ideally residence is patrilocal, after a year of bride service in which the husband works for his father-in-law to recompense the bride's family for her loss. This arrangement has emotional as well as economic functions, for the couple's first few years together are considered almost a trial marriage and their union is indeed fragile during this

---

ates as vigorously as ever at the rancho level, where curing and seasonal ceremonies occur. One has the picture of a decline in the more inclusive, less kinship-oriented *kalihué*-ranchería entity, and simultaneous fragmentation into the smaller, kin-based ranchos. Indeed all the important matters of everyday life are conducted at the rancho level, and it is in this sphere that the individual spends most of his time, finds his greatest satisfactions, and establishes his closest ties.

period. The bride is reluctant to sever ties with her family of procreation. The couple may in fact sow crops in the ranchos of both parents, distance permitting, and then decide to remain at the most compatible site. Thus the patrilocal ideal is far from rigid. Other considerations than the couple's personal preference influence their ultimate location, for example, patterns of inheritance.

Inheritance tends to be bilateral in terms of property and livestock. The land per se remains "owned" by the community but land-use rights are settled below the community level. Ritual duties accrue to the senior son, who on ascending to the position of rancho elder is expected to erect and maintain an oratory or *xíriki* of his own. (All ancestors are honored in these oratories along bilateral lines within the recollection of the present generation, but important individuals—mara'akate or political leaders—are more likely to be remembered.) Thus after the year of bride service older sons are more likely to observe the patrilocal rule.[9]

Younger sons, sons of second wives, or men whose wives come from wealthy families may affiliate themselves permanently with the bride's father, giving the latter the welcome addition of his much-needed labor.

The principle of primogeniture is present but not sufficiently strong to prevent inheritance and succession disputes. For example, if no adult rancho heir exists, the younger brothers of a deceased elder may inherit his role. Serious conflict may develop between brothers or between the younger sons of the deceased and their paternal uncle, and at this point ranchos often divide. Younger brothers and their families are

[9] Another way in which seniority among collaterals is reflected is in the religious system, where the term "elder brother" connotes affection and respect and indicates special ritual responsibilities.

most likely to depart (Weigand 1970). Females may and often do inherit the rancho, and their husbands or sons fill the leadership role. Regardless of the disposition of the rancho the elder's widow almost always remains in residence.

Huichol kinship is reckoned bilaterally, generating diffuse kindreds.[10] Inheritance occurs through both parents to children of both sexes with a male primogeniture preference in certain matters, as previously mentioned. Women can own private property in the form of household and personal effects as well as livestock. Both sexes are considered equally responsible for procreation, and children are not affiliated into corporate groups through matrilineal or patrilineal recruitment. The kinship terminology differentiates between one's children and his nieces and nephews, but in one's own generation, cousins and siblings are called by the same term. Grimes and Grimes suggest that this reflects the emphasis on cooperation among rancho age-mates in a mobile population where sibling bonds are a very important source of social cohesion and joint labor. They note:

> A Huichol child lives in a household . . . [which] usually forms part of a ranch that contains several other households of similar composition. Every few years the household as a unit may move to some other ranch within its kindred. The child thus has its parents and biological siblings as constant members of its personal community . . . and learns to adjust periodically to new sets of ranch-mates that include siblings of either of its parents and their children. Siblings are encouraged to cooperate . . . with age-mates of other households on whatever ranch they may be living [1962:105].

[10] Children clearly belong to both parents, but a patrilineal bias is evident in certain matters, such as residence, emphasis on male ancestors in ritual, and, of course, assumption of leadership roles.

The importance of peers is further reflected in the fact that collaterals may be recognized to four or five degrees and are often found in company on peyote expeditions and in cooperative labor parties (Weigand 1970).

Seniority, it has been seen, is significant as a basis of differentiation, and the age principle is used to allocate authority and respect within a single generation and between adjacent generations but is set aside between alternate generations. The grandfather-grandchild relation stresses identity, equality, and reciprocity rather than differential and asymmetrical expectations. Kinship terms used are reciprocal between alternate generations and ideally the grandfather names and "baptizes" the child. One Huichol put it thus:

Between grandfather and grandson things are strong because they are of the same flesh. Father and son and also mother are too, but between grandfather and grandson it is closer. *Neteukari* is said by the grandfather to his grandson and the grandson says the same to his grandfather, because I am the son of his son and he is the father of my father so we are the same. He gives me my name. He is the one who puts the sacred water on me from over there [Wirikuta].

Kinship terms are also used to refer to groups of deities, for example, *tateima*, our aunts, which signifies female rain and water deities; *tamatsi*, our elder brothers, usually deities depicted as deer; Tatewarí, our grandfather, designating Fire, according to Grimes (1959). In a later conversation Grimes clarified some ambiguities in connection with the relationship between ordinary kinship terms and kinship terms used in reference to deities.[11] *Tateima*, for example, is never used in everyday address, hence Grimes suggested that it be

[11] Personal communication, Mexico City, 1966.

translated as "our ritual aunts" or "our ritual mothers." *Tatewarí* is also reserved for a ritual context and may be translated as either "our ritual grandfather or "our ritual great grandfather"; evidently there are regional variations in usage. But *Tatewarí* is invariant in its reference and confinement to the First Mara'akame and to the Fire deity. Terms referring to those beyond great grandfather become metaphorical and are used to signify the "very ancient ones" or ancestors. An informant has suggested (and Grimes has confirmed) the following definitions in reference to ancestors: *nekakai wiwierí* = my great great great grandfather (meaning "my sandal strap" or the "sole of my sandal," "which is closest to the earth, it goes way down, very far back, as the sandals are the lowest level"); *netewarí* = my great grandfather usually reserved for the fire deity, but occasionally used in the plural for male deities generically; *neyeteurixa* = my great great great great grandfather (literally referring to the *yeteurixa*, a thistle plant which flowers and then becomes a dry burr), which may be rendered as the "Ancient Ones" or First Huichols.

There are some ritual kinship relations modeled on the Spanish *compadrazgo* system. Huichols prefer close relatives to fill the positions of godmother and godfather and have, in addition, *compadres* for Catholic ceremonies and events such as confirmation, and for sale of cattle. Most *compadre* relations are between Huichols and non-Huichols, where they take the form and function of asymmetrical patron-client relations.

Marriages usually occur within the extended family, that is, with a close relative in the bilateral kindred. Ideally, boys' parents arrange a match with a girl from the boy's rancho play-group but more often these days couples choose one another without parental intervention. Marriage between first cousins occurs regularly though some voice the objection that these are "too close." In any event, no distinction between cross and parallel cousins is observed in marriage regulations. The incest taboo operates only within the nuclear family, but violations of this stricture have been noted; in some cases no action was taken against the parties concerned nor was there any attempt made to sever the union.[12] Polygyny is not common nor does it appear to be associated with marked wealth; it has been estimated as occurring in approximately 5 per cent of Huichol marriages (Grimes and Hinton 1961:23). The average number of wives in polygynous unions is two, maximum reported five. A slight sororate bias has been noted in that when a man takes a second wife she is usually the first wife's sister or a close relative. This is viewed as especially desirable in the event that the first wife dies, leaving children whom the second wife is more likely to treat well since she is the children's kin. Divorce may be initiated by either partner; usual reasons are infertility or cruelty.

Technology, Material Culture, and Division of Labor

All Huichols are maize farmers and say of this, "Maize is our life." Although the rancho land is owned collectively, it is farmed and harvested by individual households. Some families cooperate in certain phases of farming. Cattle raising is practiced but is of limited economic importance. Food production is at minimum subsistence level; famines are not rare

[12] Equally strong or even stronger objections are voiced to marriage with mestizos, with whose impure blood, it is said, Huichols should not mingle their own pure blood. Indeed, there is a special torment in the afterlife for Huichols who have mated with mestizos (Furst 1967).

and malnutrition is a fact of life. There is seldom any salable surplus from any of the crops, and often all of a year's crop is consumed, leaving no seeds for the next year's planting. Land suitable for agriculture is in short supply, and the technology is very crude and ineffective. In late summer and early fall if the stored surplus of the previous year has been consumed, and the new maize is not yet ripe, hunger drives many families out of the Sierra into the towns and cities to beg for food, sell their services to mestizos, or engage in petty commerce and sale of craft goods.[13]

Such wealth as there is (usually in the form of cattle and beads) is not displayed or exploited and does not set individuals apart by fostering different ways and standards of life. Great pressure exists for sharing wealth, and the ungenerous can be made very uncomfortable (Nash 1966). Land under cultivation or used for pasture can be kept on indefinite tenure. The men of the households set out each spring to cut and burn the brush and foliage growing on the hillsides. The burning is a dangerous activity and a sacred one as well. One of the most important deities, Our Grandfather Fire, is responsible for the land clearing. Each year fires get out of hand and spread to the adjacent forests, with disastrous results for potentially valuable stands of timber.

When the grade of the land permits, cleared plots are plowed with wooden implements pulled by cattle but this is not common since most of the land is too steep and rugged. In June, after the rains have fallen, the earth is softened and

[13] Weigand observes that more recently "a modest degree of property is filtering into the Huichol area; crafts, cattle sales, and seasonal day-wage labor on the coastal plantations account for most of the new wealth" (1970:70). This wealth is invested in beads and cattle and in fiestas and ceremonies.

ready to receive the seeds. All members of the household swarm over the hillsides to begin planting with the ubiquitous digging stick. In late July and usually again in August, plots are weeded, and in November the maize crop is harvested. In the familiar Middle American pattern, beans, squash, and maize are grown together in the same plot. Other crops are raised in house gardens for family consumption, including cucumbers, amaranth, chile, tobacco, sugarcane, sweet potatoes, watermelons, bananas, and mangoes. (In these plots, peyote brought home from Wirikuta is grown.) When there is some maize left over it is marketed and profits are used to buy cattle.

Many Huichol families have a few cows and their milk and cheese are consumed during the spare summer months. A considerable portion of their diet is provided by the collection of a large variety of wild fruits and vegetables. Huichols hunt deer (primarily for its blood for ceremonial uses), peccary, and iguana. The decline of the animal population in recent years due to the introduction of the 22-caliber rifle has made hunting increasingly unrewarding. A deer is rarely hunted successfully these days. Nevertheless the men persist in spending great time and effort on unsuccessful hunts, partly for ritual purposes (Weigand 1970).

For ceremonial meals a maize beer is brewed (Huichol, *nawa;* Spanish, *tejuino*). On these special occasions maize is prepared in the form of saltless tamales and parched balls. Ordinarily maize is eaten in the form of tortillas; as elsewhere in Mexico a great number are consumed (an adult may eat up to a dozen per meal).

The Huichol tool kit is very rude, containing machete, ax, digging stick (which may or may not have a metal point), baskets for collecting wild fruits, vegetables, and seeds, *ixtle* or maguey fiber, sharpening stones, a piece of metal or bone for wrenching maize off the ears, and a maize cob disc for shelling maize. For food preparation there is the usual trough and hand stone for grinding maize into flour (*mano* and *metate*). Clay pots and metal vessels and dishes are purchased from mestizos. Galvanized metal buckets may be used to cook maize in a water and lime mixture. A stirring stick is employed, as are a stone mortar and pestle for grinding chile and a *comal* or griddle for toasting tortillas. Gourds are used for water storage and as dippers. Homemade cooking vessels of clay are very rare although some women still make pottery griddles for tortillas, as well as crudely shaped thick-walled, three-legged copal incense burners for ceremonies.

Today most Huichol dwellings are rectangular, although originally they were round, and consist of a single room from 29.5 to 49.2 square feet with hard-packed earthen floors. In every house there is a domestic fire kept on a fire platform; at one end the fire platform has built-up walls to hold the tortilla griddle and cooking vessels and at the other end there is a place for the *metate* and a tray for the maize dough.

The division of labor observed within the household is not at all complex, following age and sex lines where specialization occurs. Men clear the land, burn the brush, prepare the soil, and store the crops. Women look after the house, prepare the food, gather firewood, and tend the children. Men take care of such range animals as there may be while women look after cows, chickens, pigs, burros, and sheep. Women sew, embroider, and employ the backstrap loom with great skill. Most tasks are gladly performed by either sex if there is skill and a need. The entire household, including children, is involved in all phases of agriculture with the exception of the very strenuous initial clearing of the land and plowing, which only men perform. Also, men alone can hunt.

Although there are no full-time specialists among the Huichols, some individuals are sufficiently skilled at various crafts to earn extra income, although they do not escape the necessity of farming entirely. In fact, it is more common for special skills to be practiced as favors or in connection with ceremonial activities than for personal profit. Even the most prestigious and learned mara'akame does not devote himself exclusively to ceremony or curing, although he may earn a substantial amount of money or goods for these services. He may seek to aggrandize himself through these abilities but this is rare, and basically he, like his fellows, is a maize farmer.

Huichol social organization and technology, it can be seen, are not complex. It is in the areas of aesthetics and metaphysics that their culture is extremely intricate and original. Their oral literature, artistic skills in matters of craft and design, and their symbolic and ritual life are elaborate, profound, and subtle. Nowhere is this more evident than in their religion, and this will be discussed next.

CHAPTER 3

Huichol Religion

> If people have learned how to read and write, it should be to defend their people. Because our lands are our Mexican country. This Mexican earth, it is our land. We must defend that. We must follow our history, our customs, our stories. I do not know these things well, but I know that it is not as some say to us, that we must be like everyone else. Why should that be? Why should we all be the same? That we should not follow our history, our customs, with a good heart, with a pure heart? That is what I cannot fully understand.
>
> Ramón Medina Silva

Among the Huichols one encounters the unusual combination of rude technology and simple social organization, together with an elaborate metaphysical, ideological system.[1] In aesthetics, mythology, oral tradition, symbolism, and cosmology Huichol culture is highly developed, rich, and especially beautiful. As might be expected, Huichol religion is intricate and difficult, of all aspects of the culture one of the most rewarding and challenging for an outsider who would understand it. Religion, here especially, cannot be severed from other aspects of Huichol life. There is no distinction between

[1] Some of the finest anthropological writings on religion have concentrated on the nature of the relationship between religion and social structure. Generally speaking, French sociologists have viewed religion apart from social structure, as a structure of ideas in its own right. The British, on the other hand, have concentrated on the ways in which religion reflects social structure. Without becoming entangled in these issues here, it should be noted that in the present work a systematic study of the relationship between religion and social structure is not undertaken, not only because religion per se is not my subject but also because such an approach would not be likely to be particularly fruitful in the Huichol case. Obviously there are so-

sacred and profane, nor is there even a reliable separation between secular and sacred.[2] The good life is the religious life. The good day's work is sacred. That which is beautiful is beautiful because it is moral. An evil man is not truly Huichol, for to be Huichol is to live in the proper manner. In other words, to be Huichol is to be sacred and this applies to all behavior, objects, and ideas that make up the culture. That which is nonindigenous, not correct or unacceptable, is not merely secular or even profane. It is outside the state of being Huichol.

The Huichol notion of the sacred is elusive and in many ways difficult for a Westerner to grasp. It seems to embrace above all the concept of attaining wholeness and harmony. To be in accord with one another, with oneself, with one's customs—this is the state of being a proper Huichol and it is sacred. It is a dynamic condition of balance in which opposites exist without neutralizing each other, a tension between components that does not blur their essential separateness.

---

cieties where an understanding of social structure is indispensable to an examination of religion but there are more fruitful approaches to take in regard to the Huichols. One alternative, which is adopted here, treats religion as providing a system of meanings, hence a source of integration, primarily ideological and secondarily behavioral.

[2] The Huichols do not make distinctions between sacred and profane and sacred and secular. If these concepts are treated as continuous rather than dichotomous it can be seen that Huichol behavior does reflect degrees of religious intensity, despite the fact that such distinctions are not made explicit. The degree of intensity manifested during the peyote hunt is very great indeed, perhaps the most intense sacred experience they know. Nevertheless in their terms all of Huichol life is sacred and that which is regarded with opprobrium is not profane but non-Huichol. These matters are discussed in more depth in Chapters 5 and 6.

The concept is replicated, as will be seen, on many levels and in many forms—it appears in the mara'akame's sacred chair, which is made from "strong" and "weak" woods that together constitute a whole. It recurs in the balance maintained by the mara'akame in his flights between the layers of the cosmos, and most dramatically it is seen in the apocalyptic union of elements attained in Wirikuta during the peyote hunt. Special sacredness accrues to the combination of weak and strong; thus innocence and vulnerability are treasured and carefully protected by those who are most powerful. Children, maize, *primeros* who have never been to Wirikuta are especially sacred because they cannot take care of themselves and they are vigilantly guarded. (Perhaps this sensitivity to vulnerability is the reason the Huichols view with such distaste the aggression that they consider characteristic of mestizo interpersonal relations.)

Although being sacred is a matter of the greatest seriousness it is not monolithic. Sacred ceremonies may be conducted with flashes of humor. Deities are often regarded without awe or reverence. Improvisations and substitutions are quite acceptable and frequent in the most important religious ceremonies, but do not lessen their sacred character. The sacred is a natural condition for the "true Huichol." It flows in and out of the mundane with a continuity that seems at odds with the concept of sacred as "set apart" and "special." Here it seems to mean powerful and proper. The sacred for the Huichols is continuous with the mundane in that it is within the very fabric of everyday concerns and everyday life lived as it is supposed to be.

Inevitably, the presentation of a religion as intricate as this one would need to be simplified and limited even if it were the sole subject of discussion. In this study, nonindigenous religious features are excluded altogether. This limitation is possible because the Huichols have isolated the Catholic elements which they have accepted, distinguishing them from their own beliefs and practices. There are the Huichol myths and the Christian myths, Huichol practices and objects and the Christian; there is no genuine blending but rather a coexistence of two systems. Extensive attention to those indigenous religious matters readily available in the ethnographic literature will also be omitted.[3] One can find excellent, detailed descriptions of religious objects, iconography, and ceremonial events in Lumholtz (1902), Zingg (1938), and Furst (1968), hence those subjects will be treated less thoroughly here.

Throughout this chapter, I have tried to concentrate primarily on those features in the religion most pertinent to the deer-maize-peyote complex and to the peyote hunt, the central problems at issue here.

Major Deities

The number of deities in the Huichol pantheon cannot be determined, for the number and importance of deities vary from one community to another and from one mara'akame to another. In all likelihood, no single individual could name all the deities which have been identified. Lumholtz once counted forty-seven named gods but goes on to say, "The number is actually unlimited, since every hill and every rock of peculiar shape is considered a deity" (1900:10). Lum-

[3] The extremely complex topic of the ceremonial cycle has been omitted because it is treated in great detail in the works of Lumholtz (1902) and Furst (1968). The most important feature of the ceremonial cycle for purposes here is the manner in which each event is based on the preceding one. All the events ultimately require peyote gathered by pilgrims in Wirkiuta; this feature of the ceremonial cycle is discussed in Chapters 4, 5, and 6.

holtz also points out that not all gods are "in reality" different, and that there are a few principal deities which may have as many as eight to ten different names.

Ultimately, such reductions of the deities to a few convenient categories is a subjective process dictated by the needs of each investigator and the particular interpretations held by the people among whom he worked. In the case of the present study, four large categories seem adequate: Tatewarí (Our Grandfather Fire); Tayaupá (Our Father Sun); Tamatsi Maxa Kwaxí-Kauyumari-Wawatsari (Our Elder Brother Deer Tail); and the many water, maize, and earth goddesses known collectively as Tateima (Our Mothers).

Tatewarí, Our Grandfather (Fire)

Tatewarí is perhaps the oldest god among the Huichols and is sometimes referred to as the "Old God." He was the first Huichol mara'akame and accordingly is the special deity of all mara'akate. Although all gods may be prayed to for all purposes, some deities have special powers which cause them to be favored by certain individuals for particular purposes; the association of the mara'akame with Tatewarí is perhaps the most important. Tatewarí reveals the messages and wishes of all the deities to the mara'akame, either directly in dreams and visions or indirectly through Kauyumari, the Sacred Deer Person and culture hero. Tatewarí is, in fact, the mara'akame of the gods, for he led them on the first peyote hunt and thus provided the ceremonies and myths for that event in "Ancient Times." He built the first *tuki*, or community temple, and taught the Huichols how to make proper offerings and how to behave in ways pleasing to the gods.

Tatewarí is the special protector of man. He provided the fundamentals of religious beliefs and practices and continues his benevolent services to the Huichols in multiple capacities. Through the mara'akame, he provides essential information to them concerning the wishes and predispositions of other deities, enabling man to avoid the displeasure of the gods. Tatewarí gives the mara'akame his powers to cure and retrieve lost souls. Also, Tatewarí cleanses man, returning him to his original condition of innocence and purity, the condition which must be regained before the peyote can be found. And Tatewarí sends the deer to man.

The significance of Tatewarí is moral and practical as well as spiritual and religious. Practically, Tatewarí provides warmth, makes the cooking of food possible, and he clears the fields for planting. Symbolically, he stands for companionship and security afforded by the presence of other Huichols. The Huichols' active affection for him is readily apparent; not only do they make offerings to him diligently and speak of him with reverence and gratitude, but they cherish him as well, and it is not unusual to hear a Huichol address him affectionately using the diminutives usually reserved for children. He is regarded as a Huichol possession, and when a party of Huichols sees fire being used by mestizos, Tatewarí is hailed like a companion unexpectedly encountered in a strange place, and comments are heard to the effect that "those others are borrowing the Huichol fire."

The following text was offered by Ramón to explain the significance of Tatewarí to the Huichols; it reveals the multiple functions and some of the feelings and attitudes typically associated with this major deity:

Why do we adore the one who is not of this world, whom we call Tatewarí, the one who is the Fire? We have him because we believe in him in this form. *Tai*, that is fire, only fire, flames. Tatewarí that is the Fire. That is the mara'akame from ancient times, the one who warms us, who burns the brush, who cooks our food, who hunted the deer, the peyote, that one who is with Kauyumari. We believe in him. Without him, where would we get warmth? How would we cook? All would be cold. To keep warm Our Sun Father would have to come close to the earth. And that cannot be so.

Imagine. One is in the Sierra, there where we Huichols live. One walks, one follows one's paths. Then it becomes dark. One is alone there walking, one sees nothing. What is it there in the dark? One hears something? It is not to be seen. All is cold. Then one makes camp there. One gathers a little wood, food for Tatewarí. One strikes a light. One brings out Tatewarí. Ah, what a fine thing! What warmth! What light! The darkness disappears. It is safe. Tatewarí is there to protect one. Far away, another walks. He sees it. There he is, walking all alone in the darkness, afraid perhaps. Then he sees it from far away, that light, that friendly light. A friendly thing in the dark. He says, "I am not alone. There is another Huichol. There is someone. Perhaps he has a place for me there, a little warmth." So he speaks. Tatewarí is there in the dark, making it light, making one warm, guarding one. Is it possible to live without such a thing, without Tatewarí? No, it is not possible.

Or if it is a matter of working to produce maize, squash, beans, melon. Working is not enough. We need Tatewarí. If one has a wife, she wishes to cook for one. How can one satisfy one's hunger with a pot of raw beans? With raw maize? It does not satisfy. But give these things into the hands of Tatewarí, let them be warmed by the flower of his flames, then it is well. In Ancient Times he was transformed. When the Ancient Ones brought him out, he came out as mara'akame, transformed, so that all could see him as he was. So that he could embrace Our Father when he was born. So that he could lead those Ancient Ones who were not of this world to hunt the deer, to hunt peyote. So that Kauyumari and he became companions, so that our life, our customs could be established there from Ancient Times, so long ago that no one can remember when it was.

That is why we adore him, why we have him in the center, that one who is Our Grandfather.

Tayaupá, Our Father (Sun)

In certain regions within the Huichol territory, particularly in the western section, Tayaupá, the Sun deity, is said to be at least as important as Tatewarí. Even in those areas where Tatewarí is considered more significant, the statement is frequently heard that Tayaupá is a very powerful deity. But in fact, in ceremonial behavior (such as making offerings) and in general discussions of religious matters, acknowledgment of Tayaupá is frequently absent. The situation suggests a distinctly ambivalent attitude toward this deity. Tayaupá, it seems, is considered extraordinarily potent, even dangerous to man, and he is not approached with the same easy familiarity and enthusiasm seen in the behaviors directed toward Tatewarí. Overt statements concerning the dangerous attributes of Tayaupá are heard from informants and can be found in the mythology as well. Father Sun must be kept away from the earth, it is said, for if he comes too close, he would burn it up.

The theme is by no means unique, as Lévi-Strauss points out in his discussion of the significance of fire. The cooking fire, he observes, is often regarded as a link between the sky and the earth, which prevents them from coming too close together. If man did not have fire, he suggests, the sun would have to be closer to the earth to provide heat. The conflagration which would result from the contact between celestial fire and the earth is avoided because the domestic fire mediates between the sky above and the earth below and thus saves man from the excesses of the sun (1969:298–29; first published in 1964).

It is the specific duty of Tatewarí and all the mara'akate who came after him to see to it that Father Sun stays in his place, properly distant from the earth. To ensure this, Tatewarí erected the five Brazil trees which support the four corners of the earth and the center of heaven.

Although the mara'akame has special powers which he receives from the Sun, he is not immune from its dangers. He may be harmed by the Sun, for example, when he journeys to the sky to retrieve a soul. Further, the Sun has various animals which are sacred to him but dangerous to man, particularly different kinds of poisonous snakes. Of all the deities, only the Sun sends misfortunes to man in the form of illness (especially smallpox) either as punishment or warning. This contrasts sharply with the behavior of Tatewarí, of whom it is said, "He may warn us by sending little sparks, but they are sparks that never burn one."

The Sun was born in Ancient Times to light and warm the earth by day, as Tatewarí lighted and warmed it by night. Tatewarí was already born when the ancient Animal People seized a beautiful little Huichol boy and threw him into the water to become the Sun.[4] As the boy was thrown in, the water rose up and blood came to the surface. The boy traveled down the five levels to the underworld and eventually emerged to the east in a violent burst of volcanic activity

[4] Lumholtz (1902:108) recorded a version of this story in which the young boy is thrown into the fire instead of water. This suggests that the Huichol myth concerning the origin of the Sun is, in this regard at least, similar to that found among the ancient Aztecs. Further discussion of this follows.

from the mountain called Hunaxu. It was very beautiful but very dangerous and all the animals were frightened and ran away. Tayaupá's emergence from the mountain is described by Ramón.

Ah, in those days it was if to melt the earth, when he was born. When the Sun, Our Father, was born, he was strong, he was shining, hot. When he was born, the stones began to come up, fly up, the earth was flying up, the trees were flying up. A great roaring came there on Hunaxu, the mountain that burned. He was born and the mountain exploded and the earth was shaking.

The trip from the lake through the underworld to the mountain was very dangerous for the Sun, for he had to defend himself against great serpents from the underworld who meant to devour him. The Sun was received after his birth by the First Mara'akame, who made him his sacred chair so that he could rise to the sky. The mara'akame raised the chair by his singing until the Sun was in his proper place, and then he put the sacred Brazil trees in their places at the corners and center of heaven to keep the sky and Sun where they belong. The souls of mara'akate journey after death to the heavens to live with the Sun, to protect him from dangerous animals and help assure that "Our Father travels well" in his passage through the underworld between dusk and dawn.

In the respective births of Fire and Sun one sees the previously noted ambivalence reappearing. Thus Tatewarí is brought into being gently and beautifully, as a tiny spark which grows like a flower when two sticks are rubbed together. Tayaupá, however, is born with a bloody human sacrifice and ends in a burst of volcanic violence. And Tatewarí may send sparks to touch those men who do not have pure thoughts or pure hearts, while Tayaupá may destroy the entire world.

In part this ambivalence can be interpreted as reflecting the different attitudes man has toward different states of natural forces, one beyond his control and the other domesticated. But it may also be related to historical factors, that is, to the temporal order of the arrival of the two gods in the Huichol pantheon. Tatewarí precedes the Sun; among the Huichols as in many parts of preclassic Mexico, the oldest deity identifiable is the Old Fire God represented as a wizened old man with a brazier on his head.

The possibility that the concept of the Sun deity was borrowed by the Huichols from the southern agriculturalists cannot be overlooked. The similarity between certain elements of belief and practice with regard to the Sun among the Huichols and the Aztecs is striking, especially the sacrifice of a human victim whose blood is necessary to the Sun, and the mutual dependence of man and the Sun whereby human offerings keep the Sun in the sky and in return the sun assures good crops. Further, at certain ceremonies in the spring a bull is sacrificed and his blood and heart offered to the Sun. Some elements of this ceremony, such as the eating by the mara'akame of a small portion of the bull's heart just after it has been removed from the animal, suggest that a substitution of animal for human sacrifice has occurred. The Huichols have a tradition that at the birth of the Sun deity a child had to be sacrificed to give the new-born Sun strength. This is reminiscent of Aztec practices, it may be noted. Deer blood is also offered to the Sun and images of the Sun deity and offerings intended solely for the Sun are smeared with deer blood on certain ceremonial occasions. Although it is clear from other texts that the Huichols generally regard bones as the source and focus of life, in these sacrificial ceremonies the victim's blood is the most important offering.

If the Sun deity was borrowed from the Aztecs, the ambivalence associated with the Sun would not be surprising, for he would have been a foreign element in an exceptionally well-integrated system.[5] Such an interpretation is in accord with that offered earlier which suggested that the Huichols made a relatively recent and incomplete shift to agriculture from hunting, and to the Sierra from the desert. The sun is of course a more important natural element for agriculturalists, to whose life and livelihood it is more visibly tied, than to hunters, who are more independent of seasonal changes. The scorching desert sun is a trial to hunters while the campfire in the chill night is a blessing.

Tamatsi Maxa Kwaxí-Kauyumari (Wawatsari): Our Elder Brother Deer Tail[6]

Although this interesting figure is not equivalent in importance to Tatewarí and Tayaupá, he is included in this discussion because of his significance in the deer-maize-peyote complex. Occasionally he appears as a distinct personage and at

[5] Further indication of the negative attitudes associated with the Sun deity emerges clearly in the myth cycle concerning Kieri Tewíyari, an evil datura-using sorcerer and antagonist of Kauyumari. Their epic confrontation is described in Furst and Myerhoff (1966).

[6] Wawatsari was not consistently included in these manifestations of the deer, indeed, his name was not mentioned by Ramón until 1968. It seems that Wawatsari represents the Guardian of the Deer, referred to as the "Principal Deer," and he is important as a guide to Wirikuta. Kauyumari, on the other hand, is fundamentally the deer as mediator between the mara'akame and Tatewarí; he is "chief interpreter." His affinity with the mara'akame accounts for Ramón's emphasis on him at the cost of Wawatsari. The latter might have been regarded as more important by someone who was not himself a mara'akame. Wawatsari appears very little in this account because he was not "present" on my trip to Wirikuta in 1966. Wawatsari figures more prominently in Furst's account (1972) of his peyote journey in 1968.

other times he merges with Kauyumari, the Huichol culture hero and trickster.

Kauyumari is roughly translatable as "one who does not know himself" or "one who makes others crazy."[7] There is reason to believe that he is closely modeled on an actual historical personage, perhaps an important early mara'akame who later merged with the Sacred Deer Person. The exploits of Kauyumari are often distinctly human. He is courageous but frail, and the comment is often added to myths in which his behavior is anything but admirable, "Well, of course, that happened in those days before he became sacred." In this condition Kauyumari manifests aspects of the typical American trickster-culture hero. His exploits are often irreverent, almost always clever and frequently amusing, recounted with great delight. One story described how he made possible the first sexual relationship between man and woman, thus assuring the perpetuation of the Huichol people. Kauyumari is a semidivine figure, possessing magical powers, but not a deity to be venerated or given offerings. He often appears as a trickster engaging in extravagant sexual exploits "before he became sacred." He is an inexhaustible source of humor and entertainment and in his own way is regarded as responsible for several important Huichol characteristics and practices.

Tamatsi Maxa Kwaxí alone—that is, without the appellation of Kauyumari—is one of the most important of the deities, a major participant in the original First Hunt of the gods and also the principal deity of that group collectively

[7] This translation may refer to an actual mara'akame who was unstable, epileptic, or given to fits. This would be quite possible in view of the very common manifestation of nervous disorders among shamans in general. Some authorities have even regarded such instability as the necessary condition for becoming a shaman. See Eliade (1964) and Silverman (1968).

known as Our Elder Brothers, primarily associated with hunting, and particularly with hunting of the deer. Tamatsi Maxa Kwaxí is symbolized by the deer tail which is frequently placed in family oratories (*xíriki*) and community temples (*tuki*), along with the deer horns of Kauyumari. Together the horns and the tail of the deer symbolize Maxa Kwaxí-Kauyumari, but Kauyumari alone is thought of as the Sacred Deer Person, the anthropomorphized tutelary animal of mara'akame. One of the most important tasks of Kauyumari is his service as intermediary between the mara'akame and the gods.

As a culture hero, Maxa Kwaxí-Kauyumari gave many important gifts to the Huichols, protected them against enemies and evil sorcerers, and aided them in obtaining the peyote and the deer in the First Times.

Kauyumari, it is related in Huichol myths, appeared first as Maxa Kwaxí but lacking his horns. These he received when the sacred feathers of Tatewarí were placed on his head and subsequently became antlers. For this reason sacred arrows are worn on the head and equated with horns on many ritual occasions. It is through the arrow horns that Huichols on the peyote hunt communicate with those remaining at home and through them that the mara'akame communicates with the deities, especially Tatewarí. Maxa Kwaxí learned the shamanic arts of curing, soul retrieval, and magical flight from Tatewarí and in turn uses them on behalf of his people.

The many manifestations of Kauyumari and Maxa Kwaxí can be quite perplexing to the non-Huichol. Kauyumari is embodied in the mara'akame's basket of sacred objects, which in this context is known as Takwatsi Kauyumari. He may be represented as a pair of deer horns literally or figuratively placed on or tied around the mara'akame's basket. Or the deer horns may appear alone, tied to some part of an individual's costume or gear, as when they are attached to the mara'akame's bags and baskets containing offerings for the peyote. Here they serve as a guide, bringing information from Tatewarí to the mara'akame as to where to find the peyote. A deer tail may also be used in art or ritual to indicate the presence of Maxa Kwaxí, and in the construction of the *tuki* when deer horns are mounted on the roof for protection, with a deer tail placed between the horns.

Several writers have spoken somewhat loosely of these associations involving Maxa Kwaxí as the Sacred Deer Person, Kauyumari and the mara'akame as "transformations" or "transfigurations." Such terms are misleading, for this is not a case of one object or person becoming another by changing form but rather a case of differing manifestations of the same phenomenon.[8] No essential change is involved, only an altered appearance. The matter is explained thus:

> We call him Kauyumari. We call him Maxa Kwaxí. It is all one. Kauyumari aids Tatewarí. He aids Tayaupá. He guides the mara'akame in what must be done. So that the peyote can be hunted. So that the mara'akame can take the peyote from the horns of the deer, there in Wirikuta. Ah, the horns of Kauyumari, those are the arrows of Tatewarí. They are the same. When the mara'akame calls him, he comes. He is there, in the mountains. He is called with the arrows. He awakens, he comes when the mara'akame calls him, as the deer, as the Takwatsi, as the arrows. Kauyumari, that is the Sacred Deer Person, the companion of Tatewarí.

One of the most interesting aspects of this chimeral figure is his strong resemblance to the Master or Owner of the Spe-

[8] On the peyote hunt, both Tamatsi Maxa Kwaxí and Kauyumari participate, the former identity assumed by one of the peyote pilgrims and the latter manifested in the deer horns carried by the leader of the hunt.

cies found so often among hunting peoples; he is examined in this light later in the discussion.

Other Lesser Male Deities

Numerous other male deities hold less important places in the pantheon as a whole but they figure significantly in the deer-maize-peyote complex and are frequently represented by the pilgrims in the peyote hunt.

Tsakaimuka is a patron deity of the deer hunt, the "Snarer of the Deer," and was among those Ancient Ones present during the First Deer Hunt. Watákame, who was also present, is the Clearer of the Fields, the Sower, the Burner for the Second Time, the Cleaner of the Maize. It was he who was saved by Nakawé, Our Grandmother Growth, when the deluge swept all others away, and who through his labors and his marriage to 'Xuturi Iwiékame, Our Mother of the Children, replenishes the land and its people. Another figure always represented on the peyote journey is Tatutsí, Our Great Grandfather. During the peyote hunt he is a principal assistant to Tatewarí in the latter's role as First Mara'akame. As such, Tatutsí walks directly behind or sits to the left of the mara'akame who is Tatewarí.[9] And Tatutsí administers to the mara'akame all the rituals which the mara'akame has first administered to the peyote pilgrims.

[9] The Huichols generally equate the left side with the sinister, the underworld, the dangerous, and so forth. The location of the principal assistant on the mara'akame's left during the peyote hunt is probably a reversal of ordinary location, just as on the peyote hunt the fire is circled to the left, or counterclockwise, whereas it is ordinarily circled to the right. This reversal is compounded when the pilgrims say that they are circling "to the right, always to the right" although in their actions they can be observed to be circling to the left. Fur-

Tateima, Our Mothers, Female Deities

Of the female deities, called "goddesses of earth and water" by Lumholtz, the major figure is Nakawé, and the lesser, numerous water and rain deities are collectively known as Tateima, Our Mothers. All the female gods, together, are responsible for rain, earth, growth, and maize.

Nakawé, the One Who Came First, has engendered much confusion among ethnographers and linguists. Her name has been translated as Our Grandmother Growth, but this may be a proper name which cannot be translated. Nakawé was present at the beginning of the world before the others appeared and it was she who remade the world after the deluge, first by sending the macaw to scoop up the mountains with his beak while the earth was still soft, and then, with her magical staff, by recreating all the animals and plants which had been drowned in the flood. At that time she saved a single man, Watákame, the Clearer of the Fields, along with a little black She-Dog. With both of these she shared her canoe. After the flood, the little dog turned into a girl, who became Tatei Xuturi Iwiékame, a water deity and goddess of children. Watákame and Xuturi Iwiékame then became the parents of the new people who came to populate the world. Nakawé is depicted as a very old woman with long hair who walks all alone in the barrancas of the Sierra, leaning on her staff. Pilgrims may visit her home in a sacred cave near Santa Catarina asking for long life, the health of children, and good crops.[10]

---

ther discussion of the significance of these reversals of ordinary placement is found in Chapters 5 and 6.

[10] Nakawé is probably the female counterpart of Tatewarí in that both are the oldest, perhaps original and principal, deities in the Huichol pantheon.

Tatei 'Utuanaka may be seen as the major Maize Mother and is especially important here for her participation in the First Peyote Hunt. Nakawé and Tatei 'Utuanaka, along with Tatei Yurienaka, Our Mother Earth Softened by Rain, are associated with maize and earth. These may be usefully distinguished from the many female rain and water deities, the most important of whom are collectively called Tatei Matinieri, Where Our Mothers Dwell, a cluster of permanent water holes in the desert of Zacatecas, close to Wirikuta, containing the Sacred Water which must be gathered in the course of the peyote hunt. At this place are found the dwellings of Tatei Kaxiwarí, Tatei Hamuxa and Tatei Xapawiyékame, all of whom are represented in the form of snakes and all of whom were participants in the First Peyote Hunt. The Huichols distinguish between these freshwater deities who dwell in water holes in the high deserts, springs, and rivers, and Tatei Haramara, the deified Pacific Ocean. The latter figures primarily in those ceremonies which do not concern us here; indeed, salt water and salt in all forms is strictly and specifically excluded from all events and to all participants even remotely connected with the success of the peyote hunt.

Other female deities include: Tatei Kúkurú 'Uimari, Our Mother Dove Girl, who was also mother of the boy who became the Sun; Tatei Wérika 'Uimari, Our Mother Eagle Girl; Tatei Nétsika, the five maize girls who are the daughters of Kúkurú 'Uimari; Tatei Wérika, associated with the Sun and often depicted as a two-headed eagle; Tatei Niwetúkame, patroness of children, who determines the sex of a child before it is born and gives it its soul (*kupuri*).

The few moon and stellar deities are weakly developed compared with those associated with the sun, fire, maize, deer, peyote, water, earth, and growth. The deities discussed thus far are those who are central to the deer-maize-peyote complex and are represented by peyote pilgrims in their annual recapitulation of the First Hunt.

Relationships among the Deities

Although nearly all deities are referred to and addressed by kinship terms, it may not be assumed that any strict genealogical relations are thought to exist among them or between them and living men by the Huichols.[11] As previously mentioned, most of the terms used in connection with the deities are employed only in a ritual context and differ from the everyday kinship terms used among men with each other. The relationship terms used in sacred contexts may be understood as the "Ancient Ones" or "Our Venerated Ancestors" (Grimes and Grimes 1962). Urukame and Kakauyarixi are two generic terms meaning Ancient Ancestors. Before the ancestors were the Héwixi, the mythological Animal People who were destroyed in the great flood. Apii was the shaman-chief who "brought out" Tatewarí from wood, in which he existed before he was made manifest.

The Huichols provide a warning against the practice used by some anthropologists of attempting to find a one-to-one

[11] It should be emphasized that the relationship terms used in a sacred setting have been rendered as "deities" and "gods" for lack of a more suitable English or Huichol equivalent. There is no indigenous term for deity and, as will be seen, these supernatural figures are not "deified" in the sense of being greatly removed from man and everyday life, nor are they worshiped. Like "praying" and "acknowledging" the four directions, the problems of translation for culturally nonequivalent concepts are formidable. For convenience, "deities" and "gods" are used throughout this text but they should be understood by reference to their context as much as possible.

relationship between social organization and ideology or mythology, with the latter seen as a direct and exact projection of the former. Not only are kinship terms used quite figuratively by the Huichols toward their deities but distinctions which are not important in what Geertz (1965) would call the "lived-in-order" are quite significant in the "thought-of" order. Thus the principle of age or seniority is stressed in Huichol social organization but not as much as in religion, where "Elder Brothers" constitute an important category of deities.[12] On other occasions the categories "grandfathers" and "great grandfathers" are collapsed or used interchangeably depending on the context.

Earlier I touched on the affinity between grandfather and grandchild and pointed out that the Fire, toward whom the Huichols have positive emotions, is known as Our Grandfather, while the Sun, toward whom they have ambivalent feelings, is Our Father. The ambivalence toward the father reappears in what might be called the "orphan" theme, which is evident in a number of myths. In many Huichol texts the young boy heroes are described as "orphans," which usually means they have no father and live alone with the mother. Such is the condition of the boy who sacrificed himself to become the Sun, the boy who saved his mother and all the Huichols from starvation by obtaining maize from Tatei Kúkurú Uimari, the boy who obtained fire from the Animal People. It is said that most mara'akate are also orphans.

A number of interpretations of these features may be offered, one of them historical. Probably Huichol women and children were often left alone in camp by their hunting hus-

[12] Succession to the position of elder of a rancho is usually determined on the basis of seniority, but in other matters concerning inheritance of property and authority age is not consistently stressed.

bands in precontact times.[13] The only older men with whom the children would have sustained relations would be their grandfathers, or men in their grandfathers' generation. During the colonial period this condition would have been exacerbated when the Spanish removed adult Indian men from their families for enforced labor or killed parties of hunters or insurgents whom they encountered. Under these circumstances, the Huichol "orphan boy" would naturally have closer, more sustained relations with his grandfather and could be expected to have rather vague and ambivalent attitudes concerning his missing father.

Another interpretation may be suggested on the basis of Radcliffe-Brown's (1950) well-known observations concerning the merging of alternate generations and the antagonism between adjacent generations. He has observed that in Africa and many other parts of the world children are expected to demonstrate reserved, formal behavior in the presence of the father but are permitted more informal, familiar behavior toward the grandfather. Radcliffe-Brown finds that the relationship between grandparent and grandchild stresses an affectionate rather than authoritative component; it may even approach equality and this is often indicated by reciprocal kinship terms. Such is the case among the Huichols, where "grandfather gives the grandchild his name," where they "call each other the same, for are they not of the same flesh?" Thus it is not surprising that the much-loved Tatewarí is known as Our Grandfather while Tayaupá, Our Father, inspires more fear and respect than affection.

[13] When specifically questioned on this point, Ramón said that in the old days of hunting, the men were gone for perhaps a month at a time. On what kind of evidence he bases this opinion is not clear, however.

The deities are not specialized in the sense that one must pray to one for one thing and to another for something else. Naturally, individual Huichols and mara'akate have favorites among the gods, and in the various regions the gods differ in importance to some degree. But any deity may be asked for all that is necessary to life. Requests are usually specific and basic, for good health, good fortune, children, safety, and so forth. A cumulative principle here is detectable in that the more deities one addresses and gives offerings to, the better one's chances for success.

The Mara'akame

There seems to be an inverse relationship between the simplicity of the religious division of labor and the large size of the Huichol pantheon, for only one religious specialist is truly significant—the mara'akame. He acts as, and is variously referred to as, shaman, priest, healer, and leader. As will be seen, he fills all these roles, and any single nonindigenous term for his role is incomplete and occasionally misleading.

The Huichol mara'akame has been a key figure in maintaining the integrity of his society. He is the principal actor in the drama of Huichol survival. His part in Huichol life transcends the usual shamanic functions found in primitive societies and approaches the more public, formal activities associated with the role of priest. The mara'akame attends the sick, divining the causes of illness with the assistance of Kauyumari, who acts as his tutelary spirit. The standard shamanic techniques are employed—blowing smoke, spitting, sucking, massaging, and so forth. His powers of curing are the result of the special relations which obtain between him and the deities. The mara'akame, like all classical shamans, has the gift of access to the other worlds. He is able to transform himself into various animals; he has the power to make the magical flight to the land of the gods and can follow the souls of the dead to the underworld. All these magical skills are used on behalf of an individual patient in curing ceremonies or for the welfare of all his people on more public occasions. In these ways the Huichol mara'akame is a typical shaman.

But in the Huichol *tuki* services, in the annual ceremonial cycle, in the making of offerings, in presiding over life crises, he acts more as priest than as shaman, for here he is officiating at recurrent, ritualized public events on behalf of the entire group. On these occasions he performs as "singer-priest," embodying and promoting traditional values, jealously guarding the Huichol cultural heritage and identity—admonishing, teaching, modeling, explaining, and advocating "all that it means to be Huichol."

Eliade (1964) defines the shaman as a magicoreligious specialist in the sacred who acts primarily on behalf of the individual at times of private misfortune, illness, and unscheduled crises and who derives his special powers from an intimate, informal relationship with the spirits whose assistance is given through the mediation of a tutelary animal. The mara'akame is a shaman, according to this definition. And if we use Eliade's (1964) characterization of a priest as a religious specialist who serves a congregated public on recurring occasions of general concern, acting as formal and official intermediary between man and the deities, then the mara'akame is also a priest. This unique figure, then, is a shaman-priest, or mara'akame.

There have been varying estimates concerning the number of mara'akate practicing among the Huichols. At one time Lumholtz (1902:21) stated that one fourth of all Huichol men were shamans. Estimates made by mara'akate themselves are probably more reliable and reasonable. One widely respected mara'akame stated that there are nine mara'akate in the community San Andrés Cohamiata or about one for every eight or ten ranchos, which he felt was probably not atypical. This means there would be around eight to ten per community, or fifty in all. But one cannot place too much faith in even these figures since the term mara'akame is sometimes used loosely to refer to individuals who are at varying stages of completion of the minimal five-year period of preparation required to be a full-fledged shaman-priest.

Each of the five Huichol regions in the Sierra has the services of several recognized full-fledged mara'akate, individuals who enjoy great prestige and who conduct the ceremonies and rituals during the annual cycle of religious events. In the course of these ceremonies their main task is the chanting of an enormous body of sacred myths, which may last several days and nights. The leading mara'akame also functions as the priest at the main *tuki* in the region, officiating at the offering of sacrifices. And of course, a mara'akame leads the pilgrims on the annual journey to Wirikuta.

The manner of selection of a mara'akame is not entirely clear; however, there appear to be certain "tendencies" which on further study might turn out to be valid generalizations. For example, while the office is described by informants and in the literature on the Huichols as not inherited, it appears to run in families, often in alternate generations. Long-range observation alone would make it possible to ascertain the degree and kind of patterning. Individuals of either sex may become mara'akate, for although females in this position are encountered relatively rarely, at least one is presently practicing and others are recalled. Informants note other tendencies—the mara'akame is usually an orphan (meaning he has no father), and is frequently the youngest or an only child. All these features are typical of shamans, according to Eliade (1964). But above all, the mara'akame must be qualified as an individual. Obviously the candidate needs great intelligence, strength, and endurance. One mara'akame (the woman shaman previously referred to) was observed to chant without stopping for thirty-six hours, a feat which evidently is not unusual. And all mara'akate must go without sleep and consume a bare minimum of food and water while enduring great physical exertion during the peyote hunt. The candidate must have an extraordinary memory to command the incredible number of songs, myths, and chants. Great social sensitivity and a deep and detailed knowledge of psychology, social relations, and medicine are necessary for his success in curing. The aspiring mara'akame is profoundly spiritual, and willing to sacrifice the physical and material satisfactions available to others in return for a life of intense dedication and religious service. The enormous social prestige and sense of uniqueness enjoyed by the mara'akame, however, offsets the many required sacrifices. This was succinctly put by Ramón: "The mara'akame is rich, very rich, the most fortunate man of all, but he has very few things. He is a poor man, but he is rich."

Another attribute described as essential for a successful mara'akame is his self-control and psychological equilibrium. Eliade (1964) specifies the shaman's need for psychological control and self-mastery, for his profession requires continual and intense attainment of abnormal psychological states, namely, magical activities, trances, and visions. Eliade is convincing in arguing against the common view that shamans are usually neurotic, unstable, epileptic, and so forth. Eliade points out that in the course of rigorous training and dedication the person who was perhaps initially neurotic learns to control his frenzy, to manipulate his proclivity to visions, fits, and trances, and to use it in service of his group. Thus he can no longer be regarded as "sick," for his profession constitutes his cure.[14]

Eliade describes the shaman as one who is above all a "connecting" figure, bridging several worlds for his people. He travels between this world and the underworld and the heavens. He transforms himself into an animal, talks with ghosts, the dead, the deities. He dies and revives. He brings back knowledge from the shadow realm, thus linking his people to the spirits and places which were once accessible to them but from which they have been severed.

The mara'akame like most shamans is chosen by divine election. The method of selection is typical; a call is received from one of the deities, usually Tatewarí. The call is most likely to come to a young boy, often an orphan, solitary and unusual even though still a child. The myth which describes the boy chosen to become the Sun also contains this description of a boy likely to become a mara'akame.

Ah, that little boy, he knew something. He was very pleasing, that boy, for he was already chosen, he had a sign. He was made for that. Those others did not know this, that is why they were

[14] The same point has been made by a psychiatrist (Silverman 1968) who compares the shaman in a primitive society with the schizophrenic in our own and finds very similar cognitive processes with entirely different psychological and social outcomes. The shaman becomes a useful citizen in a community which provides him with a socially acceptable role for the expression and utilization of his peculiarities. This provision completely alters the development of what remains a serious impediment in our society, which instead of providing roles for the unstable, systematically retracts them by removing the schizophrenic from the social structure.

rejected. He, that one, he knew something. He was an orphan. He had no father, just a mother. He was poor. And look where he came to be—the best in the world. He was very much alone, he walked alone. Very serious. He spoke to no one. He played only for himself. He was already chosen for this. He would eat and play and go into the fields all by himself. He loved his mother but he was by himself. He hardly spoke. That is how he was. He looked into himself.

The call comes to the young boy spontaneously in a vision or dream, without any physiological inducement, without deprivation or drugs.[15] But his success in fulfilling the call is far from assured, and actual assumption of the office may not occur until he is well into middle age.

As a boy and young man the aspirant mara'akame acquires extensive religious knowledge informally, as do most of his fellows. There is no apprenticeship as such, although he may seek knowledge of songs and myths from older mara'akate, especially if there is one in his family. He witnesses many cures and participates in many ceremonies, often assisting with the chanting and preparations. Many Huichols have extensive religious knowledge, but the mara'akame must master a truly enormous body of material. He must enjoy the esteem of his society. He must be respected, a man of intellect, self-control, judgment, and in addition, should have considerable skills in singing, storytelling, and playing the violin. Ability in the plastic arts is also appropriate, for he alone decorates

[15] Ramón's "call," described in the first chapter, came when he was about eight years old, in the form of a miraculous recovery from a snake bite. At this time he did indeed become more solitary, reflective, and grave, more oriented to spiritual than mundane affairs. The same pattern was identified in the "call" and response of a Luiseño shaman, described in "Shaman of Rincon" (Myerhoff 1966).

the deer horns, and his ritual offerings should be especially well made.[16]

The man who wishes to become a mara'akame begins a specific probation period when he feels ready to undertake five consecutive years of making certain sacrifices and leading a group of pilgrims to Wirikuta in a successful search for peyote. His sacrifices include five years of fidelity to his wife, during which time he foregoes all love affairs. He undertakes frequent fasts and abstentions from salt and sleep, according to instructions he receives from Tatewarí in his visions.[17]

The hardships involved in becoming a mara'akame are severe, particularly the leadership of the peyote hunts, each of which is more taxing and strenuous than the last because each year he "takes on more of the weight of his people." To vow to become a mara'akame and fail is a serious matter, jeopardizing the aspirant and those around him. Those who fail are in danger of becoming sorcerers, for they have acquired some magical power but have not demonstrated the strength and knowledge to control it. The pressure to complete training once undertaken is great, internally and externally, and that

[16] To these requirements which represent conventional Huichol values, Ramón added his own provisos; the mara'akame these days should be bilingual and, if possible, literate, to protect his people from "those land-grabbing Spaniards with their maps and titles." He should learn the ways of the city and the outside world because he needs to be as proficient in that realm as in the realm of the dead and the gods, in order to protect and serve his people.

[17] A mara'akame needs special strength, obviously, and he is aided in this by the endowment of five souls instead of the usual one. He is given these additional souls when he is chosen by Tatewarí as a small child; without this gift, he would not have the power to undertake the duties associated with the role. When he dies, his souls may be passed on to another emergent mara'akame, thus a continuity is maintained. This is analogous to the reincarnation of mara'akate from each other's bones in the form of rock crystals discussed in detail by Furst (1967).

few succeed compared with those who aspire is due to the great intellectual, psychological, and social demands made of this sacred leader of the Huichols.[18]

Ritual Elements [19]

Among the Huichols, as perhaps among most deeply religious peoples, ritual elements are nearly endless in number and few are unitary. It is almost always possible to break

[18] Ramón consistently described the mara'akame's training period as five years, that is, five successful trips as leader of peyote pilgrims.

In the spring of 1971, however, Ramón and Lupe visited the Los Angeles County Museum of Natural History to demonstrate their arts and crafts, and I had the opportunity to share my home with them for a short time and to have uninterrupted talk about matters I had been pondering since our first meeting. I uncovered some unexpected layers of Ramón's religious philosophy. Some of this material, I suspect, he had simply been unwilling to discuss earlier, but I believe that he had developed or learned some ideas only recently. He spoke for the first time of the end of the world, when Wirikuta would be regained permanently. He elaborated on the relations between peyote pilgrims, and he discussed the advanced training of the mara'akame after he had completed five successful peyote hunts. We went over my texts and pictures from the peyote hunt we had undertaken together and he explicated many matters and offered additional interpretations and corrections. At that time he explained that there was another "level" of the mara'akame's training, that after an additional five years of study, primarily through peyote visions in Wirikuta, he would "understand more." Perhaps this is why he included Wawatsari in the 1968 trip but not in 1966, and gave more attention to the passage into Wirikuta in the later journey. Evidently his knowledge was growing, but this would not continue indefinitely —after ten years "all was known," he said.

[19] The theoretical problems of defining, delimiting, and identifying a ritual and separating it from ceremony and symbol are enormous and are taken up further in the last chapter of this work. A working definition of ritual is used here as follows: a particular action embedded in a sacred context, employing a symbol or symbolic object and set apart from ordinary actions by its rigid, repetitive, unvarying character. This definition was drawn primarily from Goody (1961).

them down into smaller and more numerous constituent actions. Therefore, I will apply here the same principle of selection employed throughout this work—and will consider only those rituals observed to be most relevant in the peyote-deer-maize complex.

Three rituals concerning the fire are especially prominent: circling, cleansing, and feeding. Circling the fire is from left to right in single file, led by the mara'akame. Whenever the fire is circled, those present maintain a precise order. This theme of ordering and placement occurs again and again and is closely associated with the Huichol sense of propriety and balance. The reason for the circuit was explained by Ramón this way:

> We all form a circle around Tatewarí. One who wishes to have more life, who wishes to show love for Tatewarí, who wishes to venerate well, circles around Tatewarí. And why do we venerate him? Because he is Fire, because he is the First Mara'akame. It was he who was there when the Sun was born. He taught those Ancient Ones everything. He led them on that journey to Wirikuta. He makes warmth and cooks our food.

In other words, the circling ritual is an act of gratitude, affection, and respect like a genuflection or clasped hands in our usage. Tatewarí can cleanse and purify. Peyote pilgrims and all those who wish to be in a state of purity pass their clothing over the fire, turning their cuffs and pockets inside out. The mara'akame may brush them with his sacred plumes, motioning the accumulated filth into the fire, where it is destroyed. This ritual is also employed during the pre-peyote hunt "confession" (described in Chapter 4) when all sexual transgressions are revealed so that the mara'akame may brush these events into the fire. At the same time, he places a knot

The pilgrims circling Tatewarí, venerating him. "We all form a circle around Tatewarí, so one walks around him, venerating him." So say the pilgrims, for whom circling the fire is a prominent ritual and an expression of devotion.

in a cord, one for each transgression, and destroys these events by burning the cord, thus returning the confessant to a state of ritual cleanliness and innocence.

Feeding Tatewarí may be regarded either as communion or as an offering and partakes of both of these more general categories. A small part of all that is eaten, drunk, consumed, or used when away from home on a sacred mission, such as the deer hunt or the search for peyote, is preserved and shared with Tatewarí on returning. In addition, twigs from the place to which one has traveled are saved and given to Tatewarí on reentering the home territory, and this too is called feeding Tatewarí.[20]

Sharing and communion rituals are very common among the Huichols and at every ceremony all participants distribute food to each other. The point was much stressed during the peyote hunt—everything which passed one's lips was shared three ways: some for the four directions and the center, some for Tatewarí, and some for each of the people present.[21] This sharing may be done quite casually and gaily—during feasts, for example—or with the utmost formality as when during the peyote hunt each of the participants carefully selected his finest specimen of peyote and placed a small piece of it in the mouth of each of his companions. The same pattern recurs frequently and in many forms. The function of this ritual sharing is a basic one; as stated by Ramón, "We do this because now we are one, now we are in accord." The "we" here refers to Tatewarí, the cardinal directions of the cosmos, the peyote-deer, the mara'akame, and the *peyoteros*, all of whom constitute a momentary community by virtue of the ritual.

Offering and sacrifices take many forms; the most dramatic, the sacrifice of animals on major ceremonial occasions, has been mentioned. In addition, one may classify as an offering the many sacrifices and privations undergone for various occasions. All those who go on the peyote hunt give up salt from the time they start preparations for the trip until the

[20] Returning to the fire remnants of all one has eaten while in Wirikuta has considerable symbolic importance and is discussed in more detail later.

[21] This emphasis on sharing may be still another indication of a recent hunting past for the Huichol. The importance of sharing among hunters is self-evident in view of the relative infrequency with which large game is encountered among most hunting peoples and in view of the impossibility of storing large quantities of meat.

end of the dry season ceremonies. Extramarital sexual relations are forsworn for various lengths of time, by the aspirant mara'akame as well as by the entire group of *peyoteros*, and also before planting and during the deer hunt. This is a grave deprivation for the generally permissive and affectionate Huichols. And the peyote pilgrims forego all but the bare minimum of food, sleep, bathing, water, and rest during this arduous undertaking. Even those who remain behind are bound by some of these strictures—forswearing salt, sex, and hearty meals.

More ordinary offerings are made in the innumerable forms of sacred objects, foods, and beverages offered to the deities in the *xíriki:* among the more common are *nawa*, deer soup, deer tamales, peyote, chocolate, candles, decorated coins, votive gourd bowls, tobacco, maize, sacred arrows, plumes, sacred water, and wool-yarn paintings.

Another very common ritual action is the "acknowledging" of the four cardinal directions and the center (usually up, sometimes up and down). This may be done by waving ceremonial plumes in the four directions and center or by spraying or scattering food and drink in each direction. The gesture looks very much like censing and occasionally like making the sign of the Christian cross in the air or on the human body. On the peyote hunt, for example, the plant is held up to the cardinal directions on the body (touching forehead, eyes, throat and breast) and though it very much resembles Christian crossing, it cannot be interpreted as related to it in any way.[22]

Several interpretations of the significance of the directions

[22] In addition to signifying "directions" on the body, each of these parts—forehead (specifically the fontanelle), eyes, throat (specifically voice box), and breast (specifically heart)—has further symbolic significance; this is discussed later.

in Huichol religion are possible. Concern with the directions has long been prevalent throughout Meso America and in American Indian cultures. The Huichols, too, believe that four sacred Brazil trees hold up the corners of the world and keep the sun from falling into the earth. The inclusion of the center along with the four directions probably accounts for or at least is related to the sacred Huichol number five. Naturally this directional orientation is expressed in many forms, resulting in the replication and intertwining so characteristic of ritual and belief. For example, the Huichols achieve the proper arrangement of the fire by crossing two logs on east-west and north-south axes. At the center, where the logs intersect, they carve a small shallow depression out of the earth. This is spoken of by the Huichol pilgrims as "the cavity of the world." It is a doorway to the center, and Ancient Ones come and go through it. One may see this interest in the center as a manifestation of the ubiquitous *axis mundi*, the pole which pierces the layers of the cosmos, a theme with which shamans all over the world are concerned since in their magical flight they ascend and descend these connecting rods. Or, following the suggestion concerning the shaman's professional concern with being balanced between two points—that is, at the center—the center here appears to symbolize the conjunction of the layers of the world.

On another level, there are rituals in various parts of the world whose purpose is more narrowly "placement" or "location," and Huichol rituals concerning the directions may be one of these. Such rituals structure and define an otherwise limitless and chaotic universe and go farther than mere delimitation; in this case, they place the Huichol in the center of it all. It is possible that this ritual—like that of carefully placing individuals in a particular order for ceremonial processions, fire circling, placing offerings in their proper places before the deities—achieves a kind of resting state, a sense of completion and precision. Perhaps it was something like this that Lévi-Strauss referred to when he said:

> The thought we call primitive is founded on this demand for order. . . .
>
> It could even be said that being in their place is what makes [things] sacred for if they were taken out of their place, even in thought, the entire order of the universe would be destroyed. Sacred objects therefore contribute to the maintenance of order in the universe by occupying the place allocated them [1966:10; first published 1962].

Lévi-Strauss's analysis of objects applies equally to individuals and deities in the Huichol case. Another related example is found in Douglas' (1966) discussion of the sense of purity achieved by observing the proper placement of objects. We reorder our environment to make it conform to our ideas, to make unity of experience. That which is out of place is contaminated, and impure, she points out. It follows that putting things in their proper place will be an important ritual in establishing them as sacred.

Of all Huichol ritual behaviors, fire circling and acknowledgment of the four cardinal directions and the center seemed the most frequently enacted, at times operating as what might be called "filler"—bridging the end of one part of a ceremony and the beginning of the next. These rituals opened and closed major ceremonies, tied the parts together, and provided something to do to get through occasional awkward pauses when it was not clear exactly what was to happen next.

Major Huichol religious rituals involve singing, dancing,

chanting, and perhaps praying. Singing and chanting are important in every ceremony; anyone may sing, accompanying himself or others on violin, rattle, or guitar, and anyone may dance. Frequently, the mara'akame is especially skilled in these matters and will lead the activities, but everyone seems to know all the songs and stories, none of which are secular. At times the mara'akame, seated in his sacred chair and aided by one or two assistants, chants the myths which justify and explain the ceremonies being performed; in these instances participation is less general and the tone more formal. Whether something which might be called "praying" actually occurs is open to question. There is oral communication between man and the deities but it is not in the form of supplication, and the attitude with which it is undertaken is not one of humility or awe, though it is often solemn. Our term "prayer" is perhaps better replaced by "invocation," "acknowledgment," or "communication." The Huichols use terms such as "adoration" and "veneration" in Spanish but these also seem rather inappropriate to the nature of the activity for which they are used. "Prayer" is used in what follows for lack of a more precise term.

Another form of relating to the gods will be discussed at length later, that is, "becoming the gods," representing the most intense form of human-supernatural communication possible. So much of Huichol religion eludes our Western vocabulary, based as it is on profoundly different premises and goals, that semantics is a perpetual problem.

Sacred Objects and Religious Paraphernalia

The Huichols erect two types of religious buildings—the small oratories, *xíriki*, (local or family god houses) and the *tuki* (community temple). The *xíriki* resembles an ordinary

Huichol house, and there may be one or more on each rancho. Here offerings are made and the souls of deceased relatives who have returned as rock crystals are kept; here one finds the gourds of sacred water, offerings, deer horns and tails, musical instruments, staffs of civil officials, and the like. Evidently, the sacredness of the *xíriki* is not affected by the presence of strangers, for it may be used as a guesthouse for passersby. The *xíriki* have no furnishings except for the *niwetari* or ceremonial shelf which serves as a kind of altar for sacred objects and offerings. Offerings are also stuck into the walls and roof. The entrance to the *xíriki* often faces east. On individual ranchos, a *xíriki* may be used for any deity or ceremony, but in association with the *tuki* in the larger community centers each one is dedicated to a particular deity.

The *tuki* is constructed along the same lines as the *xíriki* but is generally much larger, typically thirty to forty feet in diameter.[23] There are only about fifteen to twenty of these large temples in the Huichol territory, while there are hundreds of local *xíriki*. For the large, community-wide ceremonies during which the *tuki* is used, several temporary *xíriki* are erected in a semicircle to the east side of the *tuki*. The principal guardian of the *tuki* is Tatewarí, whose fireplace stands between the entrance on the east side of the temple and the "sacred cavity" in the center. While chanting inside the *tuki*, the mara'akame keeps the fire between himself and the rising sun, representing the distance necessary to keep the sun in its place.

On top of the *tuki* and *xíriki* are deer horns of Kauyumari.

[23] The *tuki* has sometimes been called the *calihuey*, a Spanish corruption of the Aztec *huei-calli*, meaning big house or temple. The term was evidently picked up by the Huichols from Spanish missionaries.

The mara'akame chanting inside the structure communicates with the deities by means of these horns, which are placed "so that one can hear what Kauyumari says and follow his instructions, because without that the mara'akame would be completely in the dark, there inside."

The *'uweni* or shamanic chair provides the mara'akame with his "sacred place" during his chants at ceremonies. This round seat with a backrest bordered with deerskin displays woven designs which represent the five-petaled "flower" that is the symbol for peyote. The chair is made of bamboo strips attached to a base with large chunks of resin. While seated in this chair, the mara'akame gazes into the fire and has his visions from Tatewarí. To facilitate this communication, the Huichols may provide the deities with identical miniature chairs and lay offerings upon them.

The chair has additional power because the branches of different trees are used for its four supports; the alternation of "strong" and "weak" trees constitutes a closed circle which connects these opposed properties so that together they form a balanced whole. The *'uweni* is the only indigenous and usually the sole piece of furniture found among the Huichols. When traveling to various ranchos to conduct ceremonies, the mara'akate carry their chair on their backs. Their assistants sometimes sit on backless bamboo stools. The *takwatsi* (Kauyumari) is the basket in which the mara'akame keeps his "utensils," an oblong, woven basket with a fitted lid, approximately a foot long, three or four inches deep and wide, and large enough to accommodate his plumes and arrows snugly.

The mara'akame's plumes or ceremonial arrows (*muvieri*), like the *takwatsi* and *'uweni*, have a secular counterpart, nearly identical in appearance with the sacred object. The ordinary hunting arrow is feathered longitudinally, but the ceremonial arrow has a bundle of hawk, eagle, or turkey feathers tied to it. Power objects such as rattles from rattlesnakes or miniature deer snares may also be attached to the feathers. The arrows are used also in cleansing rituals and in curing.

There are ten arrows in the full complement of the mara'akame's utensils, five major ones for singing ceremonies and five minor ones for curing. Like most sacred objects these were "people" in ancient times.

The pervasiveness of the arrow suggests that it has a generalized or multiple-purpose power, for it is used on many occasions with different effects. For example, people stick arrows in the headbands of women and children for protection. They are left behind in sacred places such as Wirikuta, caves, water holes, and roofs of *tukis* or *xírikis*, and Huichols use them to signify the presence of Kauyumari. Mara'akate may use the arrow to bring rain or to remove the spell of a sorcerer. The arrow is explicitly identified with the horns of Kauyumari. The latter, the myths tell, first got his horns when Tatewarí placed his ceremonial arrows on Kauyumari's head, and it is through these arrows and horns that Kauyumari communicates with Tatewarí. The association between arrows, feather, and flight symbolism so often found in a shamanic complex is clear.

One of the most significant aspects of any religion is the world view it formulates, implicitly and explicitly. Such formulations are most conspicuous in major rituals and in particular in the symbols around which they are built. I now turn to one ritual, the peyote hunt, to examine the events which comprise it and ultimately the meanings it conveys through the deer, the maize, and the peyote symbols which figure so prominently in that event.

CHAPTER 4

The Peyote Hunt as an Event

And as it is a unity that Uru 'Tsata and Tsinurawe wanted, those names that we call them through Tatewarí, we want to give them the offerings so that they will know everything, so that they will see everything as it is. Because they like it, they like it very much, our story, our symbols, our customs, everything. If it is that they are of another race, that does not interest us. What interests us is that they are a part of us, that they have become this way among us indigenous Huichols of Mexico.

Ramón Medina Silva

The peyote hunt is the central ceremony in the Huichol religious calendar and the pivotal event which unites the Huichols with one another, with their deities, and forges into a single complex the deer, the maize, and the peyote. The peyote hunt is presented here from two points of view, my own as a participant-observer (in 1966), and a mythological account provided by Ramón. Detailed descriptions of the peyote hunt are available in the works of Lumholtz (1902), Zingg (1938), Furst (1972b), and Benítez (1968a and 1970); congruencies and discrepancies between this version and those of Furst and Zingg are indicated throughout this chapter. Considering the differences in time, training, and culture of the various authors and the different mara'akate involved, the peyote hunt appears as a remarkably stable ceremony. I have also indicated some corrections and reinterpretations made in my account after discussing the 1966 peyote hunt with Ramón during his 1971 visit to Los Angeles.

My own observations are given in the first person and are

specific and subjective. A more formal, third-person treatment would have lent a timeless, objective, and generalized tone that would have been misleading. The peyote hunt is a complicated event, the full meaning of which might or might not be absolutely clear to an outsider after a lifetime of work among the Huichols. Certainly, the first time witnessed, it raises as many questions as it answers. Moreover, it is not presently possible to make sound judgments about the typicality of the event. My description of the peyote hunt represents a chronological, detailed personal account of that which I witnessed others doing and that which I did myself. I have tried to stress this by giving attention to the particular group of pilgrims involved, their motives for going, their relationships with one another, their moods and attitudes.[1]

Ramón's text, "When the Mara'akame Plays the Drum and Flies the Children to the Land of the Peyote," provides a

[1] The difficulties of comprehending the peyote hunt, or any Huichol ceremonies, without a knowledge of their mythology are formidable. Zingg also found this to be so, commenting: "It wasn't intentionally for a 'pure induction' that I went to these ceremonies with a blank mind, and left them but little more enlightened. Native onlookers, or even Indian friends, will not tell the meaning of the simplest point, so strong is the tribal sanction against divulging tribal secrets to foreigners. . . . I would not have learned the first elements of the subjective culture of the Huichols, had I not been successful after months of patient kindness, to get a native informant who would brave the displeasure of his fellows in giving me the mythology, in which it is all explained" (1938:411).

In addition to the mythical version of the peyote hunt as given by Ramón, I would have liked to obtain a version of the myth and event as interpreted by an ordinary pilgrim participant, since the views of religious specialist and outsider-anthropologist are obviously quite atypical. But it was not possible to gather a layman's point of view on the journey without offending Ramón, who claimed (justifiably, I felt) the right to provide the correct and official version of the event.

mythological account of the pilgrimage. This rather lengthy text is valuable for several reasons. First, it provides the depiction of an "inner map," a cognitive and spatial plan transmitted from one generation of Huichols to the next; second, it includes some of the mara'akame's feelings, aspirations, and experiences during the ceremony. Finally, it closely parallels and explains many of the actual events I observed during the peyote hunt. The second part of the text is not a myth per se but an explanation of "How the Names of Things Are Changed on the Peyote Journey." It provides information critical to the interpretation of the overall significance of the peyote hunt, as given in Chapters 5 and 6.

Several points about Ramón's text deserve comment. First, this version was dictated by Ramón when he was still a novice, lacking one year to complete his training. In statements such as, "I will do it there; I have a good heart; I will guard them well," he is anticipating his duties and behaviors on the forthcoming peyote hunt. In the myth he takes a magical trip, rehearsing the future, actual trip. At the same time it is the mara'akame's affirmation or pledge to himself and to his people of his faith and determination. In this text, one sees him equating himself with the First Mara'akame of those Ancient Times and linking his present and future roles. He obliterates time and merges the primordial, archaic, and the mythic with the yet-to-come, the world at the end of time, creating a sense of the eternal nature of these rites—for himself and for his listeners.

Another noteworthy feature of this text which sets it apart from other myths and chants is its unusual explicitness. As stated earlier, in most myths, names of places, deities, and sacred objects are referred to vaguely, since ordinary adults know them well, making it superfluous, even burdensome, to go through the entire story with beginning, middle, and end intact. The storyteller can refer to a relevant fragment without regard for its position vis-à-vis other sections, but Ramón here was addressing children, many under five years old, who were receiving their first exposure to "the heart of the Huichol." Thus Ramón related the story in chronological sequence, carefully providing details, explanations, translations. The style, accordingly, is less allegorical, less obscure, and more precise than most Huichol oral literature. Ramón wanted to leave nothing in doubt, hence the frequency of statements such as, "We do this because our ancestors traveled this way"; "We follow in their footsteps so that our traditions will not die"; "We gather the peyote so that we may have life," and so forth. At one point, for example, the narrator describes how in flying, a little girl loses her wing which is replaced by the mara'akame so that she may rejoin the others. Ordinary style would have portrayed that same incident something like this: "One went up. No, it was not so. Something was missing, something fell down. He replaced it, saying, 'Being as you are, you are like that.' She said, 'They who are in their places, they did this.' His heart is good."

The myth is related as the central part of the Drum and Calabash ceremony, which is a kind of "first fruits" festival, held before the peyote hunt so that the children "will understand all." It takes place during the dry season, usually late fall when the maize is still green but the squash is ripe. At this time, the mara'akame plays the drum, beating the deerskin head with his palms while he and his assistants chant. During the chant, he "transforms" the children into a flock of little birds and leads them in magical flight from the Sierra to the land of peyote. The row of bird-children is symbolized by a fiber cord to which bunches of cotton have been tied, one for each child. One end of the string is attached to the drum, the other to the sacred chair of Kauyumari on which the mara'akame is seated.

Ramón had prepared me for the peyote hunt in the summers of 1965 and 1966. Such understanding as I did attain of the event and, subsequently, of the deer-maize-peyote symbol complex was due to my participation in the hunt, along with the extensive preparatory coaching and ex post facto explanation and interpretation provided by Ramón. Despite the fact that I had heard about the peyote hunt for over a year before I witnessed it, and had read about it, I saw much that puzzled me. Similarly, I had heard much in the myths that was not meaningful until I witnessed the peyote hunt myself. Without this combination of mythology, interpretation, and participation, I believe, the event is incomprehensible. Accordingly, I have provided both my version of the peyote hunt and Ramón's mythological version, which taken together provide a complementary picture of the event and its meaning and an interpretation unattainable by a consideration of one without the other.

As mentioned earlier, other anthropologists who worked among the Huichols did not undertake this journey, possibly because there is no place for nonparticipants in the rituals. It was my impression that Ramón solved the problem of what to do with outsiders only after we were en route to Wirikuta. Impulsively, it seemed, he invited Furst and me to drink Holy Water and view the Sacred Land along with the other pilgrims just as we approached Wirikuta. From then on, barriers between "us" and "them" faded and our participation was profound and exacting. We were no longer exempt from the ritual prescriptions and proscriptions which applied to the other pilgrims. Nor were we given the privilege of attending to our work first. Previously, we had been allowed time to change film, make notes, operate the tape recorder and ask questions, but after drinking the Holy Water, Ramón treated us like fledgling Huichols who needed patience, urging, reprimanding, and reminding. For the first time, Ramón seemed more concerned that we "learn our lessons well" than that we make a technically sound and accurate record of Huichol religion. In Wirikuta we were active novitiates instead of passive recipients and much was expected of us. As always, Ramón was gentle but not permissive.

Each year parties of pilgrims set out from all over the Huichol country for individual and collective benefits. The journey takes place in the dry season between October and February. It must follow the Drum and Calabash ceremony and precede the spring ceremonies to bring rain. Theoretically, the more journeys one can make the better but practical limitations keep the size of the parties down. Above all, the trip is expensive. Ceremonial offerings must be gathered and prepared. The family remaining behind must keep the fire going night and day, which requires a sizable fuel supply. Food provisions have to be taken along, and if possible the pilgrims should have new and magnificent clothing for the trip. (Being away from the fields cannot be considered "an expense" at this time of year when the crops need no tending.) Other kinds of hardships exist for those who remain behind as well as for those who endure the strains of the trip. Salt, washing, sexual intercourse, full meals, ample sleep, for example—are forbidden to all those involved, whether staying behind or going.

The composition of the party and the choice of a leader are handled rather informally. At the right time of year those who wish to go to Wirikuta inform others and together they decide upon a desirable leader, who need not be from their region, rancho, or kinship group, although in fact pilgrims are usually close genealogically and geographically.

My Version of the Peyote Hunt

Members of the Pilgrimage

Ramón, Lupe, and her niece, Lucia, were living on a small rancho on the outskirts of Guadalajara when one of the pilgrims came down from the Sierra and requested that Ramón lead a group to Wirikuta in December 1966, a few weeks later. Since it was known in the mountains that Ramón would be going and that he had already established a reputation as an able and successful leader on three previous trips, he was sought out by those of his kinsmen and acquaintances who had the means and desire to make the journey.

The entire party, the *hikuritámete* or peyote companions, involved thirteen people, including four "who remained behind" but who were nevertheless participants, and two North American anthropologists, Furst and myself. (According to Lumholtz [1902:127] the average number of pilgrims is between eight and twelve.) The pilgrims arrived at Ramón's rancho a few days before the scheduled departure. The group was typical in its wide age range and inclusion of both sexes, according to Ramón and Lupe, and also typical were the reasons which prompted them to undertake the trip.[2]

In addition to Ramón and Lupe, the pilgrims in the party are described below. Their ages are only approximate, and

[2] Lumholtz (1902:135) states that women do not go to Wirikuta but none of the informants consulted agreed with this. It is also considered very desirable to have young children along, even infants in arms, "because they are pure and make things more beautiful."

Spanish or baptismal names are given here for convenience, although Spanish names were not used consistently or exclusively on the trip. All names except those of Ramón and Lupe have been changed.

Francisco was "more or less eighty years old." His age was given as between seventy and 110; the variations seemed to depend on the point being emphasized at a given moment: that he was really not too old or that he was really very ancient indeed. For any age he was a man of vitality, lithe and lean, commanding his body astonishingly, now telescoping it into an impossibly small space, then leaping about with sudden grace and precision. He capered and twinkled and made others laugh easily and he was responsible for many of the lighthearted moments on the trip. That Francisco was quite poor was indicated by the fact that he had no wife to embroider his costume and that his *manta* pants and shirts still carried the labels from the flour company of whose cloth bags his garments had been made. He had decided to take the trip to Wirikuta because the previous year one of his cows had been struck by lightning. Perhaps it was a message from Tatewarí, since despite his age and religiosity Francisco had never been to Wirikuta. He was one of four *primeros* on the trip, a *matewame* (plural *matewámete*) or pilgrim who goes for the first time to Wirikuta and for whom the trip is especially important. Never again is it so dangerous, for one who has never been to Wirikuta can easily lose his soul there and the mara'akame must take special precautions with *primeros*.

Sebastián was Lupe's brother-in-law, perhaps forty-five years old, father of her two nieces Victoria and Lucia. Victoria and Sebastián had walked in from their rancho in the Sierra. Sebastián's reasons for going were complex. He was worried about Lucia, who was showing signs of alienation from traditional culture, and had evidently hoped to induce her to accompany him and Victoria on the journey. He was a learned and serious man, reserved and intense. This was his eighth trip and it was disclosed that in his youth he had aspired to become a mara'akame but had failed. He was fearful of becoming a sorcerer or being driven mad by sorcerers, dangers considered common to one who sets out but falls short of becoming a mara'akame. Whether primarily to prove his virtue in his own eyes or the eyes of his fellows, Sebastián was intensely involved in the ritual of the pilgrimage throughout.

Carlos, perhaps fifty years old, was Ramón's paternal uncle and elder of the Las Cuevas rancho from which most of the pilgrims had come. Carlos went to Wirikuta as often as he could, and this was his ninth time. As a senior figure in terms of religious experience and social position, he was the logical person to perform the important duties as assistant to the mara'akame. Neither as given to frivolity as Francisco, nor as reserved and fervent as Sebastián, Carlos kept to himself and his devotions.

Pablo was a younger man, around thirty. He had recently married Carlos' daughter and lived at their rancho, but he and his wife were in that stage when newlyweds decide with whose parents they will throw in their lot. Pablo and Carlos were taking the opportunity to feel each other out during this important event. Although there is no formal attempt to consolidate and perpetuate the social bonds established among *peyoteros* after returning home, there is a deepening of spiritual and emotional ties which can certainly enrich previously existing or anticipated relationships. It is advantageous for everyone if those who travel together to Wirikuta are kin, for the camaraderie fostered by sharing this ritual experience coincides with and reinforces extant important social ties. Pablo was quiet, soft-spoken, and rather deferential to the three older men. He performed many small duties for them and listened attentively when they played the violin or sang and chanted. It was his first trip and he was an eager if somewhat apprehensive student. He followed directions well and quickly but was unmistakably the least sophisticated in religious and aesthetic matters among the men present. Pablo, it was my impression, wanted to learn and wanted to make a good showing, and he was aware that the older men were watching him closely.

Victoria, the only female member of our group besides Lupe and myself, was a sweet and pliant adolescent very unlike her independent, occasionally defiant older sister, Lucia. She was always eager to please and her timidity did not mask her delight and interest in the events taking place around her. It was her first trip not only to Wirikuta but also out of the Sierra, so that everything she encountered was new. During the journey her large eyes often opened so wide with speechless wonder that those about her laughed. One of her reasons for taking the trip was to make up for her sister's defections and thus to help assuage her father's disappointment with his older daughter. Several pilgrims hinted that this compensation would also be well received by the deities. Victoria was a model Huichol girl and very irksome to Lucia with whom she was inevitably compared.

Besides the actual pilgrims, "those remaining behind" are also considered participants. These are the friends and family who gather at the rancho from which the others depart, and throughout the *peyoteros*' absence, "those remaining behind" tend the fire, observe many of the same ritual pro- and prescriptions, stay in close spiritual communication with the travelers, and "tend the *peyoteros* with their hearts and affection." Although the mara'akame is not accorded more social prestige for leading a large party, the more people who are involved and who give him faith, support, and affection during this dangerous period, the more able he is to protect the pilgrims and support the spiritual burdens he must sustain on their behalf.

"Those remaining behind" on this occasion were, besides Lucia, Ramón's half-brother Fernando, who had been residing temporarily in Guadalajara, and a poor female relative and her young son from Carlos' rancho. The woman and son were both deaf-mutes without any independent means of support and were probably obliged to fill Carlos' request that they accompany him to Guadalajara and remain behind while he went to Wirikuta. It was general knowledge that Fernando and Lucia were becoming acculturated and therefore could not be trusted with the sole responsibility for keeping the fire lit and observing the rituals necessary for the well-being of the pilgrims.

Among the pilgrims several informal groupings emerged which could be observed whenever ritual considerations did not determine interpersonal relations. To some extent male and female divisions of labor were detectable, in food preparation and distribution particularly. Lupe was in charge, with Victoria assisting. The three men, Francisco, Sebastián, and Carlos, interacted primarily with each other though Francisco occasionally seemed to find their company tedious and sought out someone else. Pablo associated with these three men too, but rather from a distance, often as observer, occasionally as errand-runner. He was clearly not yet one of them but the barrier was not rigid. Ramón was set apart naturally, and when he was not engaged in his nearly interminable tasks, he would explain and interpret matters at hand to us outsiders. The amount of time not structured by ritual was amazingly little. Nearly always everyone had his place, his duty, his attitude, and activity provided for him by events. The releases from this structure when informal social and personal behavior could emerge were few.

As indicated, the pilgrims varied widely in degrees of acculturation and amount of experience outside the Huichol territory. Of the four men from the Sierra, all but Francisco had been to a city before, and Pablo had had only the most limited contact with non-Huichols. Francisco and Pablo spoke no Spanish, had never worn "Spanish" (mestizo) clothing, and had not personally encountered such phenomena as cameras, tape recorders, restaurants, packaged food, or bottled soda pop. None had been in a motor vehicle except rarely in a truck or country bus. Victoria was completely unfamiliar with mestizo ways. Lupe, Ramón, Fernando, and Lucia spoke some Spanish and were quite accustomed to city life and outsiders. Fernando and Lucia, though very learned and skilled in Huichol stories, arts, mythology, religion, songs, and dances, showed indications that they would probably not remain with their people when they were older.

Preparation and Rehearsal

Pilgrims and myths describe the trip to and from Wirikuta from the Sierra on foot as taking forty to forty-five days, approximately twenty days of straight walking, with additional time spent in preparations and post-Wirikuta ceremonies at home. Wirikuta is located just outside the former colonial mining town of Real de Catorce in the state of San Luis Potosí, perhaps three hundred miles away from the Huichol region of the Sierra. How one gets to Wirikuta is considered irrelevant by Huichols, and these days more and more pilgrims take buses or the train to the outside of the sacred area. Wirikuta proper is demarcated by boundaries invisible to an outsider. A flat stretch at the base of two sacred mountains, it is largely uninhabited, a featureless brush desert of creosote and cactus. The heart of Wirikuta where the peyote grows can only be reached on foot, for there are no roads or even paths into the center of the region. Walking the entire way from the Huichol Sierra to the desert is preferred, "because it is more beautiful." No matter how one travels to Wirikuta, the pilgrimage is sacred if all the necessary stops are made and the appropriate rituals are performed along the way. For this pilgrimage we arranged to travel by camper to the edge of Wirikuta, in order to accommodate our camera and recording equipment. There we made camp and hiked the rest of the way into the sacred area.

Because the camper was an unusual element in the pilgrimage, it had to be incorporated into the ritual, and this necessitated a number of innovations and special preparations. First, smooth entrance into and exit from the vehicle had to be achieved, and this was rehearsed several times under Ramón's direction so that everyone could get in and out easily, without talking and without awkward pauses or confusion. Second, everyone's place in the camper had to be established, where his gear was to be kept, where he was to sit, in what direction he was to face, and so forth. The essential problem here was to establish and preserve the order of the pilgrims walking in single file. Finally a place had to be found for the horns of Kauyumari, the decorated deer horns which the mara'akame ordinarily carries on his person so that Tatewarí can lead the group to the peyote with Kauyumari as his helper. Ramón eventually decided to tie the horns to the front of the camper to give them the most frontal, guiding position possible since he felt that wearing them inside the camper would be less advantageous. The decision was reached after much consultation and experimentation, and ultimately everyone agreed that this was the most desirable solution to a difficult problem. (This ability of the Huichols to accommodate to new situations, innovate accordingly, yet preserve a consistently religious attitude and intent may be counted as endowing their religion with a flexibility that in no small way contributes to its durability and resistance to outside corrosion. This is seen in small matters and large, for example in substituting bull for deer blood when the latter, now nearly unavailable, is called for in rituals.)

The party members arrived at Ramón's little rancho outside Guadalajara within two days of each other. Francisco, Carlos, Sebastián, Pablo, Victoria, and the deaf-mute woman and her son came down together from the Sierra, and Fernado came from somewhere in the city. Lucia, Ramón, and Lupe were living at the Guadalajara rancho at the time. All came in their ordinary dress, a mixture in some cases of Western and Huichol items, carrying bundles with the makings of their ceremonial costumes and offerings which they would assemble in the next few days.

Much washing of costumes and some last-minute embroidery and decoration were done by Lupe and Lucia. New sandals were made, hats adorned, beads strung, until the transformation of the tired, dirty, poor group from the city and mountains into properly adorned Huichols was complete. For the next two days and nights everyone sat around in Ramón's patio preparing the offerings to be left in Wirikuta. Gourds were cut and cleaned and bead and yarn designs pressed into them. Coins (intrinsically worthless without adornment) were covered with wax, string, and beads. Other sacred objects were made and empty bottles were brought in and cleaned of their labels to be used as sacred water containers. Ramón himself concentrated his efforts on adorning the horns of Kauyumari, wrapping colored yarn around the central part of a small pair of deer horns, then tying on three of his ceremonial arrows in the middle with the bunches of eagle and hawk feathers hanging freely so that they could blow in the wind. He sat on his *'uweni* or shamanic chair as he did this, working carefully and slowly, enjoying as everyone did the violin playing by the older men. Several times as Ramón "prepared Kauyumari" he put his hands to his mouth and made the call or whistle of the deer. He made also several new arrows of Brazil wood and bamboo, decorating the shafts with yarn and hanging from them miniature deer snares.

One of the older men produced several small packages of *yé (Nicotiana rustica)*, the tobacco of Tatewarí which grows wild and is said to give one visions. It is sacred and only used ceremonially when all the men smoke in unison. Rolled into maize husk cigarettes, the tobacco is carried to Wirikuta in the sacred wart gourds (*yékwei*) worn by older men and experienced *peyoteros*. Ramón did not have a tobacco gourd but kept his supply in a small woven neck bag exactly like those worn around the waist and over the shoulder but much smaller. In this bag, too, he kept all those things to be given to Tatewarí on returning home—ends of cigarettes, matches, pieces of tortilla, candy wrappers, bottle caps, orange peels—bits from all that passed his lips. The others kept similar remnants in their ordinary bags. (The Huichols have a great predilection for bags as part of their costume. Zingg [1938] states they are worn for "pure swank" and certainly much justifiable pride is taken in these magnificently decorated objects. But it is also possible that the bags are valued as a sign of religious devotion, showing that the wearer is dutiful in carrying a great many things back to Tatewarí, just as the number of tobacco gourds a man wears is sometimes operative as a badge of his ritual status.) Only Ramón carried in one of his bags the matches and candles for the trip since only the mara'akame can "bring out" Tatewarí.

Taking the Names of the Deities

In the course of the preparations, Ramón revealed that on the previous night he had dreamed the names to be taken by the *peyoteros* for the journey and had told them which of the deities they were to "become" until we returned from Wirikuta. The names of the *hikuritámete* were neither completely arbitrary nor systematic. Victoria was named for a particular offering she brought which was most suitable for the Goddess of Children. Lupe was named for her favorite, a maize deity. Carlos was Tayaupá because he was knowledgeable and had made many trips to Wirikuta. Francisco, because of his advanced age, was "Our Great Grandfather."

The peyote names given to the pilgrims were as follows: Ramón, of course, was Tatewarí, as the mara'akame leading the group must be always. Following him in order and importance were Carlos as Tayaupá (Our Father Sun). Sebastián as Tsakaimuka (Snarer of the Deer); Tatutsí (Our Great Grandfather) in the person of Francisco. Lupe came next as Tatei 'Utuanaka (Our Mother Maize), and Victoria was 'Xuturi Iwiékame (Our Mother of the Children).[3] The last

[3] In the account of the First Peyote Hunt given by Ramón, the female deities did not start out with the males but joined them later, at Tatei Matinieri, arising from the springs there. The primordial model

man, Pablo, was Tamatsi Maxa Kwaxí (Elder Brother Deer Tail). Finally, myself, first as Yoawima 'Uimari and then as Tsinurawe, and then Furst as Uru 'Tsata.[4]

Some comments on order and division of labor are needed here.[5] On this journey Tayaupá-Carlos performed as the mara'akame's assistant. On Furst's subsequent (1968) trip and in Ramón's official ideal account given below, it is Tatutsí who fills this role. Here it was clear that Carlos was the most appropriate person to serve as Tatusí, in fact the only suitable pilgrim, since of the males he was the most experienced and respected in religious matters. Why, one wonders, was he not

---

was not followed on the pilgrimages witnessed by Furst and myself; in these the women were included from the beginning. Perhaps this discrepancy is a reflection of the lesser social and economic importance of women in Ancient Times and historically, compared to their significance as members of a society of sedentary agriculturalists.

[4] When we started out for Wirikuta, I was called Yoawima 'Uimari, Growing Purple Maize Girl, an affectionate but not especially sacred appellation. During the peyote hunt, Ramón endowed Furst and me with the more sacred peyote-seeker names (Tsinurawe and Uru 'Tsata) indicating our changed status as a result of our incorporation into a state of unity with the others. That we were not given peyote names earlier, along with the rest of the party, suggests to me that Ramón did not originally anticipate the depth of our involvement in the ensuing ceremonies, and only after he realized how much we had been drawn into the peyote hunt did he find it necessary to identify us accordingly.

[5] In 1971, Ramón discoursed about the order of the 1966 pilgrims in more detail, explaining that there were many specialized tasks allotted the participants which were not evident to us. For example, Tatutsí was responsible for guarding us from the rear against sorcerers or evil winds. It was Tayaupá's duty to protect the vulnerable *primeros* and he carried special offerings to achieve this. In discussing the 1966 trip in 1971, Ramón remembered perfectly all the participants, their order, their deity names, and their reasons for going although three additional trips and five years intervened.

simply given the role of Tatutsí instead of Tayaupá, since names of pilgrims are changeable from one year to the next? Perhaps Tatutsí, Our Great Grandfather, was obviously more suitable for old Francisco, who, as a *primero*, could not possibly have acted as Ramón's assistant.

The order of the pilgrims was significant. To some extent it expresses ranking of a person's ritual standing and of the importance of the deity with whom he is identified. These two features do not entirely coincide, however. Though some deities are more important than others, not all deities can be ranked in relation to each other, nor is an individual's ritual ranking precise enough to make the ordering on the journey a dependable or stable indicator of his status. Obviously, many subjective and arbitrary factors enter into a mara'akame's final decisions in these delicate matters of precedence.

What seems at least as important as the ranking indicated by the pilgrims' order is the fact of order per se. As in the case of acknowledgment of the four directions and the center, the carrying out of rituals with fixed arrangement of personnel serves to locate spatially the individuals involved. Such "placement rituals" delimit the universe and give boundaries to the chaos of the noncultural world. Throughout the peyote hunt in every movement, at every pause, placement of the pilgrims was maintained consistently, regardless of the awkwardness it caused occasionally.

The circumstances surrounding the anthropologists' names were interesting. Mine was related to what was seen by Ramón as my being young and inexperienced; Yoawima 'Uimari is one of the five innocent, protected maize daughters. The reason for my second name, Tsinurawe, was less clear except that it was a name belonging to a *hikuritámete*.

Tsinurawe, translated as "eyebrow of the peyote," refers to the hairlike fuzz on the center of each peyote button which "senses" the ritual condition of the seeker. Uru 'Tsata was translated as "the arrow which guards us," specifying Furst's role as driver of the vehicle which got us safely to Wirikuta and back.

Here are some of Ramón's comments explaining how the names occurred to him.

When I dreamed the names for you, the names that you were given there in Wirikuta, I did not see those names as though written, as one says. I saw these visions and heard them. It was when the colors exploded there, those colors of Tatewarí, and it was Tatewarí who spoke these names. Those names came in colors, very brilliant, red, red, blue, blue, very deep and rich. They were bright, so bright those colors, that they almost blinded me by so much brilliance.

You do not put a name to these *peyoteros* just for the sake of giving a name. No. That is not how it is. It is because the Ancient Ones have given it this way with the peyote. That is how they appeared to me, so that I could tell each one his name. I was made to see all that with the peyote.

No special names were mentioned for "those who remained behind."

After two and a half days of naming, rehearsing, sewing and preparing offerings, Lupe and Lucia served a ceremonial "last meal" to all present, consisting of tortillas and water. Everyone prayed aloud, offering bits of the tortilla and water to the four directions and the fire at the beginning of, during, and after the meal. From this moment on many restrictions were in effect without further rituals to establish them.

The mara'akame, Ramón stated, had the most severe requirements to endure—Ramón, in fact, had not slept for

Three pilgrims eating their last meal before setting out for Wirikuta. After this ceremonial "last meal" of tortillas and water is served to the pilgrims, many restrictions are in effect, and the pilgrims are permitted only the minimum of food and drink until the end of the pilgrimage.

the previous three nights or eaten a full meal three days prior to the arrival of the others.

Preparing the Fire and "Confessions"

On the afternoon of the third day, Ramón led the party of pilgrims out of his patio and into the fields to gather sacred food for Tatewarí, who would have to be fed the whole time that our party was away. In single file and silently, all departed, and when they returned each had a large load of wood tied to his back. Ramón prayed over the large pile of wood, holding each piece aloft to the four directions with one hand, clutching his Brazil wood bow and deerskin quiver in the other. Everyone chanted with him and the mood became very solemn. His prayers were for success in the venture "to find our life, that which we need to live, the *híkuri*." Ramón then took from his hut a small round stone disc (*nearika*) about two feet across and two inches deep, used to cover "the hole, the sacred cavity" that goes down to the center of the earth, from which Tatewarí was born. He scooped a small declivity in the ashes, then squatting beside the fire, assumed a circular shape himself, holding his arms in a large "O" over his head, himself taking the form of a *nearika*, while speaking quietly and soothingly to the fire. Several large pieces of wood were placed over the cavity, one carefully pointing east and west, the other north and south, and everyone in his proper order, single file, made the ceremonial circuit around the fire.

Evening found everyone seated around the fire "in his proper place," with the four who were to remain behind looking on as a cleansing ritual began. This event, well reported in the literature on the peyote pilgrimage of the Huichols, is often referred to as a confession but that term is misleading insofar as it connotes the confession in Western religious tradition. The Huichol ceremony is conducted without shame, embarrassment, contrition, or intention to repent. It provides neither profound catharsis nor religious absolution, though no doubt it does give some relief to troubled consciences and provides social absolution of sorts. But these functions are secondary to its major purpose which is to transform the participants spiritually by making them "new." The only actions "confessed" are sexual misdeeds, this though the Huichols are known to be flexible and casual in forming sexual liaisons. Other transgressions considered far more heinous are not included. Further, small children and even infants who will undertake the pilgrimage must participate though they cannot be said to have had illicit sexual romances. And too, all the sexual transgressions of an individual's lifetime must be named anew with each ceremony, even though they had been removed by a prior cleansing. It appears that, for this ritual, sexuality is used to symbolize the mortal condition which must be set aside for the peyote pilgrims to become the deities.

And the ceremony serves social purposes as well. The peyote companions must be in a state of utter accord and trust for the pilgrimage to succeed. Adulterous relations, known and suspected, are revealed and forgiven during this ritual. Those who persist in harboring resentment after this ceremony risk supernatural sanctions in the form of terrifying peyote visions and even insanity in Wirikuta.[6] Accordingly, the tone during the event was one of lightheartedness and affection, marked by frequent teasing, boasting, and joking. Only with this context in mind, and lacking a suitable English term, can this ritual be referred to as a confession. The ritual is the first step toward attaining the ultimate goal of the peyote hunt, the return to the innocence and Paradise of the First Time.

[6] After the pilgrimage, conflicts can and do erupt as a result of disclosures made during this ritual; but it would be wrong to assume that the requirement of goodwill for the journey merely delays inevitable discord. In the interim, injured parties have been united in an intensely spiritual and emotional union which ultimately assuages some lingering resentments. And the joking and badinage that occur during the event release tension and ease the humiliation which offended spouses would undoubtedly feel more keenly under other circumstances.

One at a time, in their proper order, each of the pilgrims came forward, acknowledged the four directions and then in a highly formalized speech stated the names of all those persons with whom he or she had ever had illicit sexual relations. For each name mentioned a knot was tied by Ramón in a husk fiber cord he brought forth from his deerskin quiver. The participants' mood was especially gay when old Francisco came forward to name his amours. Ramón was directed by the others to make one knot for each five names because the old man had had such a long life and so many romances that to make a knot for each name would leave no one else room on the cord. At the conclusion of each person's statement Ramón with his plumes brushed the pilgrim from the head downward, making a motion of shaking into the fire the individual's sexual experience. Before returning to his seat each pilgrim paused to shake and brush his clothing meticulously into the fire, turning his bags inside out, shaking his cape and hat, cleansing his clothing as well as himself, then circling the fire and returning to his proper place among the other *peyoteros*.

When it was Lupe's turn to come forward she did not confess for she asserted she had never transgressed. Instead she made a speech on the role of the mara'akame's wife, what a good woman she must be, how she must be strong, must help her husband and must guard his back from evil and sorcerers. Everyone solemnly agreed and Lupe was cleansed despite her purity before returning to her place. The pilgrims were finished and Ramón himself stood to make his confession to Carlos, seated on his left, handing him the cord. Ramón prayed aloud then mentioned a few names. Lupe sternly reminded him of a few more, which he agreed solemnly should indeed be added to the cord. After Ramón's cleansing by Carlos all the pilgrims were new, leaving only "those who remain" to be called up. The same procedure was followed, even with the deaf-mute who could make only barely intelligible sounds, and her eight-year-old son, whom it may be presumed was sexually innocent.

The smooth and easy progression of the ceremony ended abruptly when Lucia, the last of those to be called up, came forward, docilely enough, but then stood in silence before Ramón, refusing to speak. Everyone began to address her in tones varying from gentle urging, to imploring, to chiding and scolding and finally warning. Long silences alternated with sharp outbursts of anger but for fifty minutes the girl stood with her head hanging and would not speak. From time to time she looked around as though seeking an escape but she made no attempt to move. At last Lupe made a long and impassioned speech to her while the girl twisted miserably from side to side. "Don't you see what you are doing to us? Why do you do this thing? Don't you know that we cannot drink the Sacred Water, we cannot find the peyote? We cannot find our life unless you do confess." When Lucia could bear it no longer she began to mumble, mentioned three names which were knotted into the cord, circled the fire, and left the group to stand by herself. She alone was not cleansed with the arrows and she stood apart in the shadows in silence for the rest of the night.

Later Ramón explained that her action had jeopardized the entire journey, that had she not at last relented the trip could not have been undertaken that year, for "all must be of one heart, there must be complete unity among us," and Lucia was withholding her good will by refusing to be cleansed. In view of the enormity of the consequences of not making the trip, the strength of the group's antagonism and agitation was not surprising. All the dry season ceremonies were impaired by Lucia's reticence since these ceremonies cannot be held without peyote from Wirikuta, preferably obtained in person by members of the community conducting the ceremonies.

Lucia's motives were not entirely clear to anyone except that all agreed, "She was not a good girl," and it was hinted that her defiance was due to her acculturation and deviation from Huichol ways. It is also possible that there were more immediate and personal motives. There was no love lost between Lucia and Lupe and on many occasions the latter's authority seemed to chafe the girl.

The knotted string was held up, prayers were said over it by Ramón, and it was burned in the fire. The life experience represented by the cord was destroyed. The *peyoteros* were now pure, made new. They were no longer mortal. It was from this moment that the pilgrims became and were known to each other as the Ancient Ones.

Ramón then placed one end of his deerskin bow in his mouth, using his mouth for a sounding chamber and holding the other end between his toes, and began twanging rhythmically on the string with the side of an arrow. The sound emitted was telling Tatewarí that the *peyoteros* were leaving for Wirikuta, that everything was in readiness. He removed from his quiver a piece of cactus fiber cord, the *kaunari*, which he passed over and through his bow. Then resuming the rhythmic beating on the bowstring, he gave the end of the cord to Francisco. Everyone in turn grasped the cord as it came to him so that it passed first in front, then behind all the pilgrims. The cord was returned to Ramón, who scorched it in the fire and replaced it in his quiver.

The *yé* cigarettes were taken out and all the men smoked,

Circulating the sacred cord, which symbolizes the pilgrims' unity. Ramón takes a cactus fiber cord from his quiver and passes it to each of the pilgrims in a circle, then returns it to his quiver after scorching it over the fire. Later, in Wirikuta, the cord will be knotted by each pilgrim, then unknotted at the end of the journey.

talked, and laughed and the convivial mood which prevailed prior to Lucia's defiance was restored. In the course of the smoking of the *yé*, Ramón blew smoke on the knees of the women, vigorously rubbing it in. This, he later related, was not part of the peyote ceremony but was his own special secret used to give the women strength for the difficult journey; it was their first trip and they were fearful and apprehensive.

The atmosphere was relaxed and happy as Ramón sounded his horn and everyone began to shout and chant together. Ramón took up the violin and began a little song, one of the songs that "belong to the peyote journey," which Tatewarí sang on the first trip, for now Ramón was Tatewarí. The group responded by starting a dance around the fire, singing, turning, dipping, spinning in the flickering light. The song told of the many fine offerings that would be given for the *híkuri.* At last, as the night sky began to lighten, the group became silent, with everyone wrapped in his blanket staring fixedly at Tatewarí alone with his thoughts.

Departure for Wirikuta

At dawn everyone was up, packing his belongings, trying on costumes, gathering together his offerings, packing them in large wicker and reed baskets which were worn on the back by ropes over the shoulders or tumplines.

When everyone was ready Ramón inspected and adjusted costumes, smoothing the material, examining the packing of the offerings. (Much care was always taken with the proper arrangement of belongings, and packing and repacking occurred continually throughout the trip. This seemed related to the general value on order and proper placement.) When all was judged to be well arranged, Ramón indicated that the group should gather around the fire which had been kept alive all night and would be so kept until the *peyoteros'* return. Candles were taken from bundles, lighted, and held as everyone began to pray and weep; the prayers concerned the fervent desire to arrive safely at Wirikuta and find the *híkuri.* Those to remain at home stood in a single line also holding candles, along the path which the pilgrims would take when leaving. At last the departure began and the *hikuritámete,* led by Ramón twanging on his bow and holding their candles carefully in their left hands, passed by those staying behind. One by one each silently placed his right hand on the left shoulder of those remaining, then went on down the path to the camper. Everyone entered and quickly found his appointed place. Ramón settled in front to direct things and remained vigilant at this post for the entire journey.

The first days were easy traveling, primarily on roads, northward on the Saltillo highway. Ramón twanged on his bowstring as we arrived at each sacred place. Near Salinas del Piñón Blanco (Huichol, Paxturi) we cut off the road onto the brush-desert wastelands. Ramón directed us carefully for it is very difficult to find these places by car. (Walking *is* much easier and more beautiful, given the terrain.) As we came to each site, Ramón indicated fragments of the myths in which it was mentioned; most places were included in the myth which recounts the telling of the peyote journey to the children. Many of the features he pointed out were inconspicuous and even invisible to an untrained observer—heaps of pebbles, tiny water holes, tree stumps, small caves, hillocks, and little clumps of rocks.

As we approached Zacatecas, Ramón told us that it would be necessary to draw the curtains in the camper because those who are *matewámete*, going to Wirikuta for the first time, had to be properly prepared before seeing the sacred places. This danger first occurred at the place called La Puerta in Spanish; in Huichol it is the "Vagina," the passage into the Land of Our Origins, the Place of Beginning.

A short way past La Puerta in an open, empty field, Ramón directed everyone to leave the car. Rapidly, with downcast eyes, he led the group into the middle of an utterly desolate but holy place. The companions knelt in a semicircle and Ramón prayed over them, sweeping them with the sacred plumes which he then swung about in the air. Then over each *primero* in turn he prayed and brushed and when he finished he blindfolded each with a scarf. The *primeros* were especially solemn now, and some tearful, "because it is the first time we will see our lives, because we are coming to pay our debts, there in the sacred land." [7] The first pilgrims in Ancient Times also cried in this place, Ramón said. All those who came here would surely receive absolution and strength, he explained, but one could only come when bidden by the gods. One cannot simply go whenever he feels like it and some Huichols die without ever being called to Wirikuta, he explained later.

Back in the camper, we continued precariously through the desert, passing thick jungles of spiny cactus groves, past veritable forests of nopal and sunbaked desert villages rising suddenly out of the dust. The region was utterly bleak and empty except for an occasional forlorn mestizo or a wagon laboriously pulled by grim mules through the underbrush. It was here that Rabbit Person and Hummingbird Person and other of the Ancient Ones had dropped out of the First Peyote Hunt from hunger and fatigue. The place remained sacred and Ramón stopped to leave them some offerings. The dust was so thick in and outside of the car that the windows had to be kept closed. "Those blindfolded ones," wordless and sightless, tightly held their lighted candles and despite their obvious discomfort sat silent and still. With the onset of

[7] In 1968 the blindfolding of the *primeros* at La Puerta was immediately followed by another elaborate ceremony of entrance into the Land of Our Origins, although it was not in 1966. In the later trip as reported by Furst (1972), the pilgrims were led through a place called the Clashing Clouds. The clouds open and close and the entrance must be held open by the mara'akame for all to pass through. It is evidently a very dangerous passage for everyone but especially so for the *primeros*.

The blindfolded *primeros* circling the fire. "Those blindfolded ones," wordless and sightless, tightly hold their lighted candles and circle the fire with nearly as much assurance as the other pilgrims.

evening we made arrangements to pass the night in the desert so as to arrive next day at the place of the Sacred Water, which should be visited at dawn.

We stopped on a relatively level place and gathered sufficient brush to keep the fire going all night. The blindfolded ones walked to the campsite with nearly as much assurance as the others. Ramón soon had started a small fire and everyone circled it, each drawing from the fire a piece of smoldering wood and holding it aloft to the four directions as Ramón prayed ardently. No one had eaten all day and neither supper nor water were taken now. It became evident that no one intended to sleep. The *peyoteros* wrapped their blankets about them and huddled close to the fire. The night was bitterly cold and the gift of the warmth from the fire was so welcome that an attitude of awe and veneration toward Tatewarí seemed most appropriate. Ramón began to chant and tell the myths of the peyote, of the deer hunt, and sang the peyote songs. Alternately, the companions dozed a bit during the night in a sitting or squatting position, never actually lying down or sleeping. At any one time, two or three were always awake, singing, chanting, and tending the fire. It seemed that, like Tatewarí, the ceremony had to be tended perpetually and was never allowed completely to subside. And so we passed our first night out.

Arrival at Tatei Matinieri

Camp was broken before the sky had lightened so that everyone would be at Tatei Matinieri by dawn, "in order to help Tayaupá come up." We crossed more desert, a grueling trip in the half-light, progressing slowly over the low, dense growth of desert laurel, barrel cactus, jumping cholla, rabbit ear cactus, creosote bushes, and agave. At Ramón's direction the camper bumped to a stop at a place undistinguished to a non-Huichol but known, relevant, and obvious to the *peyoteros.* As the sky passed from black to gray to a luminous pink Ramón hastily directed everyone out of the vehicle with his bundles of offerings. The *primeros* though still blindfolded managed with a minimum of direction to assume their places in line and then the group set out toward a series of tiny water holes about a quarter of a mile away, at a pace between a brisk walk and an outright run. Tatei Matinieri consisted of about a dozen little dirty puddles, a series of permanent springs beside a small marsh, punctuated by a solitary stunted tree.[8]

The *peyoteros* assembled in a line, in their proper order, facing the ever-brightening eastern sky while Ramón chanted, prayed, and gestured with his plumes, until he directed them to set down their bundles. Ramón, at the head of the line, then beckoned forward the first pilgrim, Carlos.[9] Ramón squatted beside the largest water hole and taking up some in his gourd bowl removed Carlos' hat and poured water into it. He then touched both of Carlos' eyes with his plumes, sprinkled water on his head, and had him drink that remaining in the bowl. The ritual varied somewhat for the *primeros*. Ramón took more time and care with them, praying over them longer. After they had drunk the Sacred Water instead of sending them immediately back to their places in line he removed their blindfolds and urged them to gaze up and behold the sacred place to which they had returned as gods. He pointed out the important features of the landscape, the places the gods had stopped and rested, eaten, sung, or talked with the animals while traveling back to their homeland. Especially affecting were Ramón's ministrations over Lupe at this time. He carefully led her from her place to the water and she remained motionless for a moment after he

[8] The significance of permanent springs would certainly have been greater to people living in the desert than to those living in the mountains. That the springs are so inconspicuous but nonetheless known, named, venerated, integrated into the mythology, lends support to the interpretation of the Huichol as originally having come from this region historically, as well as mythologically.

[9] Ramón's manner of directing the movements of the *peyoteros* was fascinating, always nonverbal, often so subtle as to be completely invisible to an outsider. At important times, the pilgrims watched him intensely and the resultant activities seemed choreographed—simple, natural, and somehow inevitable in their order and grace.

Ramón pointing out Wirikuta to Lupe after removing her blindfold. Ramón leads Lupe from the line of pilgrims and anoints her with Sacred Water. He then raises her blindfold and points out the important features of Wirikuta. She hesitates a moment before raising her eyes and seems almost reluctant to behold such an awesome sight.

The pilgrims displaying the offerings they have brought to the peyote. Each pilgrim lays out his offerings for the peyote while holding candles toward the ascending sun. Ramón chants and prays with great emotion as the pilgrims weep and urge the deities to accept their offerings.

had removed her blindfold. He bade her to lift her eyes, to behold the place of the Ancient Ones, where it all began, and she did so slowly, almost reluctantly. The sun struck her face fully. She seemed transfixed and tears spread evenly down the wrinkles of her rapturous face. Seeing her thus no one could help but know that she found the Sacred Land to be as beautiful as she had been told all her life. Ramón grasped her arm and led her back to the line with apparent satisfaction; all was as he had said. He had brought her here safely, and that she was his wife and so moved by the experience which he had made possible for her unquestionably intensified the meaning of the moment for both of them. The man Ramón for an instant was transcendent over the mara'akame. When Ramón had completed the ritual for each *peyotero*, Carlos administered the Sacred Water to Ramón, sprinkling it on his head and giving him the remainder to drink.

Offerings were then spread out by each pilgrim, lined up, and displayed—including the deer horns which had been removed from the camper temporarily for this purpose. With great care, each *peyotero* laid out or held heavenward his treasures, displaying them to the ascending sun. Impassioned prayers by Ramón told the gods that these were the offerings being brought for the *híkuri*. Ramón drew from his bags tortillas which he blended in his gourd bowl with some of the Sacred Water, stirring the mixture with the end of his candle, and then placed some of the resultant paste in each pilgrim's mouth. This was the sacred food of the First People. All prayed aloud but independently with great emotion, weeping and shouting, waving plumes and feathers and candles toward the sky and in the four directions, pointing out the beauty of their gifts to the gods. Even the shyest and youngest among them, Victoria and Pablo, were outspoken and animated, imploring the deities to give them success in their quest.

At this point, quite unexpectedly, Ramón called forward Furst and then me and administered the Sacred Water and blessing to each of us, telling us, "Now you are in accord and of one heart with your brothers, the Huichols." He directed us as we clumsily imitated the movements of sprinkling the water and tortilla mixture to the four directions.

The mood changed after the consumption of the sacred food. Laughter and shouts of joy replaced the weeping and praying, this because the "deities" had glimpsed their homeland and had been promised a successful return and peyote hunt. There was now much capering and cavorting. Francisco leaped about the springs like a rabbit, dazzling everyone with his agility. He had the gift of surprising people usually by looking at one moment like a wizened fragile old man who would break if he moved, then suddenly and without warning leaping straight up into the air or dancing a little jig without reason. The bottles and gourds were brought out and everyone moved among the springs to gather the Sacred Water they needed for various purposes, since each of the Rain Mothers is especially good for a particular kind of favor or blessing. (Francisco, for example, primarily because he wanted protection for his cattle, gathered water to take home from one of the holes representing a deity known to protect animals.) The Sacred Water was also used to sprinkle and bathe all the offerings. They were made sacred by anointment with these waters, just as on other occasions, when they are smeared with deer blood, they become acceptable to the gods. Without this ritual, they are merely beautiful but not sacred or suitable as offerings.

Establishing the Reversals

Containers of water and offerings were returned to the bundles, horns were replaced on the camper, and everyone resumed his place as we headed toward "Where the *Uxa* Grows." [10] Merriment and excitement filled the car and animated chatter and laughter. By way of explaining the laughter, Ramón reached over and taking some of my hair in his hand said that now it was cactus fiber. Pointing to himself, he said that he was the Pope, that Lupe was "an ugly boy," Victoria a *gringa*, and Francisco a *nunutsi* (little child). Thus I

[10] *Uxa* is desert laurel, a yellow root used in subsequent peyote ceremonies for face-painting; this plot of *uxa* is near a lake known as Agua Perdida.

knew the reversals which he had previously described had been put into effect. Someone sneezed and the laughter was uproarious; according to one of the conventions of the reversals, the nose had become the penis, thus a sneeze was a delightful off-color joke.

According to both Lumholtz (1902) and Zingg (1938) and Ramón's earlier statements, the reversals should have been instituted much earlier, before the *peyoteros* had actually left home. But if the reversals were operating before this time, I found no indication of it. Ramón had attempted to explain the reversals to me on several occasions previously, stating, "On the peyote hunt, we change the names of things because when we cross over there, into Wirikuta, things are so sacred that all is reversed." Now two matters were clear which had previously been obscure in discussing reversals. First, Ramón had originally stressed the fact that the mara'akame dreams new names for things each year, an arrangement which seems merely to disguise the sacred places. In fact, dreaming was only one source of inspiration for providing reversals; some are accidental and many are conventional and recurrent. Nearly all of the examples provided by Ramón at home in fact were used during this trip. Nevertheless, there was much improvisation, particularly pertaining to matters that were unusual this year, such as the presence of the outsiders, their equipment, and the camper. The camper became the "burro," who would stop "if he ran out of tequila" and who was traveling along a fine highway instead of the miserable ruts that passed as roads, and would eventually take us home "to Los Angeles." Interestingly enough, although these reversals were often offered in jest, and some by accident or mistake, once instituted they were no less serious and obligatory than the more conventional ones. All mistakes were persistently and firmly corrected by everyone.

The reversals applied to behaviors as much as to people and objects, thus one addressed someone in front of him by turning to the rear and one accepted something from another by telling him, "You are welcome," so that the giver replied, "Thank you." How greatly and extensively the reversals altered our subsequent activities will be apparent later. A second point is significant here, that while occasional substitutions occurred actual oppositions were more desirable. This was not always possible, for example, where no clear opposite existed no immediate antonym sprung to mind, and substitutions were inevitable. But, just as Ramón had said, it could be seen that whenever possible, "everything should be upside down and backward," and not merely different.

An aesthetic principle was involved as well. If one could compound the reversals, devising a whole series of them, this was reckoned as especially satisfying. All would nod with approval when one made a comment such as was made at the end of the extremely successful peyote trip, that "here we all were in the middle of the city, beneath the moon, having failed to bring back *híkuri*, having only baskets full of flowers because there was no *híkuri*." This was said as we stood in the hot sun in the empty desert with our baskets heaped high with peyote. Sudden switches in emotion must also be explained at least in part by the reversals, as when the heavy, almost grief-stricken atmosphere of the journey prior to the undoing of the blindfolds and the arrival at the Sacred Water abruptly gave way to conviviality, joy and a sense of high anticipation as we approached Wirikuta itself. The significance and function of these reversals are discussed in greater detail elsewhere.

We traveled north through San Luis Potosí and more reversals were suggested. Tangerines became lemons. We passed a dry salt lake which was sugar and a pond that was filled with tequila. At last we turned north and finally reached the desolate district of Real de Catorce. Ramón indicated that here we had to stop and look for deer tracks, for unless there were deer tracks there would be no peyote. (According to the mythology the first peyote appeared in the tracks left by the first deer.) Everyone fanned over the countryside, carefully and quietly searching the ground for an indication of deer tracks. After several hours the group gravely returned. No sign of the deer had been discernible but this was not definitive of failure since we were still outside of Wirikuta proper. It grew dark. We quickly found a place to leave the camper and began preparations to camp for the night.

Everyone gathered creosote brush for the fire (which Ramón lighted) and, after placing a piece of brush on the fire and circling, assumed his proper place before it. Then each *peyotero* brought forth remnants of what little he had eaten during the day and gave them as offerings to the fire. Clothing was shaken and brushed over the fire with each person getting as close to it as possible, holding up legs and arms, hands, and feet, leaving behind the pungent odor of seared cloth and hair.

Arrival at Wirikuta—the "Knotting-in"

Brush was heaped high around the *hikuritámete* thus forming a series of concentric circles, the fire in the center, the pilgrims surrounding it, they, in turn surrounded by a high wall of brush which served as a windbreak and provided food for the fire during the cold dark hours.

As before, no preparations were made for sleeping. Violins were brought out and an interlude of quiet praying, talking, and singing ensued. After a time Ramón removed the *kaunari,* the sacred string, from his quiver. This was the cord which had been used to circle the group before leaving for Wirikuta. In the same manner as noted in the first circling, the bowstring twanging, the *kaunari* was handed about in a circle, first in front, then in back of all the *peyoteros.* Then Ramón held the end of the string while he prayed and called each pilgrim to his side one by one. Each one knelt before him, holding the other end of the string, as Ramón made a knot, symbolizing the presence of the pilgrim on the journey, so that there was finally a knot for each person. As before, Carlos tied the knot for Ramón when the latter had finished with the others. On this occasion and for all those which subsequently occurred on the trip, he beckoned to Furst and to me and indicated that we should follow the same procedure. We joined the circle and knelt, holding the string, while he "knotted us into the unity," saying, "Now we are all of one faith, of one affection, of one heart." The others showed no discernible reaction to the extraordinary arrangement of including non-Huichols in the unity. (Here, as so frequently, one could not fail to be impressed with these people's poise in the face of the unfamiliar, a poise which was particularly interesting in view of the fact that they are very expressive, even emotional, and readily given to laughter and tears when in familiar surroundings.) The "knotting-in," Ramón later disclosed, must be done only after arriving in the peyote country. The ritual is not mentioned in any of the previous ethnographic descriptions of the Huichol peyote pilgrimage. Of all that had occurred before, this ceremony seemed most important to Ramón in altering our status from that of "men of another country, another religion, another race" to "Huichol brothers." Ramón made it a special point to tell us that we should not sleep that night but should remain alert and awake, holding the right thoughts, so that we would all be of one mind, have the right will, thinking of Our Father, Our Grandfather, and giving the *mara'akame* and our brothers strength which we would need the next day, in the land of Wirikuta, where we were born."

Before dawn we broke camp, the night having been passed in the usual way, with a minimum of sleeping and eating.

We passed *'Unaxa*, the "Burnt Mountain Where the Sun Was Born," mentioned in the mythical trip. The sunrise was glorious and was greeted boisterously with shouts of, "Look how ugly it is, how terrible the day will be. Our Father does not like to see us!"—another occasion when we were witness to the reversals.

In a few hours we arrived at the railroad tracks to Estación de Catorce and went on to a tiny grove of stunted trees, barely jutting over the high creosote on a vast semidesert which ended several miles away in the foothills of a small mountain range. The trees marked the perimeter of the sacred place of Wirikuta, and it was here we would make our camp, here that Tatewarí would await us while we walked eastward toward the mountains and sought the *híkuri.* The small fire was started immediately and as always each person brought a stick to feed it. Offerings were unpacked and repacked and everything except that which was to be offered to the peyote was left behind.

The *hikuritámete* set out across the desert, moving briskly toward the mountains but fanning out instead of following the single file usually observed for ritual processions. Everyone was completely quiet and grave, looking closely at the ground for tracks. As they approached the mountains, the *peyoteros'* pace slackened for peyote was more likely to be found here and the tension mounted. Their behavior was precisely that of stalking an animal. There were no sudden movements, no talking. The pilgrims bent over close to the ground, moved in the brush on tiptoe, gingerly raising a branch or poking under a cactus in hopes of catching sight of the small gray-green peyote plant which is so inconspicuous, growing nearly parallel to the earth's surface and exactly the same color as the surrounding vegetation in this region. Ramón finally decided that the area was not promising for there were signs that other Huichol parties had been here already and gathered much peyote. "We must move on," he indicated, farther east toward the mountains. We assembled this time in single file and followed Ramón for three hours of rapid walking until he gave the signal to fan out and search once more. As before, all this was in complete silence.

Finally Ramón beckoned everyone to his side—he had found peyote, seen the deer. Quickly we all gathered behind him as he drew his arrow and readied the bow. We peered down at the barely noticeable round flat-topped plant, two inches in diameter, segregated into eight sections. Everyone prayed quietly as Ramón began to stalk it, moving ever closer until when he was only a few feet away he aimed and shot one arrow into the base of the plant toward the east and crossed it quickly with another arrow pointing north so that the peyote was impaled in the center. The peyote-deer was thus secured and unable to escape.[11] Ramón drew nearer, placing his horns of Kauyumari beside it, to the west of the plant. He cleared the ground all around the plant with his knife and beckoned everyone to come forward to stand

[11] Lumholtz (1902:133) reports that the mara'akame is careful not to hit the plant with his arrows as it must be taken alive; this was not the case here.

Ramón stalking the peyote in Wirikuta. On sighting the first peyote, the pilgrims gather around Ramón in complete silence. He approaches it on tiptoe, soundlessly parting the branches, so as not to frighten it away.

closely around it. From his *takwatsi*, or sacred basket, he took his plumes and swept downward and over the peyote. This was because the first arrow in penetrating the peyote had caused rays of colors to spurt upward, like a rainbow; the rays had to be stroked and coaxed back into the peyote-deer. The colored rays are the *kupuri*, soul or life-blood of the deer, the life-blood of the *híkuri*, and must be preserved.[12]

[12] A great many plants and animals and all people have this *kupuri* or soul-essence; it is ordinarily visible only to the mara'akame. Ramón has depicted it in his yarn paintings as multicolored wavy lines connecting a person's head or the top of an object with a deity. Verbally he described *kupuri* as rays or fuzzy hairs.

The *hikuritámete* surrounded the peyote with their offerings and the plant was soon ringed with lighted candles, bottles and gourds of sacred water, the *takwatsi*, ceremonial arrows, tiny bowls, yarn paintings, deer horns, miniature deer snares, beads, decorated coins. In a long chant the pilgrims named all the deities they represented in their order—"Tatewarí, Tayaupá, Tsakaimuka, Tatutsí, Tatei 'Utuanaka, 'Xuturi Iwiékame, Tamatsi Maxa Kwaxí, all are here." Everyone wept silently, kneeling in a circle as Ramón took his arrows in each hand, dipped the tips into the "peyote-blood"; with this substance visible only to the mara'akame he anointed all those present by stroking first their foreheads, cheeks, and then their eyes and breast. Ramón carefully began to dig out the peyote with his knife, cutting it so as to leave some of the root in the ground, "So that the deer could grow again from his bones." He sliced it from the center outward along the grooves of each segment. Into each pilgrim's mouth he placed a segment of it after first touching it to the pilgrim's forehead, cheeks, and eyes. Last, Ramón was given his piece by Carlos, and finally the two new Huichol companions, the anthropologists, were beckoned forward to receive peyote in the prescribed manner.

The little group was sharply etched against the desert in the late afternoon sun—motionless, soundless, the once-bright colors of their costumes now muted under layers of dust—chewing, chewing the bitter plant. So Sahagún described the ancient Indians who wept in the desert over the plant they esteemed so greatly. The success of the undertaking was unquestionable and the faces changed from quiet wonder to rapture to exaltation all without words, all at the same moment, expressive of a synchronized harmony, perhaps called forth by some gesture of Ramón's unseen by me. Their cama-

Lupe brushed with the sacred arrows. Ramón dips the plumes of his arrows in the "peyote blood" and anoints the pilgrims by brushing their faces and breasts.

raderie, the completeness of their communion with one another was self-evident. The companions were radiant. Their love for their life and for one another was palpable. Though they did not speak and barely moved, no one seeing them there could call the experience anything less than collective ecstasy.

The hole where the peyote had been was covered completely by the offerings.[13] Ramón asked Furst and me to remain behind to watch over the cavity and offerings while the rest of the party again searched the desert for more *híkuri*. Although subsequently discovered peyotes were not venerated to this extent, for none is as sacred as the first, each time one was found it was carefully lifted, touched to the forehead and eyes and held for a moment solemnly in both hands against the throat and then pressed to the heart before being placed in the *peyotero's* basket.[14]

Furst and I remained behind on guard while the others hunted until, still whispering and moving stealthily, they reassembled after several hours, baskets heavy with cactus. The offerings were moved from the site of the first peyote and hidden in a nearby bush. Ramón repacked his *takwatsi* with its arrows and replaced the deer horns on his basket. Now, he admonished, we must all leave as quickly as possible, to return to our place beside Tatewarí, for, "It is very danger-

[13] In 1968, reports Furst (1972:177), the offerings left for the first peyote were burned. I have no explanation for this omission in 1966.

[14] The forehead or fontanelle as the opening in the embryo's skull where Tatei Niwetúkame inserts the soul of the unborn child, is considered the source and location of life. The eyes, "to see our life," the voice box, to speak with, "to tell our symbols," and the heart, the source of emotions, are the other vital organs brought in contact with the peyote. Throughout the trip, this contact ritual preceded eating or touching peyote.

The pilgrims returning to camp with twigs to feed Tatewarí. As the pilgrims approach the campfire, each cuts twigs and branches to use to revive Tatewarí.

ous to remain here." We outsiders were puzzled but fell into our places at the end of the line and found ourselves barely able to keep up, for the group was nearly running. This pace was kept up all the way back; despite the difficulty of the terrain we literally raced out, as though pursued and in great peril.[15]

[15] Furst in his 1968 trip does not report running out of Wirikuta. When I queried Ramón about this in 1971 he explained that the earlier trip had been more dangerous because there were so many *primeros*. It was my impression that Ramón himself was less afraid or less in danger in the later trip due to his increased experience.

We arrived back at camp to find that Tatewarí, which had been properly banked, was still aglow underneath a pile of ashes. Breaking twigs as we reentered the cleared area, we circled, feeding the fire, and cleansing ourselves before it in the usual fashion. Ramón further purified each of us with his sacred arrows dipped into the water from Tatei Matinieri. The Sacred Water was offered to the four directions, the fire, then to all of us to drink from a small gourd.

At last we broke formation and the tension which had been unrelenting since dawn was also broken. We could eat now and rest. The meal was far from elaborate but very welcome —tortillas, tangerines, and cigarettes. Then Ramón himself along with Pablo, Lupe, and Victoria went out to gather firewood for the night, leaving the three older men behind, saying they must not gather brush, "for it is not right for little children to do the work of grownups." The reversals became increasingly demanding, complex, and binding, necessitating so much verbal and behavioral change that everyone had difficulty following their strictures. At dusk all gathered around the fire, each wrapped in his blanket. Ramón sighed and muttered, "Ah, how bad it is here. How ugly, there is only the cold sun. We are wide awake and we found no peyote, only flowers. Tomorrow we must set out very early to find more flowers since there is no peyote."

That night no peyote was eaten but there was more sleeping than had occurred previously. The worst dangers had been avoided, the climax passed, and the sacred purpose of the trip fulfilled.

Collection of More Peyote and Visions

After a breakfast of tortillas and Sacred Water everyone set out toward the mountains to gather more peyote to take

The pilgrims at dusk, wrapped in their blankets, after the first day of gathering peyote. No peyote is eaten that night. Everyone is very quiet, very tired, but relieved that the worst dangers are over.

home for the others. The peyote would be shared with "those who remained behind" and some of it would be sold or traded to the Cora Indians, who use but do not gather peyote. Most of it would be transplanted in rancho house gardens or saved for the subsequent dry-season ceremonies, the success of which depends on the return of *hikuritámete* with sufficient peyote. The pilgrims set off with empty baskets, marching very quickly in single file to the area visited the previous day. There were no special rituals and the day seemed like time out of the usual mood of the trip thus far. Still behavior was not "ordinary" in that no one spoke aloud, there was no laughter, no eating, only the steady gathering of peyote until the baskets were completely filled. The group once more filed out of the sacred land as quickly as possible, reentering the campsite in the usual manner—feeding the fire, circling, cleansing, and praying before sitting down to rest or talk.

Everyone proceeded to sort through his peyote, selecting and setting aside those plants that pleased him especially. All were different—which Ramón revealed by scraping the stem of the peyote with his knife; the flesh of the peyote can be any of the five colors of maize, and the taste and texture vary accordingly.[16] "Here, this one is red maize. It is sweet and delicate. This one is yellow maize, hot and flaming." The pilgrims "cleaned" the selected peyote by severing the lowermost portion of the root and scraping off some of

[16] It is true that all were different but all were so sour that the mouth immediately begins to water and shrivel on contact with them. "They are very sweet, good, like tortillas, delicious, chew them well," one is urged. Yet there is reason to believe that this statement was a reversal, for though quite accustomed to the taste of peyote, the Huichols made dour faces and grimaced as they chewed.

the dirt, then cutting some of the plant along the segments. The scrapings were always saved in a piece of clothing, usually a cape, and not the smallest piece was permitted to touch the ground. The qualities of the peyote plants were discussed with great intensity. "Look here is one that is very old, here is a short, fat one. Look how sweet—this is a baby. Ah, how beautiful, this is especially sacred, for it has five sections." The plants were addressed in fond terms, the women occasionally talking baby talk to them, fondling them and devoting much attention to their diverse charms. Then under Ramón's direction each person took the sections from his chosen peyote and going to each of the others, touched the bud to forehead, cheek, throat, and eyes, then put it directly into the mouth.

The sorting, cleaning, and packing of the peyote was time-consuming, painstaking work. After the plants had been cleaned, they were arranged in the baskets, the best ones perfectly symmetrical and consisting of five sections, placed in the center of the basket, the others arranged around them in concentric circles. Layer upon layer was thus built up to the basket's brim. No empty spaces were allowed, no way for the peyotes to move on the trip home. They were not to be jostled about; peyote is very delicate and cannot stand that kind of treatment. "It must be carried back, gently, gently." When the baskets were filled, cloth covers were tied over the top. All the scrapings and leavings were gathered in one cape which Pablo then deposited in the bushes some distance from the camp, well off the ground, protected from animals. These were the bones of the peyote from which new ones will grow. Ramón had set aside five peyotes, each with five sections, graduated in size. They were strung together into a

Huichol violin with basket of cleaned, prepared peyote. Peyote plants were arranged in baskets, carefully packed so that none would be jarred or jostled during the trip home.

necklace and hung over the horns of Kauyumari, swinging between the ceremonial arrows.

This night for the first time on the trip there was much eating of peyote, in quantities sufficient for visions. (Eating peyote before this time was clearly intended as a means of achieving communion rather than for inducing visions. One must eat at least a whole plant for a vision.) There was much laughter at first and discussion of how beautiful the colors were, how funny the little animals one saw, until at last everyone fell silent before the fire, quietly enjoying his own experiences.[17] Only Ramón never joked or spoke about what he saw. Wrapped in his blanket up to his nose, he stared intensely into the fire and remained motionless for many hours. Only the mara'akame's visions have deep meaning, the others are primarily "for beauty." Ordinary people when they eat peyote hear music and see little animals, beautiful colors, and occasionally some of the creatures told of in the myths. The mara'akame receives his messages from the gods when he has eaten peyote. Then he sees and speaks with Tatewarí, Tay-

[17] Lumholtz (1902:134) states that peyote pilgrims ask the peyote not to make them crazy. This seems odd in view of the restrained behavior manifested by everyone throughout the trip, a restraint which was not less marked when they were actually under the influence of peyote. This is not to say that they were unemotional or inexpressive; on the contrary, it is evident that there was much weeping, laughter, dancing, singing, rejoicing, grieving, and so forth. But there was never the slightest indication of loss of self-control. In fact one reason the Huichols value peyote over datura is that peyote never causes one to "become crazy" if taken in the proper manner. Datura, on the contrary, is often associated with loss of control. According to Schultes (1972:47–48) violent intoxication frequently accompanies the ingestion of datura. Another discrepancy with Lumholtz' (1902:134) account of the peyote hunt appears. He states that all pilgrims see the deer when they eat peyote. According to Ramón only the mara'akame sees the deer; all the others see only deer tracks.

Ramón awaiting his peyote vision. The other pilgrims laugh and joke after taking peyote, but Ramón is silent, wrapped in his blanket, staring intensely into the fire. He remains thus motionless for many hours.

aupá, learns the names of things, the meanings of things, receives important messages, warnings and so forth. (But it is not only with the aid of peyote that the mara'akame can call on the deities. He is able to do so without it, as when he drums, chants, and sings.) The night passed thus was a quiet one, without sleeping or talking. Each person was alone, engrossed in his private view of beauty and light.

Departure from Wirikuta—Peyote Names, Eating Salt, and Untying the Cord

Breaking camp in the cold, gray morning (which, following the reversals, was described as very beautiful, full of cheer and warmth) involved gathering together belongings and baskets filled to the top with peyote, cleansing and finally circling the fire, which was banked for the last time. Everyone was very tired, dirty, and contented. It was a time of the greatest gravity and all were reluctant to leave. They wept aloud and mourned and lamented that having suffered much in regaining Wirikuta after so short a time, they had to depart. But after a while, Ramón signaled, and resigned, still in order, the companions filed into the camper. It was a quiet, peaceful time. Everyone dozed most of the way home, except Ramón, who said he had to remain awake to guard those he was leading. He explained that these exertions were especially hard for him because the journey weakens the mara'akame; it takes all his strength. For this reason it is so important that all the companions are of one heart and in a unity. Without this shared belief, this state of complete accord and trust, the mara'akame has no power and even though he is favored by the Fire and the Sun, he is helpless to use their gifts. The more pilgrims the mara'akame leads, the better, because he receives proportionately more strength from their faith.[18] The mara'akame must be careful with himself throughout the journey for he is "very delicate" at this time, "like a newborn child." (The word "delicate" [Spanish, *delicado*] is often used by Huichols interchangeably with "sacred" [Spanish, *sagrado*].)

On the way home we were all very hungry, having eaten so little for so long, and decided to stop at a restaurant for dinner. It was New Year's Day and the restaurant was pretentious though empty except for a crew of very elegant, haughty waiters, who gasped at the sight of a party of filthy Indians and *gringos* entering their establishment. Indeed we must have been a ridiculous spectacle—so haggard, so exhausted yet so unspeakably happy—sharing a precious secret, giddy with our invisible treasure, realizing that no outsider could tell that we had been transformed, knowing that others only saw us as mortals. Our delight only intensified as the waiters blanched and drew themselves up when we began moving tables around to accommodate our party. Ramón grew expansive and playful after his long ordeal, and the excursion to the restaurant gave him an opportunity to indulge his flair for drama and humor. When we had seated ourselves, Ramón stood and began to chant in Huichol as he "read" from the menu. To everyone's amusement he invented a fine story about the menu listing all the foods the Ancient Ones like best, and that obviously they had been here before us and

[18] It was made very clear at this time that however great the powers endowed to man by the deities, they were useless unless he enjoyed the esteem and trust of his fellows; they, not the gods, ultimately provided and sanctioned a man's ability to perform supernatural feats on their behalf.

left the menu for us, but unfortunately the "Spaniards" couldn't read Huichol and therefore hadn't prepared these foods for us.

We ordered our food and it was agreed that Furst and I would taste everything brought to make sure there was no salt in it and this we did.[19] Francisco played with his silverware to everyone's amusement, and, although he had never held such implements in his hands before, managed them very well by imitating Ramón. When the food arrived, the companions threw little bits of everything to the four directions and up and down before eating, just as they had done throughout the trip. Bits of egg, tortilla, butter, and melon flew through the air in a sacred hail. The expressions on the waiters' faces were truly memorable. Also unforgettable was the sight of Francisco solemnly dipping his bony finger down the neck of a bottle of soda pop and spraying it about, in the proper manner.

When all could eat no more, the *hikuritámete* swept the table clean, stuffing uneaten tidbits into their many bags, putting those foods with salt into other bags, to be eaten when the stricture had been lifted. Glasses, napkins, and ashtrays also disappeared into bags; the table, when we left, was quite empty. We collapsed ourselves back into the camper like circus clowns in a trick car and in a fine humor waved goodbye to the amazed Mexican waiters.

It was late at night when we arrived in Guadalajara (still known as Los Angeles, from the reversals), and came to

[19] Though Furst and I were not supposed to eat salt because of our ritual status, it was obviously better for us, rather than one of them, to violate the proscription. Here, as in other ways, there were degrees of being in a sacred condition. We were in a sacred state, but less so than our companions.

Pilgrims with candles. On returning home, the pilgrims file into the patio, take their proper positions, silently holding their lighted candles.

Ramón's little rancho to find all in readiness. The fire burned yet and was well tended. In our proper positions we filed to our places past those who awaited us, standing as they were when we left, silent, with lighted candles in hand. No greeting was spoken and only when the fire had been circled did all the pilgrims touch with their right hands the shoulders of those four who had remained behind. These four then circled the fire, stopping before Ramón, who gave each one some Sacred Water from his gourd bowl. Ramón began to chant, thanking the deities one at a time for bringing us success, for guiding us safely home. Without ceremony or ritual, it appeared that the reversals had been set aside and that the pilgrims were no longer the deities but devout and grateful mortals. The ensuing prayers were in no way unusual except for the rapid alteration in mood, from tears to ready laughter, flowing easily between joy, solemnity, relief, and gratitude.

The baskets were set down around the fire and peyote handed out, eaten casually rather than ceremonially (that is, without touching to the body and the sharing. It is often eaten this way all during the year, apart from any ceremonial usage that may go on concurrently.)

Ramón took up his sacred arrows in one hand, removed the coals and ashes from the fire until he reached the stone disc, the seat of Tatewarí, which covered the cavity of the fire. Each male pilgrim dropped into the cavity his tiny packets of *yé* tobacco wrapped in maize husk, tied with yarn. All the bits saved in the little bags from the entire journey were also placed in the cavity. The stone was replaced and wood once more moved to cover it.

Each person present including those who remained behind came forward as Ramón dipped a small bundle of dried flowers into his gourd of Sacred Water and with it touched the top of the head, cheeks, and lips of the participants, who drank the remaining water from the flowers. Subsequently, the same ritual was performed with peyote for the ones who had stayed behind. Ramón then removed from his quiver the *kaunari*, the string with the knots representing our unity. We were all seated around the fire as the cord circled us twice. Ramón called each *peyotero* forward in order and directed as each took the string immediately to the right of the knot representing himself while Ramón slowly untied it from the other end. The string was then passed over the fire for the

Ramón anointing the pilgrims with Sacred Water from Tatei Matinieri. Each person present comes forward as Ramón dips a small bundle of dried flowers into his gourd of Sacred Water from Tatei Matinieri and sprinkles the water on the pilgrim's head and face.

last time and returned to its place in the mara'akame's basket.

Lucia brought out a small bowl of salt and Ramón lifted that proscription by calling everyone before him and placing a pinch of salt in his mouth. With this final ritual, all the strictures against washing, sexual relations, full meals, drinking, defecation, urination, and sleeping were removed.

Post-Peyote Hunt Ceremonies: Cleansing of the Spines and the Sacred Deer Hunt

The Cleansing of the Spines ceremony took place in the Sierra several weeks after the party had returned, and Furst and I did not witness it. Ramón later reported it as follows. The first post–peyote hunt ritual (literally, "flying from here to there") has as its purpose the cleansing of everything, "to take all that off," especially all the spines and earth which might have been brought back from the land of Wirikuta inadvertently. Clearly, contact between the sacred and the mundane realms was regarded as contaminating to both. The boundaries between everyday life and Wirikuta were maintained by saving remnants of food taken from home back to the home, instead of leaving or using them in Wirikuta. This separation of ordinary life and Wirikuta was furthered by the "cleansing of the spines," which removed all matter that did not belong at home and could not be allowed to persist outside of Wirikuta. In this ceremony, according to Ramón, "the mara'akame gathers together his companions. He takes them back in his songs, from where they hunted the peyote. He follows them everywhere, where they drank the sacred water, where they searched. All of this the mara'akame sings, the whole story of the trip."

The night was passed in recapitulating the journey and all the companions were given peyote to eat, but it was not prepared in the usual manner. On this occasion it was ground up and mixed with water from Tatei Matinieri in a little gourd bowl used only for this purpose. Following the ingestion of the peyote and water mixture the former pilgrims danced, prayed, and venerated on through the night. At last the mara'akame addressed the deities:

> He asks them, all those Ancient Ones, "Well, are you pleased or are you not pleased?" This he asks them. "Are you happy? Are you contented with your relatives who took offerings to you?" And they answer, "Yes." They say to him, "Next year come again. And come back the year after that, because we will give you more life, so that you will be able to live stronger this whole year and return to us at the end of the year." That is our custom.

In the morning, after the sun had risen, the *uxa* gathered during the trip was ground and mixed to make a yellow paint, applied to the cheeks with straws. The design is the emblem of the deer, a small round yellow flower, "which is the peyote."

Then under the direction of the mara'akame small portions of the fields were cleared for maize; one field was the field of Tatewarí, another of Tayaupá, and so forth, for all the deities represented on the trip. The fields, Ramón indicated, were not full sized, big enough only to produce sufficient maize of a particular color to offer to the appropriate deity.

"Five days later" (which actually means sometime later) the mara'akame announced that it was time to chase the deer. The deer must be caught in a snare and neither bow and arrow nor gun could be used on him as for other animals and birds, because one must address the living deer to be sure that he understands the nature of his sacrifice. Ramón explained it this way:

We must set snares to catch him. So that it will be difficult for us, so that he will break our hearts. So that we will think, "Ah, it is a very special thing he does for us. He makes it hard for us to catch him. . . . He does not let himself be beaten easily. He takes this path and that, he listens to the voices he hears. He doubles back, he moves through the brush. But where he goes, whether he takes this path or that, if it is ordained that he go into the net, it does not matter which path he takes. It does not matter that I have dogs with me to search out his trail. It does not matter if I am well or if I am hurt by the rocks, by the branches. If one [Tatewarí] has commanded him so, I will come up there beside him, there where the snare is. He is in the snare, he looks up at me, saying as he does so, "Ah this is the death of me." There he lies down, he stretches out before me of his own will. I speak to him, I ask that he understand. He calls to me, "I am taking leave of my life, my life is darkening." That is how it is. Here where my brother, the deer, roams, I have succeeded once again. I am able to place him on my shoulders, I have blood to place on my ceremonial objects. Once more we have our life.

And when I bring him back those others will say, "here you are with Our Brother. Now the earth will be able to bring forth once more, now it finally will." I will say, "That is what I am saying to him as I carry him here on my shoulders." I will place him gently down on the ground. The women pick him up, they lay him gently down on their capes so that he will be well honored. They give him to eat, they give him to drink. They feed him the sacred grasses which he likes. He is in his place. I skin him, I extract his heart. I cut it through the center, I cut it into pieces. I take his blood, I paint it on Tatewarí. I paint it on his house, I anoint the earth with it, I anoint the *útsa*, the arrows, all the ceremonial objects. That is how we obtain our life.

The deer must be driven into the snare only by those men who are abstinent, those "who are in love cannot participate" even though they have cleansed themselves over Tatewarí.

(This means that the party of hunters seldom includes younger men.) The hunters were to be dressed in their best clothes, "very well adorned, like beautiful Huichols."

The most important part of the deer is his blood, which is conserved in a small piece of tied intestine for the mara'akame to use to anoint the offerings to the deities.

Lumholtz (1902:43) suggests that the deer blood is the emblem of sustenance and fertility and his blood is sprinkled over the seed corn that it may become equally sustaining. The deer is the sacrifice most valued by the gods and without him rain and good crops, health and life, cannot be obtained. Zingg sees the deer hunt as a "mystic participation in the making of sunshine, because the first peyote pilgrimage enabled the sun to shine" (1938:43). Ramón's interpretation is simpler and more consistent: the deer, the peyote, and the maize are one. One is no good without the other. Deer blood is needed to make the others work. It makes them sacred, makes the offerings powerful.[20]

The Relations of the Pilgrims after the Peyote Hunt

In view of the simple, almost skeletal social organization of the Huichols, the absence of any true corporate groups, kin-

[20] In the deer hunt, and the manner of his death, one again detects evidence of the recency of the Huichols' past as hunters and their incomplete transition to agriculture. The concept that the animal is man's brother who sacrifices himself to the hunter willingly at the request of the Guardian of the Species, the fact that the deer does not die, for "his bones are given to Tatewarí, and in this manner, Tatewarí, with his power, revives the deer and a new one is born"—these are ubiquitous features of hunting ideologies. Deer hunted in this ceremonial manner are not of interest for nourishment. Lumholtz (1902:47) describes the general unconcern at the deer hunt he witnessed when the dogs made off with the cooked deer meat. The matter was unimportant because the proper offerings had already been

ship based or otherwise, the presence of loose and flexible kindreds and the absence or rarity of ramifying ties—such as those provided for among the bilateral mestizos by the *compradrazgo* or godparent system—make it surprising that the pilgrims do not attempt to establish enduring groups capable of further collective action on the basis of their shared participation on the pilgrimage.

The deliberate unknotting of the cord which had symbolized the unity and brotherhood established by and characterizing the time of the journey makes it quite specific that the intense camaraderie of the trip is *not* to be maintained afterward. It would seem that the group's unity is intentionally defined as spiritual and definitively removed from the secular realm. Like the occurrence of avoidance behaviors in kinship relationships which are too structurally significant to sustain an open breach, true peyote companions cannot disappoint each other, quarrel, or fail to meet a request for help because their companionship is strictly confined to the religious realm. No rejection can occur when no demands are made; neither can there be failure "to act in perfect accord," when the only actions taken by the group in concert have already occurred and will not be repeated.[21]

---

made. And Ramón related that the first deer caught belongs to the Sun, so eating even one piece of it will make one terribly ill. The deer hunt is in many ways a reenactment or recapitulation of the peyote trip. The parallels between the two are numerous and of course quite intentional.

[21] Some modifications of this interpretation are in order in view of Ramón's discussions of the *kaunari* in 1971. On this visit he pulled from his *takwatsi* the *kaunari* from his most recent (1970) peyote trip. It was knotted. These pilgrims had all come from one rancho and had agreed to return together again the following year and to stay together for five successive hunts, if possible. In such a case as this, a

In discussing the relation of the pilgrims to each other and the deities after their return, Ramón explained that, on the night when the first peyote had been found, while gazing into the fire he had had visions concerning the special affinity which existed between the pilgrims and the various deities. These affinities are not necessarily with the same deity whose name they took. He described my special affinity for *'Utuanaka* as based on his vision which showed us together.

This is how Ramón described the vision:

How was it when I was given Barbara's name? Tsinurawe. Well, she appeared there, Barbara stood there, all in brilliant colors, she was glowing there, glowing so very brilliantly. She appeared there next to Tatei 'Utuanaka. 'Utuanaka, holding in her arms a baby, so beautiful, a baby of maize. 'Utuanaka had that offering

---

new *peyotero* cannot be introduced nor an old one dropped from the group without permission from all the others. If one wishes to undo his unity with the group, he may request that he be unknotted but this is a disavowal of his commitment to their accord. The 1970 arrangement is very precious and very rare because usually all pilgrims cannot plan to return to Wirikuta together since all are not from the same rancho. Thus it is more common for the mara'akame to unknot them at the close of the ceremony, when all are "liberated." "They weep when they loosen this union with the others, for it is very beautiful," said Ramón. Despite this indication of greater perpetuity among the *peyoteros* than previously observed, the fact remains that the pilgrims do not form stable, utilitarian groups on the basis of a shared peyote trip. Considering that pilgrims are usually drawn from several ranchos and are often kin, these spiritual bonds buttress preexistent ties and create new ones which are undoubtedly important in view of the inter-rancho visiting patterns of the Huichols. The bonds among pilgrims constitute a network of ties which cross-cuts and reinforces other more formal, lasting relationships. Like the "submerged line" in a strongly lineal society, the ties among pilgrims are affective, ritual, and personal and kept separate from the economic-jural-political rights and duties of the "official" social structure.

in her arms, she held the maize baby, and on each ear there was this soft fuzz, that which is like that on the peyote, that which we call Tsinurawe. Barbara was holding a gourd, the sacred gourd offering to 'Utuanaka, and above the gourd was the peyote, opening its eyes, all very fuzzy and very bright. That is how she received her name, because Barbara was together with all that, they were united, she and Tatei 'Utuanaka, with the peyote, with the maize baby, with the gourd offering. The peyote opened its eyes, soft, fuzzy, new, and I heard that name from Tatewarí, from 'Utuanaka, that Barbara was to be called Tsinurawe.

This signified that I was to make offerings of maize in a *jícara* or gourd bowl to 'Utuanaka, who was in a sense a kind of patroness for me. The proper offering to be made by each pilgrim to the proper deities was "envisioned" and communicated by Ramón. Ramón stressed the fact that as outsiders it was especially important that Furst and I know about these offerings, since they would help us understand "Huichol symbols."

The offering which each pilgrim makes to his deity is different, a gourd bowl of maize, a ceremonial arrow, a yarn painting, and so forth. The offerings are good for five years, and for five years, if possible, all the pilgrims should meet and bring their offerings with them to all the major ceremonies. Pilgrims, whether or not they return together, do acknowledge each other by using their *hikuritámete* names when they meet. (Indeed, Ramón called me Tsinurawe, from the 1966 peyote hunt, throughout the rest of our relationship.) The *peyotero* men now carry tobacco gourds and wear squirrel tails on their hats and none of those who were *primeros* will ever be considered quite as vulnerable as before. Thus the peyote journey constitutes a rite of passage for *peyoteros* as well as for the mara'akame, though less structured and significant for them than for him.

Concerning one's offerings for his particular deity, Ramón said: "If at the end of five years, you do not want it any longer for any reason, it is passed on by you to another. And if you like it, if you like our story, our history, then it is kept on. The offering is always the same and the other companions, they must make offerings of other things. So that all will be in union." (This seems to indicate that for five years it is desirable for the peyote group to be together at the same festivals but there is no mention of what, if anything, occurs when they are together.) If the offering is passed on, it must go to another person who is going to Wirikuta. A male gives his offering to a male, a female to a female, corresponding to the association between sex of pilgrims and sex of deity with whom he has a particular affinity. One must give his offering to the man or woman to whom he feels "closest in his heart." Thus he passes on his successful experience in the peyote hunt to another.

Upon returning to the Sierra, Ramón explained, a small *xíriki* would be erected for each of the *peyoteros* on Ramón's rancho and would be dedicated to various deities. These *xíriki* are arranged in a circle, one for each of the pilgrims in the same order that was observed throughout the journey.

When Ramón had completed his fifth journey to Wirikuta, when he had become a full-fledged mara'akame, he would build a *tuki* in the circle of the pilgrims' *xíriki* and this would make it complete.

The Mythical Version: "When the Mara'akame Plays the Drum and Flies the Children to the Land of the Peyote"

"Look," he tells them, "it is this way. We will fly over this little mountain. We will travel to Wirikuta, where the sacred water is, where the peyote is, where Our Father comes up."

And from there they fly, like bees, straight, they go on the wind as one says, this way. As though they were a flock of doves, very beautiful, like the singing turtle doves. They fly evenly. You can see that they become as little tiny bees, very pretty. They continue from hill to hill. They fly from place to place as the mara'akame tells them. The mara'akame goes with Kauyumari, Kauyumari who tells him everything. He protects them all. A little girl is missing a wing because the father or the mother have committed many sins. If they are missing a wing, the mara'akame puts it back on. Then she flies with the rest of them.

So they continue to travel. As they come to a place, the mara'akame points it out. So that they will know of it, how it was when Our Grandfather, Our Father, Our Great Grandparent, Our Mothers, when they went to Wirikuta, when Elder Brother Deer Tail, Maxa Kwaxí-Kauyumari, crossed over there and the children of the first Huichols went there, so that they became cured.

That is what the drum says on our rancho. When it is beaten. There the children fly. The mara'akame leads them on the wind. They land on one of the rocks. It is as though they were clinging to the rock, very dangerous. The mara'akame tells them, "Look, children, you are not familiar with these paths. There are many dangers, there are many animals that eat children, that threaten people. You must not separate, you must stay close together, all of you." And the children are very glad, very happy.

They fly on to Tokuari, to Where the Arrows Are. They fly past there. *Xiuwa, xiuwa, xiuwa,* so goes the sound of their flying. Their wings. They arrive at Tskata, the Volcanic Place, where in Ancient Times, the First Mara'akame, Our Grandfather, blessed the sacred water in the caves, so that everyone could go there, our relatives, the Huichols, everyone. The mara'akame takes a gourd bowl and with it sprinkles the sacred water over them. He tells them, "I bless you in the Four Winds, to the right and to the other side, to the north, to the south, and up above." So he says to them. He prays, "Let us feed them. There where Our Grandfather is, there on the south, there on the north. You, Our Aunt, Our Mother who are there. You, Kumúkite, gather yourselves together. You, Our Grandparents, who are kept in our houses as rock crystals, gather yourselves together. Your votive bowls are in their places, there they are."

He offers them on his right, he offers them on his left, he offers them to his east, he offers them above. Also he offers them to his west, where Our Mother Haramara dwells, where Our Mother Hamuxamaka dwells. So at last he says, "We will fly on." They land at Wakanarixipa. This is a terrible mountainous country. Here the mara'akame explains to them, "That is the way we must travel, the symbols we must follow. For when someone dies, there is always someone who comes after." Then he flies on. The children fly on, to Where the Star Lives. Then they fly to a place they call Hukuta (La Ocota, Pine Grove, the Place of Kindling Wood). Now they say, "Mara'akame tell us, how will we cross that river there?" "Well," he says, "I know how." And he takes them safely.

"At last," he prays, "Our Mothers, Our Fathers, all you who are in Wirikuta, those who are eaten as peyote, we are on our way to Wirikuta." He says to the children, "Act and feel like eagles. You will go there on your wings." They give instructions to one another, they learn. One tells the other, "Light your candle," and he answers, "Yes, very well." The mara'akame takes tinder, he takes flint, he takes steel for striking fire. They do this five times and they light the candles and worship there and go on their way. They travel and come to a place they call Las Cruces, where the cross is. They exclaim, "Oh, look, we really have come far, yes we have come far. And how will we be able to go on?" And they say, "Well, it is because we are going to Wirikuta, where the peyote grows, where our ancestors traveled. We have to get rid of our sins, everything."

The mara'akame, he travels on Kauyumari, who is the Deer,

the Deer of the mara'akame, Tatewarí, he leads them all, he is the one taking care of them all. They travel to a place called Irons Flying Up and after they have passed there they arrive at Teapari. They get to know it in the daylight. Here Kauyumari grinds the roots for the colors with which the Huichols paint their faces. It is the peyote paint, the paint which they get from the yellow roots they find growing in the country of the peyote. To get to know that place, that is why Our Grandfather, Our Father, Our Mother Haramara takes hold of them as they are. This is where they painted their faces, so that they could go across. There they pick up the root, carry it with them, so that they bring it to their homes. Our Grandfather passed by here in Ancient Times; it is he who placed it here, it is in Ancient Times that it was given its name, when Our Grandfather passed by here, when Kauyumari passed by here. It is a very beautiful place, very grand. Very sacred. So they learn all that from the mara'akame.

Now comes the most mysterious thing of all the great things on that journey. They arrive at the place called Where the Vagina Is, where it is called La Puerta, the Door, the Gate, in Spanish. Kauyumari opens it with his horns and he tells the mara'akame, "Here, the way is open, we may proceed." It is a very sacred place. Where the *peyoteros* sit in their places around Our Grandfather, close to Our Grandfather, while the mara'akame tells them to name all the women they have enjoyed, one by one. They must name them by their right names, even though all the other things are transformed. Where the knots are untied, the sins are taken away by Our Grandfather.[22]

They travel on to the place called Where the Penis Hangs.[23]

[22] This is exactly what occurs on the peyote trip, as has been seen. The statement concerning the need for "right names" despite the fact that everything is transformed refers to the reversals instituted during the peyote hunt. "Confession," in this version, occurs much later than that witnessed in the actual ceremony.

[23] No explication or identification of this place was possible.

Here the mara'akame speaks to Our Mothers, Our Grandparents. "Let us see what the deer tail plumes say."

They descend holding on to one another. This place is called the Breast, that is the name it was given in Ancient Times. There, they go on. They come to the place called Where the Arrows Stand. Then to Witsexuka, where they sit in a circle. "What is this place here named?" he asks the children. So they learn. He goes on and on, until all can sleep there.

We are not eating anything to speak of on this journey. Just a few watermelons, squash, green roasting ears of maize, just something, one thing and another. Oh, we carry a real load of life! If Our Mother is thus, if Our Father there is thus, they will give it to us, they will feed us. And he goes on, to the place where Wirikuta lies, that which they call Real Catorce, there they travel. He beats the drum.

Where it is called Wirikuta, where Our Mother Peyote dwells, there they arrive. When he has beaten the drum, when he stands by the sacred pools, when he has spoken to the Mothers and the Fathers, to Our Father, to Our Grandfather, to Our Great Grandparent, when he has laid his offerings down, when their votive bowls are in their place, when their arrows are in their place, when their wristbands are in their place, when their sandals are in their place, then it will be good, then we will have life.

The children are happy, all, they are contented. Because now they are blessed. The offerings are made, the deer tail plumes are in their place, the arrows are to the south, to the north, to the east, up above. He holds them out. The horns of the deer are in their place, no matter what kind.[24] The mara'akame says, "Oh,

[24] This refers to the growing scarcity of deer in the Sierra, which often necessitates substitutions. Here it is made clear that above all location and usage determine what is really proper. Thus bull horns "become" a kind of deer horn if "they are there, in their proper place."

Our Father, Our Grandfather, Our Mothers, you all who dwell here, we have arrived to visit you, to come and see you here. We have arrived well." And when they arrive, they kneel and Our Father, Our Grandfather, Our Elder Brother, embrace them.

"What did you come for, my children?" they ask. "You have come so far, why did you travel so far?"

They answer, "We came to visit you so that we will know all, so that we will have life."

"All right," they say, "it is well," and they bless them. And there they remain but ten minutes, a very few minutes, to speak with Our Father, Our Grandfather, with all of them there. And then the Mother gives them the blessing and they leave.

While the children are magically flying, that is, listening to the chant, an ear of maize and a squash are turned to face the east as the children fly toward Wirikuta. When they are ready to return, the maize and squash are turned to face westward to assist the children in the journey home. The trip is dangerous for the children, as they may be abducted by sorcerers and must be carefully watched by the marka'akame to prevent this. His task is made easier because he keeps the children together by "stringing them on a cord like the *kaunari*" used to bind the adult *peyoteros* together on the real trip. If the mara'akame fails and a child is abducted, he must go in search of its soul at night and bring it back. If he is unsuccessful in this, the child will die. After the party has returned safely, the children are actually given a small round tortilla which "is the peyote" they have brought home and this they present proudly to their parents who have remained behind. They have thus duplicated the true adult peyote hunt in its most important particulars in a ceremony that is an impressive and subtle blending of the actual, the magical, the symbolic, and the anticipatory.

How the Names Are Changed on the Peyote Journey

Well, let's see now. I shall speak about how we change the names of everything. Because all must be done as it was laid down in the beginning, when the mara'akame who is Tatewarí led all those great ones to Wirikuta. When they crossed over there, to the peyote country. Because that is a very sacred thing, it is the most sacred. It is our life, as one says. That is why nowadays one gives things other names. One changes everything. Only when they return home, then they call everything again what it is.

When everything is ready, when all the symbols which we take with us, the gourd bowls, the *nearikas*, the arrows, everything, have been made, when all have prayed in the *tuki*, when we set out, then we must change everything, all the meanings. For instance; an *olla* which is black and round, it is called a head. It is the mara'akame who directs everything. He is the one who listens in his dream, with his power and his knowledge. He speaks to Tatewarí, he speaks to Kauyumari. Kauyumari tells him everything, how it must be. Then he says to his companions, look, now we will change everything, all the meanings, because that is the way it must be with the *hikuritámete*. As it was in Ancient Times, so that all can be united.

"Look," the mara'akame says to them, "It is when you say, 'Good morning,' you mean 'Good evening.' Everything is backward. You say, 'good-bye, I am leaving you,' but you are really coming. You do not shake hands, you shake feet. You hold out your right foot to be shaken by the foot of your companion. You say, 'Good afternoon,' yet it is only morning." So the mara'akame tells them, as he has dreamed it. He dreams it differently each time. Every year they change the names of things differently because every year the mara'akame dreams new names. Even if it is the same mara'akame who leads the journey, he still changes the names each time differently.[25]

[25] On the basis of the trip witnessed, in which many of the reversals and substitutions mentioned here were used, it would seem that the

And he watches who makes mistakes because there must be no error. One must use the names the mara'akame has dreamed. Because if one makes an error it is not right. That is how it is. It is a beautiful thing because it is right. The mara'akame says to a companion, "Look, why does that man over there watch us, why does he stare at us?" And then he says, "Look, what is it he has to stare at us with?" "His eyes," says his companion. "No," the mara'akame answers, "they are not his eyes, they are tomatoes."

When one makes cigarettes for the journey, one uses the dried husks of maize for the wrappings. And the *yé*, the tobacco, it is called the droppings of ants. Tortillas one calls bread. *Masa* one calls *pozole*. Beans one calls fruit from a tree. Maize is wheat. Water is tequila. Instead of saying, "Let us go and get water to drink," you say, "Ah, let us take tequila to eat." *Nawa* is *atole*. And *atole*, that is brains. Sandals are cactus. Fingers are sticks. Hair, that is cactus fiber. The moon, that is a cold sun.

On all the trails on which we travel to the peyote country, as we see different things we make this change. That is because the peyote is very sacred, very sacred. And the journey, when we cross over to hunt it, is very sacred. That is why it is reversed. Therefore, when we see a dog, it is a cat, or it is a coyote. Ordinarily, when we see a dog, it is just a dog, but when we walk for the peyote it is a cat or a coyote or even something else, as the mara'akame dreams it. When we see a burro, it is not a burro, it is a cow, or a horse. And when we see a horse, it is something else. When we see a dove or a small bird of some kind, is it a small bird? No, the mara'akame says, it is an eagle, it is a hawk. Or a piglet, it is not a piglet, it is an armadillo. When we hunt the deer, which is very sacred, it is not a deer, on this journey. It is a lamb, or a cat. And the nets for catching deer? They are called sewing thread.

When we say come, it means go away. When we say, "Shh,

---

names are not different each time but somewhat patterned and recurrent.

quiet," it means to shout, and when we whistle or call to the front we are really calling to a person behind us. We speak in this direction here. That one over there turns because he already knows how it is, how everything is reversed. To say, "Let us stay here," means to go, "Let us go," and when we say, "Sit down," we mean, "Stand up." It is also so when we have crossed over, when we are in the country of the peyote. Even the peyote is called by another name, as the mara'akame dreamed. Then the peyote is *tutu* or something else.

It is so with Tatewarí. The mara'akame, we call him Tatewarí. He is Tatewarí, he who leads us. But there in Wirikuta, one says something else. One calls him "the red one." And Tayaupá, he is "the shining one." So all is changed. Our companion who is old, he is called the child. Our companion who is young, he is the old one. When we want to speak of the machete, we say "hook." When one speaks of wood, one really means fish. Begging your pardon, instead of saying "to eat," we say "to defecate." And begging your pardon, "I am going to urinate," means, "I am going to drink water." When speaking of blowing one's nose, one says, "Give me the honey." "He is deaf" means "How well he hears." So everything is changed, everything is different or backward.

The mara'akame goes explaining how everything should be said, everything, many times, or his companions would forget and make errors. In the late afternoon, when all are gathered around Tatewarí, we all pray there, and the mara'akame tells how it should be. So for instance he says, "Do not speak of this one or that one as serious. Say he is a jaguar. You see an old woman and her face is all wrinkled, coming from afar, do not say, 'Ah, there is a man," say, 'Ah, here comes a wooden image. You say here comes the image of Santo Cristo.' Or if it is a woman coming, say, 'Ah, here comes the image of Guadalupe.' "

Women, you call *tutu*. For the women's skirts, you say "bush," and for her blouse you say "palm roots." And a man's clothing, that too is changed. His clothing, you call his fur. His hat, that is a mushroom. Or it is his sandal. Begging your pardon, but what we carry down here, the testicles, they are called avocados. And the penis, that is his nose. That is how it is.

When we come back with the peyote, the peyote which has been hunted, they make a ceremony and everything is changed back again.[26] And those who are at home, when one returns they all want to know what they called things. One tells them, and there is laughter. That is how it is. Because it must be as it was said in the beginning, in Ancient Times.

[26] No such ceremony was witnessed and no reference to it was made; this omission seemed odd since other ritual conditions were "undone"; that is, strictures were specifically lifted by definite ceremonies. That one so important and unusual are this was not so treated is puzzling.

CHAPTER 5

The Deer-Maize-Peyote Complex

> You have seen how it is when we walk for the peyote. How we go, not eating, not drinking, with much hunger, with much thirst. With much will. All of one heart, of one will. How one goes, being Huichol. That is our unity, our life. That is what we must defend.
>
> Ramón Medina Silva

The religion and indeed the entire culture of the Huichols are not comprehensible apart from the deer-maize-peyote complex. Ramón stated this explicitly: "Now I will tell you of the maize and the peyote and the deer. It is not our custom to tell others of these things but because you are a companion I will tell you of them. These things are one. They are a unity. They are our life. They are ourselves." The understanding of this unity, the identification of the referents of the symbols and relationship between them, the function of the identification of the symbols with each other so that they form a single complex—these matters constitute the most difficult and the inescapable challenge in a study of Huichol ideology.

But just what does such an understanding consist of? What level of explanation is satisfactory? These questions are far from clear-cut and an explanation which satisfies one investigator may be only the beginning of the investigation for another. Lumholtz (1902) and Zingg (1938) clearly recognized the centrality of the deer-maize-peyote complex, but neither seemed especially driven to inquire along the lines indicated above, that is, *why* are these three symbols a unity, to what do they refer, and what purposes are served by their unification? Lumholtz' (1902) work is descriptive rather than analytic. He does not offer a theoretical interpretation but instead gives a sound and careful ethnographic report. On occasions Lumholtz (1902:126) refers to the deer-maize-peyote complex as a "cult"; however, he does not seem to be using the term in any technical sense.

It seems important to reserve the term "peyote cult," for reference to the North American Native American church, a revitalization movement found in particular among the Navaho in reaction to acculturation pressures. There is no reason to assume any present connection or similarity between Huichol uses of peyote and that of North American Indians (although pre-Conquest connections may well have existed).

Huichol uses of peyote also appear unrelated to Aztec peyotism, which was largely confined to the priestly class; neither is it similar to peyote use among such Mexican Indian groups as the Tarahumaras and Coras. The latter are deeply frightened of peyote, whereas the Huichols expect only benevolent results from using it. Nor do the other Mexican Indian groups have comparable symbolic associations between deer, maize, and peyote. Further, they have no ritual which corresponds to the Huichol peyote hunt. The Cora and Tarahumara Indians may purchase peyote in any market or from a Huichol, whereas the Huichols are enjoined against the use of peyote gathered from anywhere but the sacred country "where it lives." For all these reasons, it seems necessary to treat the Huichol peyote uses as distinct from that of the Navahos, Aztecs, Coras, and Tarahumaras.

What assistance in understanding the deer-maize-peyote complex can be found in Zingg (1938)? His study suffers from an overabundance of that which Lumholtz' lacks entirely—theoretical orientation. Zingg's theoretical interpretation of Huichol religion draws heavily on the early French sociologists, especially Durkheim and Lévy-Bruhl and the latter's concept of "mystic participation," which unfortunately is never defined by Zingg. Evidently Zingg regards it as self-explanatory, which is far from the case. He uses the concept so extensively that it loses any explanatory value which it might have had and becomes a cliché. Zingg, like Lumholtz, agrees that the deer-maize-peyote complex is absolutely central to Huichol life but regards this linkage as "illogical" (1938:259).[1] But this does not seem to trouble him, and he does not go on to the next question which is implicit —*why* are the deer, maize, and peyote one?

Underlying this question is a point of view which must be made explicit, the conviction that human thought, especially symbolic thought is systematic rather than random. The symbol which is "illogical" within one system of thought may be consistent and orderly within another, based on a different set

[1] Possibly Lumholtz (1902) and Zingg (1938) stopped short of a more complete explanation of the deer-maize-peyote complex because neither of them witnessed the most important event (or "field of action") in which a ritual expression is given to the complex, the peyote hunt. Both writers conduct an analysis of symbols as static rather than dynamic forces, as if they were timeless entities. Turner points out the problems arising from this approach: the critical properties of a symbol become intelligible only when a symbol is conceptualized as a force in a field of social action, for "conceptualizing the symbol as if it were an object and neglecting its role in action often lead to a stress on only those aspects of symbolism which can be logically and consistently related to one another to form an abstract unitary system" (1967:44). It seems that Zingg was indeed seeking such a consistent, unitary relationship, and thus was led to regard the association between deer, maize, and peyote as illogical.

of premises. These premises must be understood in order to make the symbol intelligible to outsiders.

Symbolic thought has its own order and logic and this is true regardless of the form of its expression—visual arts, poetry, mythology, or dreams. Lévi-Strauss's (1966, 1967, 1969) works on the structural study of myth have buttressed this position greatly, demonstrating the logical nature of myth. Lévi-Strauss's studies, it might be said, by stressing the systematic nature of myth, do for myth what previously Freud had done for dreams.

Adherents of this point of view would not ask, "*Is* there a logical relationship between deer, maize, and peyote among the Huichols?" but, "What is the logic of the relationship among them?" and then go on to the implicit functional queries: "What does this presumably logical association accomplish? How does it serve the Huichols?" This is not to deny or minimize the role of the accidental, dysfunctional, random, and irrational in human and cultural affairs. Rather it is to assert that on some level to some degree all behaviors and thoughts are purposive, integrated, coherent, and comprehensible (though certainly not in all their consequences), at least in the minds of those engaged in them. Finally, it is more important, in embarking on the path of attaining an understanding of the initially strange, to begin by assuming and searching for something meaningful rather than incoherent, and thus to proceed until proved wrong. These convictions provided the motive and set of assumptions which oriented the investigation and interpretation which I have offered here. Each reader must judge for himself whether or not the level of explanation achieved satisfies his own need for understanding.

Before proceeding with the analysis, the use of the word

"complex" to refer to the associated deer-maize-peyote symbols must be clarified. One of the purposes of this study is to demonstrate that, in fact, these three symbols constitute a unity, just as the Huichols say, and to show what the unity consists of and what purposes this unification serves. The term "complex" bypasses the more culturally specific, heavily connotative alternatives such as "cult" (for example, as used by Aberle, 1966) and "trinity" (as used in Catholicism) and at the same time avoids overly general terms such as "theme" and "configuration." It is satisfactory because it does not carry undesirable meanings but at the same time it focuses attention on the close association between the individual symbols. It is used here to refer to a system of related parts, which are discrete but rendered especially meaningful and expanded when used in combination.[2]

Procedures for the Analysis of the Deer-Maize-Peyote Symbol Complex

A number of excellent theories for interpreting symbols are currently available—those of Lévi-Strauss (1963a, 1963b,

[2] Neumann, in describing the cognitive processes of the unconscious mind, suggests the following approach to a group of symbols. "Symbols gather round the thing to be explained, understood, interpreted. The act of becoming conscious consists in the concentric grouping of symbols around the object, all circumscribing and describing the unknown from many sides. Each symbol lays bare another essential side of the object to be grasped, points to another facet of meaning. Only the canon of these symbols congregating about the center in question, the coherent symbol group, can lead to an understanding of what the symbols point to and of what they are trying to express" (1954:7). This coherent symbol group "congregating about the center" is very similar to what I have in mind when speaking of a symbol complex.

1966, 1967, 1969), Geertz (1957–1958, 1960, 1964, 1965), and Turner (1962, 1967, 1968, 1969a, 1969b, 1971) are especially valuable. The choice to use these works, in part and whole, was dictated ultimately by a practical concern—which material was likely to yield the best results, given the specific problem and data available? Turner's work appeared to be most appropriate for the present investigation; it has the additional advantage of including detailed examples of the procedures he used in his analyses of Ndembu ritual symbols. Turner's general approach and specific techniques have provided a compatible and practical model for the present work. The general theories of the other writers mentioned above are used selectively rather than systematically in this and the following chapter.

Turner's general approach to symbols calls attention to the broad spectrum of meaning they convey. Symbols are by definition multireferential. Therefore, one must take great care to specify and ascertain these multiple referents. This task is inevitably difficult because symbols are highly charged emotionally as well as ambiguous. In all cases, the personal as well as shared interpretations of symbols must be explored. From this it follows that analysis of a symbol must identify its objective referents, the emotions and meanings associated with the referents, and the public and private significance of the symbols. Turner's interpretation of the functions served by symbols is anticipated by his observation that they are "multivocal," that is, they stand for many things at once; "each has a 'fan' or 'spectrum' of referents, which tend to be interlinked and which interconnect a wide variety of significata" (1967:50–51).

Turner observes that in analyzing symbols some anthropologists have attempted to confine themselves to those meanings and referents which are overt, explicit, and fully apprehended by the people employing them. While he agrees that there are grave problems in interpreting meanings which are implicit, he regards anything less as vitiating the very nature of symbols; one of their functions is to encompass ambiguities that have *not* been raised to the level of consciousness and which cannot or have not been handled by direct and rational thought. Discussing the Ndembu, who often do not recognize the discrepancies between their own interpretation of a symbol and their behavior associated with it, Turner asks:

> Does this mean that the discrepancy has no relevance for the social anthropologist? Indeed, some anthropologists claim, with Nadel (1954:108) that "uncomprehended symbols have no part in social inquiry; their social effectiveness lies in their capacity to indicate, and if they indicate nothing to the actors, they are, from our point of view, irrelevant, and indeed no longer symbols [1967:28].

Monica Wilson (1957:6) agrees with Nadel and bases her analysis of Nyakusa ritual on overt native interpretation exclusively. Turner regards this approach as much too narrow:

> In my view, these investigators go beyond the limits of salutary caution and impose serious, and even arbitrary, limitations on themselves. To some extent their difficulties derive from their failure to distinguish the concept of symbol from that of a mere sign. . . . I consider that Carl Jung (1949:601) has cleared the way for further investigation by making just this distinction. "A sign," he says, "is an analogous or abbreviated expression of a *known* thing. But a symbol is always the best possible expression of a relatively unknown fact, a fact, however, which is none the less recognized or postulated as existing." Nadel and Wilson, in treating

most ritual symbols as signs, must ignore or regard as irrelevant some of the crucial properties of such symbols [1967:26].

One must agree with Nadel that a symbol which indicates nothing is no symbol at all. Symbols by definition *are* relevant, but the degree of comprehension of the meaning of a symbol is not a given and varies in its precision and specificity. A symbol is never unambiguous, but ambiguity must be distinguished from emptiness. There are those who would carry the argument even farther than Turner and assert that a clearly comprehended symbol is no symbol at all. It is precisely because the referents of symbols are not entirely clear to those employing them that the symbols are able to mask the irreconcilable nature of the meanings they embrace. Geertz (1965) and Lévi-Strauss (1967: first published 1958–1959) feel that symbols are more than merely ambiguous and go beyond merely concealing contradictions. They actually "celebrate paradoxes," and it is this feature which endows them with their uniqueness and effectiveness.

Turner insists, and I agree, that it is not only legitimate but absolutely necessary to include as part of the meaning of a symbol those aspects which the actors themselves are not able to interpret.[3]

Drawing on Sapir (n.d.) and Durkheim (1954; first published 1915), Turner works out the following theory: First, symbols have three essential properties: *condensation,* their representation of many things and actions by a single forma-

[3] A strict psychoanalytic approach to symbols minimizes greatly the explicit and overt interpretations and meanings which are available to the actors. Turner regards this approach as just as narrow as that of anthropologists who overlook the unconscious meanings of symbols. Both levels of meaning, conscious and unconscious, must be included, according to his interpretation.

tion; *unification of disparate significata,* the connection of the differing referents because they are associated in fact or thought, and therefore felt to possess analogous qualities; and *polarization of meaning*. By the latter Turner means the existence of two clearly distinguishable poles of meaning encompassed by symbols, one *ideological*, referring to the moral and social principles and norms of the group, and the other *sensory* or physiological, representing basic, universal human characteristics. A ritual "converts the obligatory into the desirable. Within the framework of meanings, the . . . symbol brings the ethical and jural norms of society into close contact with strong emotional stimuli . . . effecting an interchange of qualities between its poles of meaning" (1967:30). Thus a union of extremes or opposites is achieved by the symbols, in which "norms and values . . . become saturated with emotion, while the gross and basic emotions become ennobled through contact with social values. The irksomeness of moral constraint is transformed into the 'love of virtue' " (1967:30).

In these few lines, one encounters a summary statement of the basic dynamic which makes all social life possible, for it can be seen to explain why individuals follow most social dictates voluntarily, even with satisfaction, and how men come to place group values above self-interest; indeed self-interest becomes inseparable from the life of the group. In other words, what is described is the process of socialization wherein values are internalized and loosened from their group origins to become a part of the individual personality itself, thus articulating culture and personality into a coordinated entity.[4]

[4] A succinct and brilliant discussion of this process described with a somewhat different vocabulary is found in Spiro (1951).

The rituals which employ symbols, Turner goes on, are to be studied as fields of action, for in each field ritual symbols assert the "situational primacy" of a few features or principles of social organization at the cost of the other which are temporarily submerged.

All the contradictions of human social life, between norms, and drives, between different drives and between different norms, between society and the individual, and between groups, are condensed and unified in a single representation, the dominant symbols. It is the task of analysis to break down this amalgam into its primary constituents [1967:44].

According to Turner, in proceeding with an analysis of a symbol, the first stage should be the identification of its spectrum of referents and subsequently the location of the constituents which are combined into one manifestation or formation. Turner provides a useful suggestion for accomplishing this task by stating that there are three levels to be considered separately in the course of the analysis: these he calls the *exegetical*, *operational*, and *positional* levels. The exegetical consists of the overt interpretations and statements made by those using the symbols, in other words, the native texts, myths, and explicit declarations by the people being studied depicting their own view of the meanings of their symbols. The operational level is arrived at by equating a symbol's meaning with its use, that is, in a field situation observing what is done with the symbol, how it is used, what behaviors are associated with it, and so forth. Finally, the positional level is the understanding achieved by a consideration of the relationship among symbols vis-à-vis each other—the juxtaposition of symbols belonging to a single gestalt or complex. Another way of describing these three levels is to state that they consist of an analysis of (1) beliefs, attitudes, and feelings, (2) behaviors, usages, and activities, and (3) juxtapositions, relationships, and shared identity.

Turner's overall conceptualization is employed in the development of the following interpretation of the Huichol deer-maize-peyote complex. The three symbols are first considered separately, analyzed in terms of the exegetical and operational levels, and then they are considered in relation to each other positionally, juxtaposing all the associated beliefs and behaviors found to be associated with each of them in order to arrive at an interpretation of their significance as a single symbol complex.

The Deer

The deer is the sacred and magical animal of the Huichols. He gave them peyote on the First Hunt and reappears during all subsequent hunts, bringing peyote, which is conceptualized as either remaining behind in his footsteps or growing from his horns and tail. When he appears at the peyote hunt only the mara'akame can see him (although, interestingly enough, all peyote pilgrims can see his tracks, since all the pilgrims on the hunt described here searched for signs of him before the first peyote was found). The deer comes down from the skies; where he alights, the peyote is found. Thus peyote must be tracked and shot.

The deer is the animal to which one is grateful. He gives the Huichol his blood as well as the peyote. Lumholtz (1902:43) has suggested that deer blood is a symbol of fertility, but in context deer blood seems to have a more general meaning. The deer blood makes the maize grow, and more important, makes the maize nourishing. Deer blood anointed on offerings makes them sacred and able to communicate with the deities. And in one myth it is said that deer blood was once smeared on ceremonial arrows thus making them strong enough to carry the desires and intentions of the Huichols to the gods. Before this anointing the arrows are only "poor weak sticks." Deer blood is more than a fertility symbol and more than a source of nourishment; it is an activating principle which gives objects their ability to carry out their sacred tasks. Stated another way, deer blood is a magical force which gives magical power.

The concept of generalized magical powers is frequently encountered. Local names for it vary—*mana*, *orenda*, *manitou*, *charisma*, *baraka*, and so forth. It is usually conceived of as impersonal, diffuse, and residing in animate as well as inanimate objects. This magical power, as suggested by the Waxes (1962), may be understood as the dynamic of nature, comparable to our view of energy or the laws of thermodynamics.

One cannot overlook the possibility that the original association of deer with power came from the deer in part because he provided the major source of food. Lumholtz recognized this but did not consider it particularly important, confining his speculations to these: "According to the Huichol myth, corn was once a deer, an idea due to the fact that, in earliest time, deer, no doubt, was the main subsistence of the tribe" (1902:45). Presently the deer is not economically significant and it has become so rare that it is occasionally replaced by other animals in the ceremonial sacrifices that provide the blood required to activate crops and magical objects. But substitution of other animals does not change the significance of the deer or its relation to the other elements in the symbolic complex. On the contrary, the rarity of the deer emphasizes its association with the Huichols' former way of life and this is significant in the present interpretation, as will be seen later.

That the deer was once the center of a fully developed hunting religion has been suggested. Among the features often found in hunting societies and also observed in Huichol culture are the following: the hunter's close identification with the deer, addressing him as brother, speaking soothingly to him before he dies, explaining to the deer that he is needed so that the latter will understand the purpose of his death; the concept that the deer appears before the hunter because he was commanded to do so by the Master of the Species (Maxa Kwaxí-Kauyumari); the notion that the success or failure of the hunt is determined by forces other than the hunter's skills and actions; the belief that the deer does not actually die but endlessly is resurrected from his bones which are carefully saved and stored for that purpose; the identification of the mara'akame with the deer and the former's ability to transform himself into the latter and understand his language; the mara'akame's use of the deer as his special tutelary; the view of the source of life as located in the bones; and the ability of the deer to fly.[5]

The Huichol conception of and behavior toward the deer, in other words, reflect and express that part of their religion—and in my opinion it is a central part—which derives from a relatively recent past as deer hunters. Thus the

[5] The features described here as typical of a hunting ideology are also closely associated with shamanism. Although there has been much argument as to whether shamanism developed originally in agricultural or in hunting societies, it is presently found more often and in more elaborated forms among hunters (Findeisen 1960, Lommel 1967, Nachtigall 1952, Paulson 1963, Schröder 1955).

place of the deer in Huichol thought is seen as determined by the animal's significance in their past life.

Another major component of Huichol attitude and belief concerning the deer issues from the association between the mara'akame and Maxa Kwaxí-Kauyumari. In his role as culture hero, Elder Brother Deer Tail gave the people peyote, protected them from the evil sorcerer, Kieri Tewíyari, and from the dangers of being driven mad by datura. And it was Kauyumari who was responsible for the first act of procreation and thus for the perpetuation of the Huichol race.

The deer, as tutelary animal and special companion and assistant to the mara'akame, provided the essential bridge between the mara'akame and Tatewarí. As such, he served as the first and closest link between a mortal and a deity.

The deer showed the Huichols how to communicate with their gods. It may be assumed that their gratitude toward him developed from feelings originally stemming from his provision of subsistence food, feelings which were subsequently generalized and displaced from the practical to the religious-spiritual level, taking the form of affection for him for establishing the way to make contact and to some extent control the nonmundane forces which determine so much of their life.[6]

Indeed the attitudes toward the deer particularly reflected in connection with Maxa Kwaxí-Kauyumari include gratitude untinged with awe or fear. Of all the sacred symbols with the possible exception of fire the Huichols are on the

[6] That Maxa Kwaxí-Kauyumari is connected with deer instead of maize is especially noteworthy in view of the widespread American theme of the culture hero as having given agriculturalists their staple crop. If the Huichols were true agriculturalists, ideologically as well as in practice, one would expect Maxa Kwaxí to have contributed maize rather than deer.

most familiar terms with the deer. This is best seen in the characteristics and activities attributed to the quasideified Elder Brother Deer Tail. In the earlier discussion of this figure it was seen that he is conceptualized as possessing distinctly human characteristics—at times clever, often cunning, bold, mischievous, vulnerable, pleasure-seeking, and occasionally foolish, not the features designed to arouse veneration in the human heart. Elder Brother Deer Tail is half-god and half-man, exactly what one would expect to find in a figure who partakes of the two worlds, mortal and divine. The deer as Maxa Kwaxí-Kauyumari stands midway between the Huichol and the gods in his duties and in the hearts of men. He is an intermediary who bridges the mundane and the ideal, transcending the merely human but not beyond human reach and comprehension. Such a figure would kindle more affection and gratitude than awe and fear.

Some of the uses of the deer in ceremonial settings have been described earlier. The deer horns were set atop the roof in the center of the *tuki* and *xíriki*, were tied onto the mara'akame's basket in order to lead the *hikuritámete* to the peyote, and were placed before the peyote as an offering. In all these contexts the deer is identified with and used to stand for Kauyumari as the tutelary to the mara'akame, who has access to the deities through the deer. The bond between mara'akame and deer is signified by the use of deerskin to provide the surface of the mara'akame's drum, quiver, and bow. Finally, the ubiquitous ceremonial arrows used in rituals to communicate with the deities are conceived as deer horns, placed by Tatewarí on the head of the First Deer whose horns they became.

The arrows worn in the hats of the *hikuritámete* are multifunctional, not only signifying the deer and the communication with the deities which he makes possible, but also serving to communicate with those remaining at home. This function is particularly important if the mara'akame's wife has stayed behind since she is his essential assistant in his role. Thus by extension the arrows as deer horns are a symbol of communication between men as well as between men and the gods.

The deer scrotum is also used to cover the tobacco gourd carried by the older or more experience male *peyoteros* on their quest for *híkuri.* The use of tobacco is generally rare among women and the use of the sacred tobacco, *yé*, seems to be the exclusive prerogative of men. It will be recalled that the participation of the women in all matters pertaining to the deer was minimal. In the deer hunt ceremonies the women assist in the preparation of the deer broth and tamales. After the deer has been brought in from the snare they lay him on their capes and feed him his favorite grasses and maize beer. But the women are far less active in connection with deer than in the ceremonial and mundane affairs having to do with peyote and maize. The women do not hunt or use items made of any part of the deer. Although there is no exegetical material which calls for or justifies the exclusion of women from extensive or significant contact with the deer in secular and ceremonial behaviors, it can be observed that that animal is entirely within the province of the masculine world.

Maize

Maize plays a highly conspicuous part in the everyday activities of the Huichols; it is, after all, their present source of life. Despite the presumably recent acquisition of maize it has become a central theme in Huichol religion and is richly elaborated in terms of belief. Its ubiquitous and mundane nature notwithstanding, it has been the source of metaphysical and speculative thought, as demonstrated by a statement made by Ramón in reply to a question concerning the meaning of a phrase he often used in recounting myths, "the spirit of maize."

What do we mean by the spirit of maize? It is the heartbeat, the spirit. There is a spirit for each of the five colors, for the purple, for the red, for the yellow, for the white, for the speckled. Each has its spirit. How? Let us say, there is the maize, it has grown, it is ripe, it is ready. It is our nourishment, our life. We say, "Ah, how beautiful." Then the weevil gets into it. The grubs the worms get into it. They eat its meat. The spirit of the maize speaks, "No, I cannot remain here. I must go, I must leave, they are killing me." The spirit says, I must go back to Our Mother Dove Girl, Tatei Kúkurú 'Uimari, the Mother of Maize. Those sorcerers, those evildoers, throw out the spirit of maize. So that there will be no life for us. So that our nourishment is cut off. It is very painful for us, because the spirit of the maize—what is it? It is its own essence. How does it take nourishment? How does it breathe? Well, it does so in the same manner as we. So the spirit of maize thinks while it is upon this earth.

The text is particularly interesting for several reasons, one being the profundity of the question it treats: what is the essence of maize? The question is unanswerable, for the maize is irreducible to anything but itself, what Turner (1967) would call a dominant value. It would be impossible to state such a condition more tersely and penetratingly—maize is "its own essence." Another important feature of this statement is its revelation of the quest for understanding of the nature of the bond between the Huichols and the maize. To paraphrase, the narrator is asking, "What do we mean when we equate ourselves with maize?" His reply is that it can be no different from ourselves.

This statement represents an intellectual impasse and the reply is adequate. Obviously the maize does not breathe and think and eat in the same way as man. The Huichol here is questioning a religious cliché, "maize is ourselves," and pushing against the limits of formulated religious dogma. Ultimately he gives an answer to his own question that indicates he is at the outer reaches of Huichol knowledge about maize. Basically, he finds no "answer."

In addition to revealing an impressive level of intellectual curiosity, the text is significant for its demonstration of some unique features in the Huichol attitude toward maize not found in their attitudes toward deer and peyote, namely the belief that maize is mysterious and ineluctable. Myths and general discussions by Ramón and other Huichols do not treat the other two symbols with comparable attention. As has been demonstrated, deer, especially in the form of Maxa Kwaxí-Kauyumari, arouses feelings of fondness and gratitude and so does peyote, as will be seen. But neither deer nor peyote is viewed as particularly mysterious or as requiring an intellectual search for its true meaning. The concern with "the spirit of maize" contrasts with the mundane role of maize in Huichol life. Unlike deer and peyote, it is all around them; it is eaten several times a day by everyone in the society. When the Huichols say of it, "It is our life," they can be taken quite literally. In this inconsistency, there is additional support for the interpretation of maize as less old than deer and peyote in Huichol life and less well embedded in Huichol religion. It is not surprising to find that maize is regarded as strange and unknowable despite its economic and material centrality to Huichol life, for maize is still an alien element in the ideology of the people.

The spirit of maize, as the myths reveal, is to be treated with the utmost care. It knows one's thoughts. It does not like to be pinched or to be neglected. It is sensitive and vulnerable and its stay among the Huichol may be cut off at any time with disastrous consequences unless certain precautions are taken. Primarily, the precautions consist of maintaining a proper attitude. Ramón explains this:

Why One Must Not Go Clearing the Fields with Bad Thoughts

When one goes with evil thoughts, when one goes thinking evil thoughts, while clearing the fields, what then? One says, "Eh-hhh, I am walking clearing the fields. When am I going to harvest? Now what if it doesn't rain, now what if I do not clear the fields well, I do not have maize with which to eat, with which to exist." If one goes thinking this, that one clearing his field, Watákame says, "No, do not be thinking about this. You work and I will help you."

Only then when he is going with bad thoughts, when he goes on thinking bad thoughts, then one is blamed. Ah—a machete cuts your foot, eh? In this life one does not go lacking for something with which to get stuck in the eye. A piece of grass, a stake, it is the same. No, that is not lacking. It is through Watákame, he is the one who makes and unmakes. For this reason there are Huichols here, who have gone using their machetes and cut their feet. They have given themselves cuts as they went clearing their fields. When they were walking with bad thoughts. They were thinking bad thoughts. One ought not to do this.

Think of him who helps us. That one who is the Clearer of the Fields, who is called Watákame. While one is clearing the brush one should think how long ago he worked. How he was doing it. How he did it before the water covered everything. How he did when Nakawé remade this world. With axes of stone, with machetes of stone. How with his power he declared everything for us, so that we could learn. That is good. No, one ought not to go thinking bad thoughts.

Bad thoughts, inattention to the task, and doubts are inappropriate states of mind when working in the field, for they are likely to offend the maize. A positive, tranquil mental condition will assure the success of the crop.

This characteristic is by no means unique to the Huichols; Evans-Pritchard (1965) has pointed out that primitive religions often embrace the notion that human emotional and moral conditions affect events in the natural world. Fertility of the fields, success in the hunt, fecundity of women, clemency of weather are all susceptible and responsive to human emotions. This view is the essence of what Freud called "omnipotent thought" and what Lévy-Bruhl meant when he said that prelogical thinking results from a prevailing "logic of participation." Mary Douglas describes this kind of world view as man-centered: "In such a universe, the elemental forces are seen as linked so closely to individual human beings that we can hardly speak of an external, physical environment. Each individual carries within himself such close links with the universe that he is like the centre of a magnetic field of force" (1966:99). Such a view assumes an affective environment in which there are no morally neutral forces, where man's inner state is the ultimate cause of events of the natural world. It is an assumption found not infrequently in primary groups of all kinds, whether in families, bands, or lineages. In such intimate situations, the inner states of individuals are not less consequential than overt forms of behavior.[7]

[7] Where social relations are basically moral matters, where the natural as well as human field is affected by the individual's motivations

That one's state of mind is more relevant in connection with maize than with peyote and deer is possible to explain. Maize came later, was brought by outsiders, and more important, a life based on maize is precarious. A combination of ecological and technological factors—poor soil, poor tools, rude techniques, and unpredictable weather—make maize in fact a touchy mistress. The Huichols love visiting, roaming, hunting, making pilgrimages. Remaining at home to watch over the crops is burdensome to them, and the necessity of doing so is an often-repeated theme. When Lupe told the story of her life, for example, she stressed as one of her most laudable virtues her willingness to stay at home and watch the crops and, as the mara'akame's wife, she was setting an example to the other Huichol women who were more carefree and mobile. Ramón agreed with this and added that a good Huichol man was one who was willing to stay home to be near his fields.

Tilling the soil has none of the excitement, honor, or prestige connected with every aspect of the deer and hunting. Maize is mundane, unpredictable, and tedious, and in its personification it is characterized as vulnerable and demanding, threatening to leave the people on slight provocation.

Another feature of Huichol attitudes toward maize not replicated in feelings concerning deer and peyote is a pronounced aesthetic interest in the plant. Its five colors are eulogized in myths, in chants and in general discussions, and each of the five is regarded as having a distinct spirit and character. The maize provides the metaphors of beauty. A person is said to be tender as new maize, and woman as beautiful, a man as straight, and so forth. Only the fire is as much

and wishes, one encounters a distinct type of society, referred to variously as "sacred," *Gemeinschaft*, community, and so forth.

admired, and the charms of the five daughters of maize surpass everything else known to the Huichols.

As Zingg (1938) pointed out so frequently, maize is associated with the feminine realm. But it is not limited to this domain. It is equally a part of all that is vulnerable, tender, sensitive, and beautiful; in particular, maize is akin to children. In all the maize ceremonies children play a dominant part. They carry the new maize, place maize offerings in the *xíriki*, stir and turn it when it is being parched, and so forth.

On the everyday level, maize production is not confined to any social group. Men and women equally work in every phase of agriculture, although the heavier work of the first clearing of the field naturally falls to the men. Children of both sexes participate and entire families go together into the milpas. The mara'akate and *gobernadores*, specialists and authorities, sacred and secular, all are agriculturalists. No one is exempt; agriculture is the great equalizer and none of the limitations found in connection with the deer appear here.

One of the most important maize myths relates the origins of maize among the Huichols and the problems attendant on living a life based on maize agriculture. The following is my shortened version of Ramón's account of the myth, although some of his phrases have been retained.

The Story of Our Roots

"This is the story of our roots. It is a story of the maize we adore, that which we hold sacred, because it is our nourishment, it is our life. That is why we must know it well." A long time ago there was a woman, who lived alone in a small rancho with her son, Werikame, Growing Boy. That mother and her son were very hungry. They had nothing to eat, no maize, no squash. Her son finds himself alone in the woods and hears the sound of the dove above him in the trees.

As he is starving he takes aim at the bird but the bird is Tatei Kúkurú 'Uimari, Our Mother Dove Girl, the Mother of Maize. She bids the boy not to shoot her but to follow her to her house, a place where maize can be found. She gives Growing Boy a gourd bowl of sour atole (*tsinari*) and then five small tortillas in a bowl. Whatever he eats from the bowls is replenished and he finds he cannot finish it all. Dove Girl had read his thoughts, he realizes with embarrassment, and had known that he was afraid that there would not be enough to fill him up. He thanks her and she agrees to give him some maize to take home to the mother. The five maize girls come forward, one for each of the five colors. "Very pretty little girls, all in their fine clothes. She said to them, 'Who will go with this boy?' They sat there embarrassed. Silence. Nobody? 'But he should not go hungry.' So spoke the Mother of the Maize."

All the girls demur and the Mother scolds them until at last Purple Maize Girl comes forward, "very beautiful with rosy cheeks, well painted, painted on her cheeks with *uxa*, with her ear ornaments, her bracelets, her sandals, beautiful." The Mother of the Maize explains to Growing Boy that he must build the girl a house with a shelf in the center, a *niwetari* on which Purple Maize Girl should be placed. He agrees and arrives home with the girl, whom he presents to his mother. She is very angry, saying, " 'Oh, you brought back a woman. Another mouth to feed. You were to bring back maize.' " The boy explains that she is maize and describes how she must be treated.

The house and shelf are constructed. The boy goes out into the field and soon "things arrived there all piled up in the house, all the colors of maize. 'Ah,' he says to the girl, 'One has given us much maize.' She says to him, 'You have found your life. You are going to start working now, seeing as it is like that.' That girl had the virtues of maize."

The boy goes out into the field to plant and instructs his mother not to make Purple Maize Girl work, not to let her grind for she is too delicate. She must stay where she is on her shelf. But as the mother is grinding, she has bad thoughts about the girl. She feels sorry for herself working so hard while the girl, a lazy person, sits up there, dressed beautifully, as she works. The poor girl is ashamed and comes down to help the mother grind. "She ground on the metate, that girl did, that girl who was Purple Maize. As she ground, all that came out was blood. Pure blood. That *masa* was blood. Because that girl, she herself was maize. She was grinding herself. Each time she pulled back, pure blood came out."

Growing Boy soon comes running back and chides his mother when he sees what has happened. The mother denies her fault and the boy, weeping, says, " 'Ah, you let it slip from our grasp. That is what you did. It all turned out for nothing.' " The boy tries to stop the bleeding of Purple Maize Girl, putting *masa* on where the blood was, where her poor arms were. During the night the girl leaves forever, saying, " 'No, I cannot remain here because there is much danger. There are many things I cannot control. I considered staying here, but no, it is best for me to return to my mother. Because I am not happy here. I am ill at ease here.' " That poor boy finds her gone and follows the girl's trail to where he had been. He asks Tatei Kúkurú 'Uimari to return the girl, but "although his heart is pure he is refused. The Mother of Maize tells him, 'No, she did not work out with you.' "

"Our Mother spoke to us like that. As she said it, some of

us have maize, others have not. They did not take care of it. They did not adore it. That is why the spirit prefers to leave the place, back to its Mother, where there is no danger. Only the shell is left, rotten. That is why this is such a sacred story among us. It is very sad, very hard, this story. Maize is our nourishment. We must work it by ourselves, we must obtain it from the earth. We must treat it well, as a sacred thing. So that it does not leave us."

Indeed all the maize stories which I encountered have this poignant quality, usually involving the loss of maize through some maltreatment or short-sightedness on the part of the Huichols. The maize cycle myths told during the maize ceremonies involve much weeping and lamentation, not characteristic of tellings of the peyote and deer myths.

Another maize myth, "How the Maize Baby Was Lost," is told during the ceremony of the Drum and Calabash. Here is an abbreviated version of Ramón's account:

How the Maize Baby Was Lost

"When maize was born it was a small baby, very small. It crawled there on the ground, in the house, outside the house. And it soiled itself very often. And because of this, the father and mother became tired. They were angry." At last the father tells his wife, " 'It is enough. I do not want this child here, let us throw it out.' That mother felt much pity. She said, 'We cannot do this thing. It must be planted well, no matter what.' " But the father prevents her and the child is thrown out.

The baby is lonely and cries by itself, thrown out behind the house, until Tatei Kúkurú 'Uimari hears it and laments, " 'Oh, they have thrown it out there. My poor child, where it is cold, where it is lonely.' And where it crawled she put flowers, beautiful flowers, yellow especially." Then she takes pity on the child, and takes it away with her. The father and mother come out to see how the baby is doing in the cold but all they find are the flowers. "They saw where it had crawled, scattering all those flowers, to this side and that. The little trail it had made. That poor little baby, it had crawled there all alone all by itself. Because its mother and father did not want it anymore, just because it soiled itself so often. Because they thought it was dirty." The parents follow the little child's trail until they arrive at the place of Tatei Kúkurú 'Uimari. " 'We came for our child.' She said to them, 'Why? You were tired of it. It is that you do not love it. You do not wish to keep it contented. You do not wish it to be living. No, I am telling you this, you will not have it any longer. You will not be able to take it because I have it here, I have it in my heart, in my feet, it came back to my body. You cannot take it.' " The parents are angry for now they wanted it. They tried to take hold of it but it dropped from their hands. "It unraveled in their hands, like pretty wool. They would take it up and try to put it over their shoulder but it would slide down again, like drops of water, like little kernels of hail." Both of them, grieving, realize it is no use and they have lost their child forever.

Then they arrived at their home. When they had left, in their house there were many ears of maize, all beautiful, all fine. "But when they returned all of it was gone. Nothing had been left. Because they had not raised it as it should be. They rejected it and threw it out."

"All that happened because they had scorned the life that was to have been theirs. This is the story as the mara'akame sings it, the story of the little baby that was maize when it came into this world."

Like that of a child, the existence of maize is provisional and can be taken away at any time. (Among the Huichols, where infant mortality is extremely high, there is often a very realistic view of children's lives as quite precarious and their stay in the world uncertain.) The Huichols have an implicit expectation that, human nature being what it is, carelessness in handling maize will occur unless people are continually reminded of the consequences of neglect. Seen thus, the attitudes required for the monotonous and often taxing demands for continual attention and unselfish care are equally appropriate and necessary for the maintenance of children as they are for maize. And the statement, repeated again and again in myths, chants, and rituals, that "maize is our life" is literally true, not symbolically as it is for deer and peyote. On the nonsymbolic level, maize and children *are* life, the perpetuation of Huichol life. Neither peyote nor deer require this solicitude and care and neither is needed for life itself, only for ceremonial anointing and ceremonial eating. The physiological requirements for maize are fixed and excessive by comparison. The ambivalence engendered by great demands on one hand and unreliable returns on the other explains the need for continual reminding of what life would be without maize. Like life without children, it would be a sad and temporary affair. Thus, the *attitude* toward maize consisting of a combination of gratitude, fear, mystery, and solicitude is seen as explicable by reference to its alien origin, recent acquisition, its role as the staple food, and its unreliability.

The Peyote

I have already discussed some of the uses of peyote, how it is gathered, and prepared, and on what occasions it is taken. Here I wish to consider who uses it, with what effects and feelings, for what explicit and implicit purposes, and how it is conceptualized.

Like deer and maize, peyote is "very delicate," that is, sacred. Unlike maize and deer it cannot be purchased, though it is readily available in Mexican markets. It is sacred only when gathered in the land of its origins, and in the appropriate ceremonial manner. Ramón said of it:

> That other peyote, that which one buys, it did not reveal itself in the Huichol manner. One did not hunt it properly, one did not make offerings to it over there. That is why it is not good for us.

In order to be sure that he always has available a supply of peyote, gathered correctly from Wirikuta, the Huichol plants some of that which was brought back from Wirikuta by pilgrims.

> When we bring it back we plant it at home, in a little earth. Any amount you bring back you can plant near your house so that it lives. In the dry season one plants it, one waters it a little with care and there it is. Then one has it whenever one wants it.

The reference to "that other peyote" which may be purchased is explained by Huichol ethnobotanical classifications which specify the existence of two kinds of peyote, "good and bad." *Híkuri* (*Lophophora williamsii*) is good peyote and is very similar in appearance to *Ariocarpus retusus*, which has been identified as "bad peyote" or *tsuwiri* (Furst 1972b). Only an experienced and observant person, usually a mara'akame among the Huichols, can be certain of collecting the good kind. One can be sure he has obtained good peyote only if he gathers it in the right place and manner. The results of eating *tsuwiri* are indeed terrible. Ramón said, "If one eats one of those, one goes mad, one goes running into the barrancas, one sees scorpions, serpents, dangerous animals.

One is unable to walk, one falls, one often kills oneself in those barrancas, falling off the rocks." The effects are similar to those attributed to datura. The kinds of hallucinations described as occurring due to eating *tsuwiri* are culturally structured and recurrent. A common one is the experience of a man encountering a huge agave cactus in the desert, thinking it is a woman and making love to it.[8]

Eating *tsuwiri* instead of peyote may occur not only as a result of mistaken identity. It may also be a supernatural sanction, punishment for going to Wirikuta without prior confession. Ramón remarked:

> If one comes there not having spoken of one's life, if one comes not having been cleansed of everything, then this false *híkuri* will discover it. It is going to bring out that which is evil in one, that which frightens one. It knows all one's bad thoughts.

The *tsuwiri* does more than read one's thoughts. The Huichols recognize that those who have not confessed honestly will probably behave peculiarly. The pilgrim who knows that he has lied to his companions will eat his peyote in secret "because he does not have good thoughts. He knows he has not spoken honestly with his companions." When such a person goes hunting for peyote, he will find the *tsuwiri*, which "only has the appearance of peyote." When he returns to his

[8] According to Ramón, the Tarahumaras are afraid of peyote because they cannot distinguish between the "good" and "bad" plants and eat the bad kind accidentally. Said Ramón, "Because of this fear they cannot sit quietly and have these visions, as we [the Huichols] have them. They are afraid to sit there and have beautiful dreams. When they eat peyote they do not sleep, they walk and walk and have much fear. Because some of them have eaten *tsuwiri* [bad peyote] and had these terrible things happen." Since the Huichol mara'akame makes a careful distinction between the different cacti and does not let his people fall into this error, his followers expect only pleasure from peyote.

companions after his harrowing visions, the mara'akame knows at once what has occurred. The man must then confess and he may be cleansed by the mara'akame.

Peyote, like maize, can read one's thoughts and can punish one for being false or evil. The interpretation previously suggested concerning an identification of the human moral and emotional condition with corresponding events in nature is also relevant for peyote, as it was for maize. The peyote rewards or punishes a man according to his inner state, his moral deserts. The sanction is immediate, just, and certain, an effective regulator of behavior in a small, well-integrated society like this.

As noted earlier, peyote is eaten or drunk ritually only during dry season ceremonies but may be eaten at any time of year. It is also used medicinally to rectify a multitude of difficulties—to assuage pains and to obtain energy, endurance, or courage. It is made into a poultice and applied to wounds. In fact, it is a panacea. When it is eaten or drunk ritually, it is usually in quantities insufficient to produce visions and in this context must be regarded as having the specific symbolic purpose of achieving a kind of communion with the deities. Partaking of peyote to obtain visions is thus but one relatively narrow part of a larger set of purposes, and although it is an important part, it is more for the mara'akame than for ordinary folk. When peyote is eaten for visions, it is in a relaxed and convivial atmosphere, much in the manner of modern Western man's use of alcohol. Peyote (that is, "good peyote") is eaten by anyone at any time—children and men and women—for a number of purposes but always with good results.

Concerning the visions obtained from eating peyote and the feelings it arouses, here is Ramón's description:

The first time one puts the peyote into one's mouth, one feels it going down into the stomach. It feels very cold, like ice. And the inside of one's mouth becomes dry, very dry. And then it becomes wet, very wet. One has much saliva then. And then, a while later one feels as if one were fainting. The body begins to feel weak. It begins to feel faint. And one begins to yawn, to feel very tired. And after a while one feels very light. The whole body begins to feel light, without sleep, without anything.

And then, when one takes enough of this, one looks upward and what does one see? One sees darkness. Only darkness. It is very dark, very black. And one feels drunk with the peyote. And when one looks up again it is total darkness except for a little bit of light, a tiny bit of light, brilliant yellow. It comes there, a brilliant yellow. And one looks into the fire. One sits there, looking into the fire which is Tatewarí. One sees the fire in colors, very many colors, five colors, different colors. The flames divide—it is all brilliant, very brilliant and very beautiful. The beauty is very great, very great. It is a beauty such as one never sees without the peyote. The flames come up, they shoot up, and each flame divides into those colors and each color is multicolored—blue, green, yellow, all those colors. The yellow appears on the tip of the flames as the flame shoots upward. And on the tips you can see little sparks in many colors coming out. And the smoke which rises from the fire, it also looks more and more yellow, more and more brilliant.

Then one sees the fire, very bright, one sees the offerings there, many arrows with feathers and they are full of color, shimmering, shimmering. That is what one sees.[9]

But the mara'akame, what does he see? He sees Tatewarí, if

[9] This vision was illustrated by Ramón in a glorious series of yarn paintings which show the fire as it appears to the mara'akame surrounded by the offerings, and discernible in the midst of the explosive colors are the eyes of Tatewarí, looking out through the five lobes of the fire.

he is chief of those who go to hunt the peyote. And he sees the Sun. He sees the mara'akame venerating the fire and he hears those prayers, like music. He hears praying and singing.

All this is necessary to understand, to comprehend, to have one's life. This we must do so that we can see what Tatewarí lets go from his heart for us. One goes understanding all that which Tatewarí has given one. That is when we understand all that, when we find our life over there. But many do not take good care. That is why they know nothing. That is why they do not understand anything. One must be attentive so that one understands that which is the Fire and the Sun. That is why one sits like that, to listen and see all of that, to understand.

Only the mara'akame hopes to achieve this deep religious understanding by eating the peyote. The others take peyote for the beauty of it, because it elevates them, takes them out of themselves, and shows them charming, beautiful, and often humorous images, flickering lights, intense colors and little animals.

If a Huichol eats peyote nonceremonially, but in sufficient quantities for visions, he takes certain precautions to avoid drowsiness or nausea. He eschews food and liquid on the day the peyote is eaten and on the previous evening and following morning as well. He is expected to be seated comfortably and quietly and to have several free hours in which he will not need to be disturbed. He should be in a dark or shady place in order to appreciate fully the intensification of colors. Here is Ramón's description of dosage and duration of effects:

That which one feels when one eats the peyote lasts from four to five hours. That is the most, and during that time one does not eat. It all depends on the amount one takes. In order to have a real effect one must take an entire peyote [from four to eight sections]. One feels better with a larger amount. One sees more things. With two or three little pieces one does not see much. One may only go to sleep, but it is not a real sleep. It is that you are sleeping but you still hear and see things.

And afterward, after one has eaten a whole peyote and has seen many things and heard many things, one remembers everything. It is a very personal thing. It is a very private thing. It is like a secret, because others have not heard or seen the same thing. That is why it is not a good thing to tell it to others.

The Relationship between Deer, Maize, and Peyote

The relationship between deer, maize, and peyote is made quite explicit on the exegetical level, "They are a unity, they are one, they are ourselves." This direct statement does not answer the question with which this inquiry began: why are they one? On the operational level, these symbols interlock so that the entire ceremonial cycle revolves around obtaining and using them in a particular sequence. The maize cannot grow without the deer blood; the deer cannot be sacrificed to the Sun until after the peyote hunt; Parching the Maize, the ceremony which brings the rains needed to make the maize grow, cannot be held without peyote from Wirikuta; the peyote may not be hunted until the maize has been cleansed and sanctified and the children told the stories of the First Peyote Hunt. Every ceremony is dependent upon the presence of the three symbolic items, and their sequential procurement makes the entire religious calendar a closed circle. Thus on both the exegetical and operational levels—as Ramón explained and as demonstrated behaviorally in the arrangement of the ceremonial cycle—deer, maize, and peyote constitute a single symbol complex.

Perhaps the question, "Why are these three symbols a

unity?" can be answered by considering the positional relationship among the symbols, by examining what Turner calls the positional level of meaning.

The Huichols do not arbitrarily insist that deer, maize, and peyote are a unity and that "they are ourselves, they are our life." Both statements must be taken at face value. They give us the key to Huichol interpretation of their history. The three symbols, identified with each other so completely as to constitute a single concept, are used by the Huichols to signify their entire lives and to achieve their highest religious goal—continuity and unity on all levels, societal, historical, temporal, ecological, and ideological. Far from illogical, inexplicable, or arbitrary, the fusion of deer, maize, and peyote is meaningful and necessary.

How this goal is achieved becomes clear by summarizing the spectrum of referents of each of the symbols, drawing upon all the information presented thus far: beliefs, behaviors, uses, associations, attitudes, and feelings evoked by each symbol.

Let us begin with the deer. The evidence for assuming a recent transition to agriculture from hunting has been cited previously. If in addition to the deer other large animals were hunted and eaten, we have heard or seen nothing of them. In any event, the deer and no other animal presently stands for the lost hunting life. The life of hunters is quite different from that of cultivators. I have speculated that the Huichols were once nomadic, probably living in small bands, moving freely from place to place, inaccessible to the influences of other more advanced peoples and the indignities of foreign conquerors. Insulated from the caprice of weather and seasonal changes, dependent primarily on their own efforts and the behavior of the animals, they would have experienced the direct and profound relationship which in hunting societies characterizes that bond between hunter and hunted animal. In this relationship man is a kind of partner, whereas the agriculturalist is the servant or caretaker of his crops. The Huichol hunter probably led a difficult life but one of comparative freedom and independence.

Another lost attraction of the Huichol past is the excitement, the sense of potence and triumph typically experienced by hunters. Thomas (1959) has stated this beautifully in her description of the Bushman hunters, for whom foraged food is most important economically but who find in the hunt unrivaled joy and passion. In his present state the Huichol is in bondage to forces nearly entirely beyond his influence. The elements are quixotic and the maize is a demanding mistress who despite his ceaseless diligence may not allow him to avert starvation throughout the year. The outsiders, the mestizos, though unpredictable as the weather, are usually ruthless and never let the Huichols forget their impotence and subordination. And finally, the Huichols are sedentary; it is a burden which they must continually abjure one another to uphold. But no Huichol needs to be urged to hunt the deer.

In reconstructing the Huichol past as hunters and the quality of this life, it must be noted that this culture was dominated by men, for hunting was then and is today the exclusive prerogative of men. Women aid and admire but do not actively participate. In agriculture female efforts are indispensable, and Huichol women are rewarded by being permitted an extensive participation in prestigious ritual and ceremonial as well as utilitarian activities. Despite the religious and economic importance of women in everyday Huichol life, they are excluded from all that pertains to the deer and the deer hunt.

Relations between the sexes have been observed to be equalitarian, affectionate, and unmarred by overt conflict; the Huichols too describe their interactions with members of the opposite sex in these terms. Yet a theme of sexual ambivalence and antagonism (though greatly overstated by Zingg) is unmistakable on a mythological level. The presence of a *vagina dentata* myth in which Kauyumari grinds away the teeth of the Wolf Girl; the existence of a tradition which says that in Ancient Times it was the custom for the husband of a woman in labor to squat on the rafters of the house with a string tied to his penis which the wife held and pulled whenever she had a pain; the myth which relates as one of the consequences of taking bad peyote that a man may have hallucinations which cause him to mistake an agave cactus for a woman and attempt to have intercourse with it; the story of the female deity in the form of a cavern closing over Kauyumari's penis and biting it off—these are only some of the examples of a pervasive theme of sexual antagonism. One can only speculate about the many questions raised by the theme, which is particularly puzzling because of the overtly harmonious relations between the sexes on the behavioral level. Is this a case of myth providing an outlet for antagonism which is thus deflected and need not be acted out? Does the theme originate from the conjectural condition of an absent hunter-husband-father and is it possibly an explanation of the importance of the grandfather in the social organization and mythology? Is this theme a "survival" on the mythological plane of interpersonal relations which might have been enacted in the past when men could better afford to exclude the women from their affairs because they needed their efforts less? Or, does the answer involve a more profound, omnipresent reciprocal sexual envy—women of the male's potence and freedom, men of the woman's procreative abilities? One cannot begin to answer these questions here. It must suffice to point out that they remain valid and at present unanswered questions. It can be said, however, that the deer is associated with a period in the history of the Huichols which was marked by masculine dominance, an arrangement which no longer characterizes the relations between the sexes. That such a condition would be capable of arousing nostalgia, at least among the Huichol males, must be seriously considered. It is this past of freedom, autonomy, potence, masculine domination and dignity, part fantasy, part reality, which the deer represents, preserves, and carries into the present as one constituent of the deer-maize-peyote complex.

Maize and its role in Huichol life contrasts sharply with that of the deer as has been pointed out. The life of the cultivator is not eulogized by the Huichols as is the hunting of the deer. And maize, one must not forget, was procured from "foreigners," the non-Huichols who are not trusted. Zingg and Lumholtz both sensed a less-than-complete incorporation of maize into Huichol life and saw a corresponding lesser intensity in the treatment of maize during the ceremonies which involved all three symbolic components of the deer-maize-peyote complex.

Nevertheless, maize belongs in the central symbol complex for it is the present reality. And at the same time, it is the antithesis of the idealized hunting past, symbolized among the Huichols by the deer.

Of the three symbols, peyote is the most interesting.[10] The role of peyote in the complex may be seen as indicative of the peculiar *Geist* or genius of the Huichols, that turn of mind which makes them distinct and sets them apart from others around them. It has been shown that peyote is construed as providing a private experience. One should not tell of one's visions; each man has his own and each is different (with the exception of the conventional visions of Tayaupá and Tatewarí experienced by the mara'akame under the influence of peyote). It is something precious and beautiful. It serves no useful purpose. It does not contribute to social solidarity and no effort is made to ritualize and exploit the camaraderie which often accompanies shared escape from reality, seen for example among the surrounding mestizos who make drinking a social ritual. Nor is it used to strengthen bonds between individuals. It is not given to one group as a reward and mark of special status as the Aztecs did with narcotics and intoxicating beverages. Peyote occupies no utilitarian place on any level of Huichol life. Even the visions obtained by it are not used for religious illumination, didactic purposes, or intensification of experiences. They are gratuitous. And because peyote produces experiences which are only uniform in being consistently pleasant, it brings to each man something unpredictable, irregular, spontaneous, and unstructured, though

[10] Craig J. Calhoun's interpretation of the relation between deer, maize, and peyote stresses the role of the latter as mediator between the past and present, eliminating a sense of time, and thus allowing the Huichols to perceive themselves as a single people, despite the profound differences in their past and present life styles. This interpretation corresponds closely with Ramón's statement, "It [the deer-maize-peyote complex] comes to us from Ancient Times, so that we could unite all that there is in our lives" (personal communication, Los Angeles, 1971).

still within limits. It permits an experience which is not completely routinized, neither is it dangerous or likely to lead to individual or societal disruption. Peyote visions provide that part of man's life which is private, beautiful, and unique, and that part of religion which has nothing to do with shared sentiments, morals, ethics, or dogma. It is within, but separate from, the religious experience, and in some philosophical systems such experiences are considered the most elevated and most intensely spiritual available to man. As such it is the very opposite of those aspects of religion which are ritualized, mechanical, and impersonal.

Peyote, then, is the Huichol provision for an unknowable and personal experience. It is intriguing that such provision should have been devised by a people so intensely concerned with order, predictability, and propriety. Spontaneity and privacy have been retained within a fixed framework of opposing values. Such an arrangement makes so much sense psychologically that one may see in it a major source of the flexibility and durability which mark Huichol life and religion. Peyote is neither mundane, like maize, nor exotic and exciting, like deer. It is that solitary, ahistorical, asocial, asexual, nonrational domain without which man is not complete, without which life is a lesser affair.

This combination of deer, maize, and peyote represents a remarkable completeness. When the Huichols juxtapose them and consider each to be an aspect of the other they are stating that man cannot live without a sense of his past, working for his living, or finding moments of solitary beauty. Surely this is an accurate statement of the life of man when it is healthy and whole. All are essential to the human condition. The three symbols represent a unity, simply, as the Huichols say: the animal represents the past—hunting, masculinity, independence, adventure, and freedom; the plant is the labor of the present—food, regularity, domesticity, sharing between the sexes, routine and persistent diligence; the cactus which grows far away is plant and animal at once—nonutilitarian, free of time, sex, and specifiable meaning, existing for its own unscrutinized, quiet gift of beauty and privacy.

CHAPTER 6

The Purpose and Meaning of the Peyote Hunt

Look, Tsinurawe, I am telling you this because I want you to be thinking about us with much will and affection. That is why we, with much love and all our will, open ourselves and give ourselves, so that you can be of a union with us. Because this beautiful unity which you have seen, this carries much responsibility, and you must know it entirely. You must think about our story, our symbols, our custom, everything. So that tomorrow or the day after we can recognize each other as being of the same blood.

Ramón Medina Silva

The deer, the maize, and the peyote become most efficacious in the peyote hunt. In the climactic moments of the rituals in Wirikuta, these symbols provide the Huichols with a formulation of the large questions dealt with by religion, the questions of ultimate meaning and purpose. In Wirikuta, a vision is attained by the operation of the deer, the maize, and the peyote; with lucidity and power, the symbols accomplish their sacred task of giving significance and order to man's life.

Theories of Myth and Symbol: Geertz, Turner, Lévi-Strauss

We may learn how and why the symbol complex accomplishes this by first turning to the work of recent theorists. Not only are Lévi-Strauss, Turner, and Geertz coordinate in specific interpretations of symbols; their general orientations and fundamental approaches are also remarkably consistent.[1]

[1] Lévi-Strauss's analysis (1967, 1969) is concerned specifically with an interpretation of symbols operating within myths. Turner (1967,

All can be regarded as part of the intellectual tradition of Durkheim and the French sociologists in their emphasis on the ways in which culture provides the forms and meanings by which men live. Accordingly, all three are interested in the relationship between culture, perception, and cognition, and all have an intellectualist or rational bias in their shared (often implicit) assumption that human mental activity is patterned, coherent, and comprehensible in its own terms. And all recognize the cogency and continuity of symbolic processes in societies simple and complex. Though each defines the symbol somewhat differently, they concur on the ultimate functions of symbols.

Geertz (1965) follows Langer (1960, first published in 1942) in defining a symbol as any "object, act, event, quality, or relation which serves as a vehicle for a conception." That conception is the symbol's meaning. A symbol is a concrete embodiment of "ideas, attitudes, judgments, longings, or beliefs" (1965:5–9). Symbols are basically sources of information, "models-of" as well as "models-for" reality; that is, they do not merely *reflect* but actually *shape* other aspects of life. This shaping occurs by inducing a set of dispositions, moods, and motivations provided by the formulation of a conception of the general order of existence. That conception is conveyed by means of symbols. Man depends on symbols because he cannot endure a threat to his powers of comprehension. Geertz suggests as a minimum definition of religion

---

1968, 1969a, 1969b, 1971) is concerned with symbols employed in ritual, and Geertz's (1957–1958, 1960, 1964, 1965) treatment of symbols occurs as part of his general discussion of religion. Despite these differences in context, their theories on symbols can be treated sensibly apart from their broader interests in myth, ritual, and religion in general. Much of Turner's theory has been discussed and will be considered in less detail in this chapter.

the "relatively modest dogma that God is not mad." Here again, Geertz follows Langer, who points out the severe anxiety which accrues when man's symbols fail him and his sense of lucidity is challenged.

Man's suspicion of prevailing moral incoherence is allayed when symbols are employed in rituals, in Geertz's view. For ritual induces a sense of reality of the moods and motivations provided by symbols. In other words, symbols convey meanings which are activated. They are *experienced* rather than merely *thought about* when used in rituals. Geertz puts it this way: "In a ritual, the world as lived and the world as imagined, fused under the agency of a single set of symbol forms, turn out to be the same world (1965:23).

Because symbols are set in a ritual context, a behavioral rather than an intellectual system, they become alive and real to those engaged in the ritual. Beyond this, however, Geertz does not go. He does not tell us how it is that rituals, and consequently the symbols they employ, promote this sense of reality. Turner and Lévi-Strauss go into the matter more closely and their positions can be seen as taking up where Geertz leaves off.

Much of Turner's theory of symbolism was discussed in Chapter 5. Here I will consider only his interpretation of *how* symbols achieve their purposes, which turns out to be how they figure in rituals. It will be recalled that Turner pointed out that among the attributes of symbols are their multireferential character and their juxtaposition of the grossly physical and the structurally normative. Put another way, symbols consist of opposed poles of meaning—organic or sensory as against social or cultural. Thus he regards symbols as fusing opposites, uniting "high and low." By doing this, symbols convert obligatory social norms and imperatives into that which is actively desired. They transform society's requirements, burdens, and duties into sources of personal motivation and satisfaction. In describing how this is achieved by ritual, Turner states:

> Within its framework of meanings, the [dominant] symbol brings the ethical and jural norms of society into close contact with strong emotional stimuli. In the action situation of ritual, with its social excitement and directly physiological stimuli, such as music, singing, dancing, alcohol, incense, and bizarre modes of dress, the ritual symbols, we may perhaps say, effect an interchange of qualities between its poles of meaning. Norms and values, on the one hand, become saturated with emotion, while the gross and basic emotions become ennobled through contact with social values [1967:30].

Turner concludes with the logical conclusion to this interpretation: symbols not only convey meaning and provide motivations (the emphasis given to them by Geertz) but also function in a regulative and constraining capacity. Ritual symbols, like Freud's dream symbols, are a compromise between two opposing tendencies, the need for social control and the innate human desires whose gratification and indulgence would result in a breakdown of that control. Ritual symbols, therefore, can be expected to refer to the basic needs and conditions of social existence (for example, technology, fertility, environment) and at the same time to those shared values on which communal life ultimately depends (friendship, cooperation, consensus, generosity, and so forth). The symbols associated with the physiological-sensory pole will refer to the basic needs of existence and symbols associated with the ideological pole will have as referents the values of communal life. By extension, the opposition can be said to occur between jural-economic (instrumental considerations) and affective-personal (expressive).

Thus, by adding Turner's approach to Geertz's, one may view symbols and the rituals in which they are embedded as providing order, meaning, and moral coherence, and at the same time providing regulation and restraint. Seen thus, the explanation for the ubiquitousness and complexity of symbols begins to emerge. Symbols perform essential and difficult social and psychological tasks, potentially achieved by few and simple forms, actions, and arrangements. Turner's analysis proves invaluable in understanding the Huichol symbol complex examined here, as will be seen shortly. Turning now to the approach taken by Lévi-Strauss (1963a, 1966, 1967, 1969), again one finds a concordant view.

In one short statement, Lévi-Strauss (1963a) analyzes a cure achieved by a South American shaman working with a woman experiencing a difficult childbirth. He illustrates many of the themes taken up at greater length by Turner and Geertz. It is especially interesting that Lévi-Strauss uses the situation of curing to expound his interpretation of the function and nature of symbols. Geertz, too, analyzed cures achieved by the Navaho "sing" to illustrate his views on how symbols provide meanings by giving the patient an interpretation, vocabulary, and context for his ailment. Geertz concludes his discussion:

> Clearly, the symbolism of the sing focuses upon the problem of human suffering and attempts to cope with it by placing it in a meaningful context, providing a mode of action through which it can be expressed, being expressed understood, and being understood, endured. The sustaining effect of the sing . . . rests ulti-

mately on its ability to give the stricken person a vocabulary in terms of which to grasp the nature of his distress and relate it to the wider world [1965:20].

Consider this alongside Lévi-Strauss's description of the cure of the laboring woman:

> The shaman provides the sick woman with a *language* by means of which unexpressed, and otherwise unexpressible, psychic states can be immediately expressed. . . . And it is the transition to this verbal expression which makes it possible to undergo in an ordered and intelligible form a real experience that would otherwise be chaotic and inexpressible [1963a:198].

The sick person in each case is given a set of meaningful categories in terms of which he can comprehend his otherwise confused and subjective experiences. The patient's private, mystifying, isolating pain and confusion are transformed into a known, shared, and intelligible set of events when described in terms of a set of collective representations. The patient is thus relocated in a world known and familiar, coherent and orderly.

In this analysis, then, one sees Geertz and Lévi-Strauss stressing the provision of meaning and order through symbols, illustrated by their examinations of why magical cures are effective. Lévi-Strauss's interpretation of the specific means by which the shaman achieves success in curing approaches Turner's analysis of how the obligatory is converted into the desirable through ritual symbols. Lévi-Strauss states that the shaman relates a myth which is intended to refer to the sick woman's body:

> A transition will thus be made from the most prosaic reality to myth, . . . from the external world to the internal body. And the

> myth being enacted in the internal body must retain throughout the vividness and the character of lived experience prescribed by the shaman in the light of the pathological state and through an appropriate obsessing technique [1963a:193].

This "obsessing technique" consists of the rapid oscillation between mythical and physiological themes "as if to abolish in the mind of the sick woman the distinction which separates them, and to make it impossible to differentiate their respective attributes" (1963a:193). The shaman alternately invokes the myth and refers to the woman's body until they converge and "the pains of the sick woman assume cosmic proportions." This cure, then, is a ritual which provides an action setting for symbols and makes them "really real," *experienced* rather than merely thought about, set in a dramatic context in which living people actively participate. The myth provided by Lévi-Strauss's shaman is analogous to Turner's ideological pole, representing that which is social, shared, publicly known and valued, while the suffering woman's pains correspond to Turner's physiological pole—gross, private, and sensory. Just as Turner's ritual symbols fuse the private with the public, the required with the desired, the cultural with the organic necessities of life, so does Lévi-Strauss's singing shaman achieve a unification of opposites, fusing the public myth with the woman's private anguish. The integration achieved is in one case a social goal and in the other an individual cure. In both, integration is the function of ritual and symbol.

The similarity between Turner and Lévi-Strauss can be found elsewhere, if less dramatically. Lévi-Strauss in several essays discusses the opposition between nature and culture and how these two poles are bridged, a formulation quite analogous to Turner's sensory-ideological dichotomy. And both are interested in the opposition between the social/affective/expressive dimension on the one hand and jural/normative/instrumental on the other, particularly as these poles express conflicts and oppositions within a single social organization. Lévi-Strauss and Turner select the identical social organizational conflict to exemplify the operation of myth, symbol, and ritual in encompassing oppositions—the case both use is that of the opposition of matrilineality and virilocality. Lévi-Strauss considers oppositions per se as originating from the very structure of the human mind; Turner is not concerned with origins, but this makes little difference in actuality. Both writers can be located in a venerable anthropological tradition concerned with the ubiquitous existence of opposites; for example, see Radcliffe-Brown (1952), Hertz (1960, first published in 1909), Durkheim and Mauss (1963, first published in 1903), Needham (1961), and so forth.

Lévi-Strauss's approach to myths, which are made up of symbols, further exemplifies his position (1967, 1969). He regards myths and symbols as constituting several levels which are transformations of each other and which have a common underlying structure. In analyzing Tsimshian myth of Asdiwal, Lévi-Strauss discovers an irresolvable paradox (virilocal marriage in a matrilineal society). He shows how the myth indicates a whole series of oppositions (man/woman, earth/heaven, west/east, elder/younger, and so forth). In several coexisting but slightly differing versions of the myth, the distance between the opposed terms dwindles gradually. The extreme positions are mediated as the various solutions are postulated and discarded as unsatisfactory. A series of failures therefore is admitted in the myths, and ironically, in this very admission of failure, the myths achieve their purpose because the solutions they offer do not depict what is real, but "justify the shortcomings of reality, since the extreme positions are only imagined in order to show that they are *untenable*" (1967:30). Lévi-Strauss feels that myths are not to be regarded as accurate depictions of reality but rather are a means of understanding unconscious categories. Myth formulates possibilities which will *not* be chosen; it shows them to be unsatisfactory, leaving behind the feeling that the existent state of affairs, with all its imperfections, is not so bad after all. But these compromises cannot be handled on the conscious level—for this would be profitless and even disruptive. The myth makes paradoxes explicit but does not risk a conscious confrontation between elements which are truly in conflict and cannot ever be resolved. Lévi-Strauss regards the myth and its symbols as formulating paradoxes without resolving them. The symbols present and at the same time screen those ineradicable features of social and historical reality which cause instability within a society.

Following these writers' theories then: symbols are conceptions made concrete and tangible, often (but not always) in the form of an object. These conceptions are of special kinds —highly emotional, of widespread importance, ambiguous —since they contain a range of referents which include differing, even opposing and contradictory, meanings and associations. In their object state these conceptions are employed in behavioral contexts or social dramas, where they can be enacted rather than contemplated. Further, social dramas or rituals exclude the possibility of reflection on and search for the meaning of the symbols employed. Meaning of symbols can be found in myth, ostensibly. Myths provide the context, settings, explanations of ritual symbols, give them a rationale and postulate their significance, but through an oral enactment of ritual, social drama on a verbal level. In fact, myths are remarkable for their ability to avoid a genuine inquiry into the meanings of symbols. Myths provide the clichés and formulas by which one person may "explain" something to another. But these explanations, because highly stereotyped, operate toward the same purpose as ritual—not to question but to persuade. The questions are rhetorical, the goals are didactic. The meanings of symbols can be experienced and apprehended but never fully and consciously understood if they are to remain effective. Because the special purpose of symbols is the encompassing of incompatible, irresolvable sets of referents, symbols must prevent the clear, undisguised recognition of the unsatisfactory nature of present arrangements, social or ideological. Enacted in ritual and "explained" in myths, symbols prevent change and at the same time prevent the accumulation of dissatisfaction with things as they are. They are like Gluckman's (1964) explanation of the purpose of rituals of rebellion which challenge the king but not the principle of kingship. Lévi-Strauss is saying much the same thing when he points out how myths postulate a series of untenable alternative solutions to an irresolvable conflict, as does Geertz in his statement that symbols embrace and even celebrate contradictions and paradox.

Myth, then, provides the fiction, the verbal counterpart of ritual, which is the enactment of symbols. One final attribute of rituals may be pointed out. These are not ordinary dramas. Nadel (1954) and Goody (1961) have indicated that rituals are typically highly rigid, characterized by exactitude, precision, and repetitiveness. In order to be considered a ritual, an action must be replicated many times, mechanically, unvaryingly, almost obsessively, with mindless attention to the smallest detail. Nadel has defined ritual this way:

> When we speak of "ritual" we have in mind . . . actions exhibiting a striking or incongruous rigidity, that is, some conspicuous regularity not accounted for by the professed aims of the action. Any type of behavior may thus be said to turn into a "ritual" when it is stylized or formalized, and made repetitive in that form [1954:99].

Ritual must take this form because of its function—which obviously differs from its professed aims—that function is to present symbols in a context such that the opposed meanings and contradictions they embrace do not and cannot become evident. The mechanical redundancy of ritual inhibits spontaneous and idiosyncratic personal response, thus assuring that the symbols employed will not be contemplated with full consciousness.

Ritual makes the symbols workable and allows them to achieve their purpose while remaining uncomprehended and unscrutinized.

Rituals occur, significantly, in dangerous situations. Their rigidity is in contrast to the vital, shifting, dynamic aspects of the symbols they embrace. Turner (1971) has likened the relationship between ritual and symbol to that of a radioactive isotope in a metal envelope. Because of ritual, the unthinkable can be approached—taking the blood and body of the gods into oneself, being reborn and entering Paradise as spirit or deity, becoming transformed into a plant or animal—none of these hazardous feats would be possible outside of the protection and predictability afforded by ritual contexts. Thus ritual controls but does not eliminate danger. A completely safe ritual is dead, and impotent; it is ritualized, reduced to mere form.[2] Such deadening occurs when the symbols contained in the ritual no longer have vital referents, or when the ritual has overwhelmed the symbolic aspect and choked back the danger entirely. A metal container which prevents one from ever attaining access to its contents is dysfunctional—it is not an envelope but a coffin.

In this view, ritual and myth provide the contexts which allow symbols to function. They are in part masking, in part rhetorical devices—persuading, disguising, coercing, and constraining. Together, myth, ritual, and symbol constitute a tripartite unity no less economical and effective in their functions than the Huichol deer-maize-peyote symbol complex itself.

The Peyote Hunt as a Return to Paradise

The theories I have examined are invaluable in attempting to understand the peyote hunt, an elaborate ritual accompanied by plentiful mythical material, and of all the major Huichol ceremonies the most conspicuous in its utilization and dramatization of the deer-maize-peyote symbol complex. In other ceremonies, one or another of the symbols is emphasized, with the others evoked or adumbrated, but only in this ceremony are all three equally significant and indispensable, so that the peyote hunt is the pivotal and most climactic of all the religious events in Huichol life.

The Huichols say that the purpose of the peyote hunt is to return to the birthplace of the gods, to Wirikuta, where all will be a unity, to gather *híkuri,* which is the maize and the deer, so that "we may have our life." In order to return, the

[2] That rituals are necessary to control but not eradicate the dangerous aspects of symbols was suggested by Craig J. Calhoun and Riv-Ellen Prell-Foldes, personal communication, Los Angeles, 1971.

pilgrims must be cleansed of all sexual experience, that, they must return to the period of innocence, before they were mature, worldly adults. And they must be in complete good faith with one another, those with whom they travel and those whom they leave at home. When they return to Wirikuta it is as the gods themselves. Here is a social drama par excellence, a reenactment of the peregrinations of the very deities.

The Huichols' statement and behaviors indicating that they *are* the gods must be taken literally, without the qualifications automatically supplied by the Western scientific tradition, without the back-of-the-mind qualification, "They *act* like the gods, they are impersonating them." The Huichols on the peyote hunt are not role-playing in a dramatic religious pageant, nor have they merely assumed the identities of the gods. During the ritual the pilgrims strive to discard their human condition and *become* their divine counterparts. The peyote seekers begin by shedding their human sexuality; past transgressions are eliminated (not forgiven, but destroyed by the fire), and in the present, complete sexual continence is required. Salt (an essential ingredient of human life, especially for life in the desert) is forsworn, along with all but the bare minimum of physiological necessities—food, water, rest, and sleep. Even human excretory functions are disguised and denied; when necessary, a pilgrim quietly drops out of his place in line and no one comments on or calls attention to his absence in any way. All ritual actions cease temporarily until he resumes his place in the activities.[3]

[3] The *hikuritámete* do not refrain from defecating in Wirikuta merely to avoid soiling their Paradise, as one might suppose. Mary Douglas (1966) has shown that defecation per se is not necessarily regarded as dirty. It is only dirty when it is out of its proper place, in

The deprivation and exertion required for the success of this ritual can be interpreted as self-induced hardships designed to bring about extraordinary experiences such as visions, vertigo, or hallucinations, and likened to the vision quests of the North American Indians. But this comparison is specious, for with peyote a vision is obtained, with or without food, rest, and water. Neither is it adequate to stress the penitential aspect of the pilgrimage, for in context this is only a minor part of the experience. Rather, the peyote seekers in this ritual are *becoming* the gods on an action level, behaving as the gods who have none of those human needs which the Huichols deny as much as possible during this event. They aspire toward a complete achievement of the godly state; they reach for communion—for the fullest communication conceivable, for a genuine transformation.

Much of the emotional tone of the journey is explicable by adopting as one's own the Huichol's literal approach. The gods have left their home and are returning there. In what frame of mind? One's home is certainly a more desirable

violation of a social boundary. Wirikuta is utterly pure; defecation is impure there because it is a conspicuously mortal activity and brings to the sacred land the other realm—home, everyday life, "reality" —which has no place there. Salt may be forbidden the pilgrims during the trip for related reasons: it is a preservative, in the body and in nature. It retains, and retention of that which existed previously creates impurity and violates the effort to shed the past and be reborn, newly made. Lot's wife, it will be remembered, was turned into a pillar of salt for looking back. Her doom came upon her for retaining the past instead of passing into that which lay ahead without taint of mortality. So too, boundaries between Wirikuta and everyday life are observed when the *hikuritámete* return to the home fire all bits of food they have consumed in the sacred land. Neither food, nor earth, nor cactus spines are permitted to leave their proper place and be contaminated by being transported into the other realm, the world of everyday life.

place than a strange, new country to which one has either wandered or been driven. Huichol myths tell over and over of the longing for this home; a text has been recorded which describes the Ancient Ones as literally sick with nostalgia on finding themselves in the mountains, far from the high desert. Ultimately they find their cure through a temporary return. The mood with which the pilgrims return to Wirikuta is at first perplexing. They go back to the sacred land in tears, in a state of profound grief until they reach a specific place, Tatei Matinieri, when they are suddenly jubilant. How is one to understand this abrupt change of mood? Why are they sad at first, instead of joyous from the start? How can we explain, once they arrive at the sacred homeland, the reversals so that everything is its opposite? Even more mysterious, why their haste in leaving their long-sought country on the grounds that it is unsafe to remain there?

The peyote seekers, as the First People, left their sacred land involuntarily, it may be assumed. Earlier it was suggested that the peyote hunt is an enactment of a historical episode, an enforced immigration of Huichols from their original homeland. The emotions displayed by the *hikuritámete* are those which their ancestors experienced on departure from Wirikuta—grief and fear. It is only on entering the sacred land at the portal of Tatei Matinieri that they have achieved their destination, and grief gives way to exultation. Many dangers remain until they attain their final goal, but the greatest is past and from this moment they are the deities returned instead of the deities being driven out. The emotions they display reflect this change dramatically.

The ritual is much more than an enactment of a historical return, it is also a mythical return. Wirikuta is not merely the homeland of the first Huichol. It is the sacred place where the gods live, where the First People originated and lived in a state of prehuman bliss and accord. In other words, Wirikuta is Paradise, Valhalla, Elysium, Eden—the land which existed before time and the world began, before Creation, before there was life and death, light and darkness. It was where animals and man lived in a state of easy companionship speaking the same language, untroubled by problems of pain and thirst, hunger, weariness, and appetite. Men knew no discord among themselves—they were innocent, sexless, without self-awareness, indeed undifferentiated from the very gods. This was the primordial *illud tempus* which could not last. Myths throughout the world may or may not give the reasons for its termination. In many traditions some sort of Fall occurred from which Man as we know him emerged: conscious, sentient, vulnerable, flawed, and fragile. For whatever reason, the state of original perfection does not (and perhaps cannot) endure. Man was divided from the deities, from the animals and ultimately from himself, sundered into two forms—male and female—then ordered to leave his home, his harmony and purity. He and his mate had to take up the burdens of being human—to reproduce by copulation, to eat, work, suffer, and die tormented by the memory of what went before. Put another way, Man was forced to leave his state of childhood, of innocence, and assume the adult condition, which is to be differentiated, specialized, isolated, afflicted, faulty, and responsible for himself—in short, to be mortal.

This loss of innocence, godhood, and prehuman bliss causes the *hikŭritámete* to weep when they set out for Wirikuta. Their grief is replaced by joy upon retrieving the homeland, and for a time they fluctuate between tears over their loss and jubilant shouts over their return at that first emotional moment when they stand at the periphery of the sacred country, in Tatei Matinieri.

This "yearning for paradise," or the "Myth of Eternal Return," as Eliade (1954, 1960) calls the nostalgic desire to return to an original place and time, is nearly panhuman, occurring in religious systems all over the world—primitive, complex, ancient, and contemporary. So ubiquitous is this yearning that Eliade concludes: "We have the right to assume that the mystical memory of a blessedness without history haunts man from the moment he becomes aware of his situation in the cosmos" (1960:73).

The vision of this paradisiacal *illud tempus* is impressively uniform. Nearly always its perfection is equated with a state of wholeness, an absence of differentiation of any kind. Not only have the divisions not yet occurred between man and god, between man and animals, between man and woman. It goes back further, before creation, before consciousness, a condition usually terminated by the separation of light from dark. The human organism is undifferentiated, part of the cosmos. This cosmic wholeness is sundered by a primordial splitting, and ever after, the individual is haunted by the remembrance of and potentially fatal attraction for his original state.

The Perils of the Return

In this vision of Paradise, one finds the clue for understanding the otherwise baffling Huichol injunction that after their arduous and faithful journey back to Wirikuta, they cannot remain there. After a short period of time, sufficient only for hunting the First Peyote and gathering the peyote needed for the rest of the yearly ceremonies, the peyote seekers must run, literally, out of the sacred land. And throughout their little time there, they are in great peril, despite all their ritual precautions.

The dangers of remaining, indeed of daring to reenter Wirikuta in the first place, occur on several levels simultaneously. Danger on the ethnographic level is explicit: if one lingers in Wirikuta, in the Land Where the Sun Was Born, he may lose his soul. This is particularly true for the *primero*, for him the mara'akame must take special precautions. As Ramón put it, the *primero* may be in good faith, "but he doesn't really know what he has come for." He thinks he is in accord with the others but he has come in part because he is curious. Dangerous winds blow and he may wander or be blown away. If this happens, his *kupuri*, the fuzzy hairy rays which attach each person to Tatei Niwetúkame, may snap and cause him to die.

On the sociological level, the temptation to remain in Paradise is due to man's desire to dwell in a permanent state of ecstasy, forever outside of social obligation and responsibility. In Wirikuta, the *hikuritámete* are in a state of intense communion with each other, where the social self is shed and men stand beside each other as totalities, in spontaneous, joyous vulnerability, without the protection or requirements of social structure. This state of fusion of the individual with the group is antithetical to everyday life and its requirements. Indeed, it is an anathema to the allocation of roles and resources, the division of labor, the organizational, restrained, rational considerations which are the inevitable accompaniments of providing the daily dole of bread. This concern cannot be suspended for long. Thus, the experience of ecstatic communion with another—something outside of the self, whether god, the cosmos or fellow mortals—is as fleeting as it is universally sought. Real life, as Turner (1969b, 1971) stresses, is inevitably a dialectical process. It is a fluctuation between, at one pole, mundane needs met through social structure and at the other, the ecstasy of communion, which Turner calls *communitas*.[4] To attempt to make either of these opposed states the whole of life is perilous. Without *communitas*—which must be periodic and short-lived—mundane considerations are overwhelming—tedious, trivial business, mere survival. The spirit starves. Without social structure, the body starves. Alternation between the two—between social organization and ecstasy, between the mundane and the spiritual, between the sensory and the ideological—without obliterating or neutralizing either extreme, is possible.[5] But it is a possibility which requires a most

[4] To be precise, Turner reserves the term *communitas* for the ecstatic communion between men, likening it to Buber's *Zwischenmenschlicheit*, a condition where social roles are suspended, leaving men to share with each other their utterly naked, trusting, total humanness, temporarily freed from social and cultural definitions and restrictions. This suspension of self is frightening, dangerous, exhilarating, and a fundamental ingredient of many religious experiences. Turner's use of the term is generally confined to interpersonal relations and the transcendence of boundaries between men. It seems to me there are several kinds of *communitas* and many paths to reach it. In Wirikuta, the pilgrims become one with each other by becoming one with the deer, the maize, and the peyote, and by returning to the place where all was One. *Communitas* can also take the form of transcending the self by becoming one with the cosmos or with the deities.

[5] The difficulties of maintaining these two poles without attempting to obliterate their contradictory features seem especially formidable to the Western mind. In discussing the differences between Nahua and Western thought, Rafael J. Gonzalez made the following observations: "In the West, the 'golden mean' is always a condition of compromise reached by reason. *Equilibrio* in the Nahua world seems to be something different, more dynamic. It is a tense balance which comes about not through compromise, but by the encounter of two

careful, informed, and dynamic balance, a vigilant perspective that is always aware of the necessity of relinquishing *communitas* at the appropriate moment. The special task of the Huichol mara'akame is to guide his people out of Wirikuta quickly and firmly, disregarding their desire to linger. His guardianship in escorting them back to reality, in persuading them to relinquish the longing for Paradise, is as important as leading them there in the first place.

There are many psychological dangers in attempting to return to and remain in Paradise. The subject has been explored fully by Jung (1946) and by some of his interpreters, particularly Neumann (1954). And several writers have been concerned with the religious and mythological implications of Jung's thought, especially Watts (1970), Campbell (1962), and Henderson and Oakes (1963). In the Jungian view, myths and their historical developments are seen as analogues or allegories for the development of the ego and consciousness. The beginning, whole and perfect, is symbolized by the uroborus, the circle made by a snake with its tail in its mouth.

---

or more unqualified forces meeting headlong and which are not so much reconciled as held teetering on the verge of chaos, not in reason but in experience. In the West the 'golden mean' achieves comfort; in the Nahua, *equilibrio* achieves meaning" (Personal communication, Los Angeles, 1970).

Watts makes essentially the same point, in his contrast of the thought of Heraclitus and Aristotle. "In the history and climate of Western thought Heraclitus stands somewhat alone, for a philosophy in which 'it is one and the same thing to be living and dead, awake or asleep, young or old' does not seem to offer any directives for action, that is, for making choices (1970:48). Western culture, Watts continues, perpetuates the illusion that one pole of an opposition can exist without the other—the illusion that there can be good without evil, lightness without dark, pleasure without pain. Thus the tension between the poles is eliminated and along with it the ability to envision the continuity underlying these dichotomies.

Perfection exists because "the opposites have not yet flown apart and the world has not yet begun. . . . It is perfect because it is autarchic. Its self-sufficiency, self-contentment, and independence of any *you* and any *other* are signs of its self-contained eternality" (Neumann 1954:8–9). Maturity and individuation require that the harsh reality of separation, awareness, and creation be accepted, bringing above all the painful knowledge of human loneliness, impotence, and pettiness. Neumann continues, "An undeniable sense of deficiency . . . attaches to the emancipated ego. Interpreted as sin, apostasy, rebellion, disobedience, this emancipation is in reality the fundamental liberating act of man which releases him from the yoke of the unconscious and establishes him as an ego, a conscious individual" (1954:120). But like all acts of liberation, this entails suffering and sacrifice. Only in the Garden of Paradise do "opposites lie down together." The mature man with a conscious and separated ego always has a sense of differentiation. The world is forever split into object and subject, good and evil, inside and outside; the mature ego's very consciousness continually reminds him that he is a divided being.

In Jungian interpretation, then, the danger of remaining in Wirikuta is akin to the conception of "uroboric incest." This signifies the individual's refusal to enter the world, encounter the universal principle of opposites, come to terms with the difference between the inner and outer worlds and thus avoid "the essential tasks of human and individual development" (Neumann 1954:35). Neumann describes the temptation and appeal of uroboric incest in this way:

> Uroboric incest is a form of entry into the mother, of union with her, and it stands in sharp contrast to other and later forms of in-

cest . . . uroboric incest . . . is . . . a desire to be absorbed; passively one lets oneself be taken, sinks into the pleroma, melts away in the ocean of pleasure—a *Liebestod*. . . . The incest we term "uroboric" is self-surrender. . . . It is a happening full of passive, childlike confidence; for the infantile ego consciousness always feels its reawakening, after having been immersed in death, as a rebirth [1954:17].

So, too, the *hikuritámete* experience the reentry into Wirikuta as a kind of rebirth, with their new names, their ritual restoration of childlike innocence and purity. And their absorption into the undifferentiated unity of Wirikuta may be interpreted as a form of indulging in uroboric incest. Herein lies its danger from the Jungian point of view, but it is danger which can be avoided through the vigilance of the mara'akame, who calls the pilgrims forth from this state at the appropriate time and forces them to reenter the mortal condition. They weep but they leave when bidden to do so, for they have the certain knowledge that they may return to Wirikuta another year.

The Freudian view would identify the dangers of remaining in Wirikuta as those of indulging in incest and failing to relinquish an infantile fantasy of the mother as mate. An orthodox psychoanalytic approach would call our attention to the overt biological and sexual symbolism of the journey to Wirikuta. The pilgrims enter a sacred region called "Where Our Mothers Dwell" through a place known as the "vagina"; they use in their rituals a knotted cord which can be seen as representing an umbilicus. In this reading Wirikuta is a symbol for the womb and the reentry is a fantasy of incest which indicates the failure to cope with or resolve the oedipal conflict. The religious layer is seen as a metaphor for the underlying physiological and psychological processes and these processes provide the clues to interpreting the meaning of the peyote hunt.[6]

Such a literal reading of the body symbolism in the peyote hunt is undeniably interesting but it is too precise and simple. Wirikuta is more than the "Great Mother" or the "Earth Mother" or any other mother in particular.[7] And it is more than happy childhood remembered, *communitas*, Eden, the womb, the Place Where the Sun Was Born, or the Home of the Ancient Ones. It is all of these and probably many more which have not yet come to light.

For the *hikuritámete*, Wirikuta is not symbolic of something else. The Western mind habitually divides reality into

[6] Recently a number of psychoanalysts have demonstrated a renewed interest in womb fantasies, and these authors view such fantasies in the context of ego theory rather than as manifestations of infantilism or unresolved oedipal yearning. Their views are in certain respects similar to those previously mentioned in connection with Jung's concept of uroboric incest. Among these writers are Fairbairn (1963), Guntrip (1968), Klein (1960), and Winnicot (1965).

Yet another psychological interpretation of the desire to return to Paradise is suggested by Schachtel, who equates Paradise with "the myth of a happy childhood," which appeals to "disappointed and suffering adults, people without hope, [who] want to believe that at least once there was a time in their life when they were happy. But the myth of happy childhood reflects also the truth that as in the myth of Paradise Lost, there was a time before animalistic innocence was lost, before pleasure-seeking nature and pleasure-forbidding culture clashed in the battle called education, a battle in which the child is always the loser" (1949:46–47).

[7] Mary Douglas has offered some trenchant arguments against this kind of body symbolism and suggests that the body should not be seen as providing symbols for societal processes but on the contrary, societal processes are symbolized by the body. "It is the duty of every craftsman," she states, "to stick to his last. The sociologists have the duty of meeting one kind of reductionism with their own. Just as it is true that everything symbolizes the body, so it is equally true . . . that the body symbolizes everything else" (1966:146).

psychology, physiology, history, ethnography, religion, and the like, each claiming its exclusive or superior explanatory values and virtues, each regarding the others as symbols and metaphors for the fundamental processes addressed by its own perspective. To a point this is interesting, then destructive, for surely these multiple viewpoints are strikingly congruent with each other. And this is not mere accident, for not only are all the perspectives mentioned above internally consistent, but none is in conflict with the others. They are different inflections of the same reality, but the Western mind often dwells more lovingly on these differences than the areas of overlap. One need not, should not, choose among them. All point to the same interpretation—a vision, an image of a timeless, placeless, undifferentiated condition of transcending beauty, in which the self as we conceive it does not exist. The self becomes merged with the oneness, that is the critical characteristic in the image.

The primordial former condition is construed as the beginning; sometimes it is seen as the future as well as the past. In some religious systems provision is made for ordinary men to retrieve this state; in others only sacred specialists can do so. In any event the journey to this place is always fraught with great dangers. Only with the utmost care and assistance can one maintain his balance in the passage and retrieve one's self once he has stepped out of it. The details of the vision differ between one religion and the next. The specific hazards of going there and returning vary but the essential story does not. There is always the promise and the threat of ecstasy, and always the cosmic unification, always the difficulties of going out and coming back.

That the Huichols do not carve their interpretation of the peyote hunt into levels of interpretation indicates only that they find symbolic exegesis less enjoyable than we do. We should not lose sight of our interpretive exercises as different from theirs in this way, that for them Wirikuta is all levels at once. It is not that for them there is congruence among several interpretive systems; it is that the systems are the same, light from a single source, refracted into different colors. Having examined all the angles, we must reassemble the vision to get back to the Huichol significance of the peyote hunt. Wirikuta for the Huichol pilgrim is not a symbol for anything else. To quote Ramón speaking in another context, "It is its own essence. It is itself."

The Unification of Opposites in Wirikuta

Wirikuta, seen as Paradise, is a return to a mythical past which in Eliade's interpretation is a panhuman conception and desire: "Among the 'primitive' peoples, just as among the saints and the Christian theologians, mystic ecstasy is a return to Paradise, expressed by the overcoming of Time and History . . . and [represents] a recovery of the primordial state of Man" (1960:72).

In shaman-dominated religions, the special responsibility of the shaman is to return to *illud tempus* on behalf of his people, to make his ecstatic journey through the assistance of animal tutelary spirits and bring back information of the other realms to ordinary mortals. As mediator, the shaman travels back and forth and, with exquisite balance, never becomes too closely tied to the mundane or to the supernatural. His soul leaves his body during trance states and by means of a magical flight he rejoins that which was once unified—man and animals, the living and the dead, man and the gods. The Huichol mara'akame does more than this for his people; he takes the pilgrims themselves to *illud tempus* as deities during the peyote hunt, sharing with them all that existed before the world began. He is guide and psychompomp when he leads the *hikuritámete* into Wirikuta but at the climactic moment of the peyote hunt he suspends this role and himself becomes one with them as they become one with the deer, the maize, and the peyote.

Surely this is one of the truly unique features of Huichol religious life. The unity sought in Wirikuta is so complete that all social distinctions are set aside, not only age and sex, but leader and led as well. When the mara'akame receives the sacramental water at Tatei Matinieri, when he, too, "confesses" and is knotted into the sacred cord, when he observes the reversals and, most dramatically, when he is given the First Peyote, he participates as intensely as the other pilgrims. He is no longer mara'akame at these moments, nor Tatewarí; he is one with all and there is no more separation.[8]

Throughout this discussion reference has been made to the

[8] Christianity, like so many religious systems, strives for intense unity among men and a corresponding suspension of social distinctions and divisions, but it does not go as far along these lines as Huichol religion. In Christianity, congregation and priest do not become one even at the most sacred moments. The sacraments are not given to the religious specialist by the flock. And while all men become one by being equally beloved by Christ regardless of social categories, the distinction between man and Christ is maintained. Douglas cites the words of St. Paul: "Baptized into Christ, you have put on Christ. There can be neither Jew, nor Greek, nor bond nor free, there can be neither male nor female, for you are all one man in Christ Jesus" (Galatians 3:28, cited in Douglas 1966:186). Among the Huichols, mara'akame and pilgrims are equal as *hikuritámete*, and all sacred elements are fused with the eating of the First Peyote in Wirikuta—the deities no longer exist as such, nor do deer, maize, and peyote or past, present, and future as distinguishable phenomena. "All is one"; all become fused, as Ramón put it, "like the rays of the sun, like a single flame."

alteration of temporal and historical order in the course of the pilgrimage. Precisely how are time and history altered, even abolished, by the peyote hunt and why is this important? The abolition of time, as Lévi-Strauss (1966) has pointed out, is a common task in religious thought, especially in primitive religions. In myth and ritual, and in what Lévi-Strauss calls "savage thought," man attempts to grasp the world all at once, as a synchronic totality. Savage thought differs from scientific thought in that it doesn't distinguish the moment of observation from the moment of interpretation. It attempts to integrate synchronic and diachronic events into one system of meaning. Thus the past and future are the same and the present but a minor deviation from "reality," a human interlude, atypical and transitory, bracketed by a beginning and final condition of Paradise.

Ramón made this theme explicit:

One day all will be as you have seen it there, in Wirikuta. The First People will come back. The fields will be pure and crystalline. All this is not clear to me but in five more years I will know it, through more revelations. The world will end and the unity will be here again. But only for pure Huichols.

Wirikuta, then, is the archetypal beginning and end. How this state of perfection will be retrieved was explained in the same discussion by Ramón.

When the world ends it will be like when the names of things are changed, during the peyote hunt. All will be different, the opposite of what is now. Now there are two eyes in the heavens, Dios Sol and Dios Fuego. Then, the moon will open his eye and become brighter. The sun will become dimmer. There will be no more difference. No more man and woman. No more child and adult. All will change places. Even the mara'akame will no longer be separate. That is why there is always a *nunutsi* when we go to Wirikuta. Because the old man and the tiny baby, they are the same.

In this remarkable text, Ramón has described the purpose of the reversals, the reasons why, in Wirikuta, the names of things are changed. Here is the ancient theme of the unification of opposites—to achieve unity, to dramatize and live in that original state of unity, the retrieval of which is the purpose of the peyote hunt.

The concern with opposition and unity appears prominently in Western Christian religions and in Eastern and primitive philosophical systems.[9] The reversals practiced on the peyote hunt are another manifestation of a fundamental feature of human perception, recurringly and prominently manifested in religious thought. Watts puts it this way:

> What, exactly, is polarity? It is something much more than simple duality or opposition. For to say that opposites are polar is to say much more than that they are far apart: it is to say that they are related and joined . . . that they are the terms, ends, or extremities of a single whole. Polar opposites are therefore inseparable opposites, like the poles of the earth or of a magnet, or the ends of a stick or the faces of a coin [1970:45].

The same theme is found in the writings of Heraclitus:

[9] Watts (1970) suggests that the symbolism of the Christian cross may be interpreted as the intersection of opposed poles, where opposites—including demons and angels, good and evil, God and Satan—are simultaneously set apart and reconciled. So too, it is possible that this insight is relevant to understanding the Huichol preoccupation with the four directions, conceived as two intersecting axes, meeting at the center which is sacred (signified by the magical number five). Seen in this light, its sacred character would be related to its unification of opposites, its signification of primordial oneness which is the essence of the vision of Wirikuta as Paradise.

> It is one and the same thing to be living or dead, awake or asleep, young or old. The former aspect in each case becomes the latter, and the latter again the former, by sudden unexpected reversal [Fragment 113, cited in Wheelwright 1971: 90–91].

And the Gospel According to Thomas:

> They said to Him: Shall we then, being children
> enter the Kingdom? Jesus said to them:
> When you make the two one, and
> when you make the inner as the outer
> and the outer as the inner and the above
> as the below, and when
> you make the male and the female into a single one,
> so that the male will not be male and
> the female [not] be female, when you make
> eyes in the place of an eye, and a hand
> in the place of a hand, and a foot in the place
> of a foot, [and] an image in the place of an image,
> then shall you enter [the Kingdom]
> [Logia 23–35, cited in Guillaumont *et al.* 1959: 17–19].

In the Book of Genesis, Graves and Patai found instances of enacting reversals in a manner reminiscent of that practiced in Wirikuta. Here is their interpretation:

> The inhabitants of Paradise stand on their heads and walk on their hands, as do the dead. If a sorcerer summons a dead spirit by conjuration, it always appears upside down, unless summoned by order of a king—as the witch of En-Dor summoned Samuel at Saul's demand—whereupon it stands on its feet to show respect for royalty [1966:73].

The reversals in Wirikuta may be interpreted as accomplishing other purposes besides that of emphasizing the essential unity of opposed poles. By postulating the domain of

Paradise as the opposite of the known world, the former becomes more vivid, tangible, and imaginable. This equation of Wirikuta with Paradise provides the concrete vocabulary of actions and names, the mnemonic, so to speak, for conceiving and behaving in Wirikuta as deities.[10]

In returning to Wirikuta as the Ancient Ones, the pilgrims do everything backward, and, in doing so, enact their sacred condition. Their return in space and time and their reversals are rituals of transformation of the mundane into the sacred. Eliade suggests this when he says, "Consequently to do away with this state [of humanity] even if only provisionally, is equivalent to reestablishing the primordial condition of man, in other words, to banish time, to go backwards, to recover the 'paradisial' *illud tempus*" (1960:72).

The Return to Origins: Transcendence of Paradox and Differentiation

Wirikuta, as the place of beginnings and a condition of unity, is regained during the peyote hunt. Here the key symbols of Huichol religion—the deer, the maize, and the peyote—become one and thus negate many of the paradoxes and contradictions of Huichol life. To recapitulate, these unifications occur simultaneously on several levels: on

[10] The extent to which an exact inversion concretizes the Huichol vision of Wirikuta was made explicit by Ramón when he said, "Everything there is just as we know it, but backward." Thus, in lieu of the vaguely conceived, brightly lighted mansion inhabited by graceful seraphim provided in the Christian fantasy of Paradise, the Huichol finds himself in possession of a very precise picture, anchored to a most concrete set of referents in his own real world. And, of course, the reversals underscore the imperfection of human life by stressing the perfection of the life of the deities, thus making the pilgrimage even more precious an undertaking, even more tantalizing a promise.

the societal level, social barriers are transcended by means of the symbol complex when the mara'akame and his group become a single entity and distinctions between leader and led are set aside; and even biological differences between male and female, old and young, disappear, as men, women, and children participate equally and completely in receiving the sacramental First Peyote eaten on the peyote hunt. Ritual status and all other forms of social distinctions are set aside so that for a little while men stand apart from their social roles and culturally provided "personalities." Frightened and elated by this freedom, unknown since the moment of birth which forever fixes one in a social matrix, the *hikuritámete* stand nakedly beside one another, undefined, vulnerable, and starkly human.[11]

On a historical and ecological level, a past life as free, autonomous desert-dwelling nomadic hunters, living in a world dominated by males, is opposed to and reconciled with the present mountain-dwelling, sedentary life, based on agriculture, requiring an equalitarian division of labor which includes and gives considerable status to the work of women. It is a way of life which necessitates ceaseless, monotonous, and often ill-rewarded attention to the crops, the seasons, and accommodation to an ill-understood, ever-threatening pressure exerted by surrounding powerful and dangerous outsiders. Ecologically, during the peyote hunt the Huichols achieve a spiritual relation to their physical environment—not a neutral setting, not a mere place to live or exploit for a living. The very landscape is sanctified—the caves, springs, mountains, rivers, cactus groves—and the features of the

[11] Riv-Ellen Prell-Foldes suggested this frightening but exciting feeling which accompanies rolelessness, personal communication, Los Angeles, 1971.

mythical world are elevated to cosmic significance. "Plants" and "animals" become only labels, conventions, mere human categories of thought. Distinctions between them are illusory. Man *is* nature, he is an extension of it. Likewise "natural" and "supernatural" are only names that conceal their basic sameness. Thus is the ordinary elevated, the lofty made concrete as the opposite poles participate in each other and merge, manifesting their true character of continuity.

In Wirikuta distinctions melt away on the psychological level as well. The mortal condition is transcended and oceanic bliss and omnipotence given again to man; whether conceived as a once-known state or an ill-remembered dream, for a moment Paradise is the human provinence. Creation has not yet occurred, bringing man consciousness of himself, of his ultimate aloneness and inevitable death. He is the Cosmos without skin or membrane, without a self to contain and separate him. He achieves ecstatic diffusion of all boundaries. The ultimate yearning for wholeness is gained in the sacred land, when the pilgrim finds the vision of Wirikuta.

In Wirikuta, there is no time, with its compartments and limitations. Public and private experiences do not exist. There are no conflicting claims and intrusions of the social order into the subjective, individual domain. The past history of discord, jealousy, ambivalence, contentiousness—all the negative aspects of the human heritage—are pared away. And there is no awareness that Huichol life was once very different from its present version, that drastic changes have occurred. The Huichols feel that they were always a single people with a distinctive, eternal way of life, despite the discontinuities of their past and present. Without past, future, or present, there is nothing to interrupt the flow and continuity. All is immortal, all is in harmony. This is the authentic mystic vision, of perfection, of Paradise. This is the moment of ecstasy and it is apocalyptic, "there in Wirikuta, where all is one, all is a unity, all is ourselves."

This is a magnificent achievement by any standard. The contradictions dealt with occur on many levels, yet are handled with a poetic parsimony and emotional forcefulness that are among the definitive characteristics of symbols. Although Turner and Lévi-Strauss focused their examinations of the role of symbols on the management of one kind of contradiction—that resulting from incompatible sociological principles—one sees here that several other kinds of contradiction can be managed simultaneously by symbols. It must be concluded that the effectiveness of symbols is even more sweeping than these writers have suggested.

In addition to achieving the resolution of many paradoxes, the deer-maize-peyote complex can be seen to function along the lines emphasized by Geertz in his discussion of the nature and purpose of religion, namely, the elimination of that most unacceptable of all aspects of human life—the unexpected, inexplicable, and the uncanny. This Huichol symbol complex takes up the problem of moral incoherence. By making possible the retention of the past as part of the present, it eliminates the need for dealing with the question of why the world changed, why the beauty and freedom of former times has passed away, why man lost touch with the gods, plants, and animals, why the Spaniards steal Huichol land, and why it is no longer possible to pursue "the perfect life—to offer to the gods and chase the deer."

These losses require a moral explanation, an answer which realigns the "ought" and the "is." A religion can provide such a justification by postulating some sin because of which man forfeited a privileged past, thus granting assurance that life as it is is deserved; whether good or bad, it is understandable. Or an afterlife may be conceived of as compensating for the sufferings of the present transient and inconsequential reality. A third alternative is that manifested in Huichol religion—denying the gratuitous and cruel losses by refusing to relinquish the past. Their most precious religious heritage—their beginnings—is idealized and recovered. Even if only for a little while, by means of the peyote hunt, Paradise may be regained. Through the deer-maize-peyote complex, the deer and a life dedicated to hunting the deer is still a fact of present-day life rather than a fading, shabby memory, chewed over by old men at the end of the day.

The Huichols are aware that they are destitute while outsiders prosper, and their religion also manages this moral paradox. In spite of great privation, they do not see themselves as victims of blind chance or of the inexorable forces of history. With rare confidence the Huichols move through the world, acknowledging no one as better or master, and this although it is hard to imagine a people with less actual control over their fate or more at the mercy of forces beyond their power and comprehension. Yet they pity those who live a life different from their own, so sure are they that their present life is beautiful and significant, just as their past life was perfect. A great part of this conviction may be attributed to the deer-maize-peyote symbol complex. The deer as the past life of perfection, the maize as the mundane, human dimension, and the peyote as the spiritual, private, and free part of life merge—the mundane is elevated and refined by its association with the divine, and the gods themselves become accessible, knowable, and even mundane. Thus the realm of the senses is refined while the spiritual realm is made tangible.

Because of the contact between these realms the dichotomy between them disappears.

Geertz (1965) says that religious symbols embody attitudes, longings, and beliefs. The Huichols' symbols embody an image of a morally closed world in which nothing is neutral or gratuitous. Even the ambiguities and puzzles of that life are given significance, put in their place, put in order. The human condition becomes lucid and more than merely bearable. During the peyote hunt the major symbols make the imaginary life the real life, and provide that fusion of the "lived-in" with the "thought-of" order which Geertz describes as one of the major tasks of religion. Wirikuta is not an imaginary place. The pilgrims need not speculate as to what it might be like. Through their own will, dedication, and virtue, they are truly there and even those who never go know it from the reports of other peyote-seekers. They touch the earth, feel the hairs of the gods brush their faces, feel the warmth of the fire as it sears their past away, taste the waters from the sacred springs, turn the peyote over in their mouths, and watch with their own eyes as the surrounding world becomes a luminous and vivid place of magic animals and plants and flowers.

Many times in the course of the peyote hunt the peyote pilgrims affirmed that while their life is poor materially, full of travail and danger, they were not to be pitied, for their symbols make them rich. And the mara'akame, who probably suffers more than most individuals in the society, is the richest one of all. The treasure of Huichol culture is aesthetic and spiritual. These people envy no one, at least that is their ideal. They have in abundance a culture's greatest gift—an utter  conviction of the meaningfulness of their life. As Ramón was fond of saying, "Our symbols—the deer, the peyote, the maize of five colors—all, all that you have seen, there in Wirikuta, when we go to hunt the peyote—these are beautiful. They are beautiful because they are right."

Bibliography

Aberle, David. 1966. The Peyote Religion among the Navaho. Chicago: Aldine.

Anderson, Edward F. 1969. The Biogeography, ecology, and taxonomy of lophophora (Cactacea). Brittonia 21 (4): 229–310.

Beals, Ralph C. 1932. The comparative ethnology of northwest Mexico before 1750. Ibero-Americana: 2. Berkeley: University of California Press.

——. 1943. Problems of Mexican Indian folklore. Journal of American Folklore 56: 8–16.

Benítez, Fernando. 1968a. En la tierra mágica del peyote. Biblioteca Era. Serie Popular. Mexico.

——. 1968b. Los Indios de México. Vol. II. Biblioteca Era. Serie Mayor. Mexico.

——. 1970. Los Indios de México. Vol. III. Biblioteca Era. Serie Mayor. Mexico.

Bennett, Wendell C., and Robert M. Zingg. 1935. The Tarahumara, an Indian Tribe of Northern Mexico. Chicago: University of Chicago Press.

Bohannan, Paul J. 1957. Justice and Judgment among the Tiv. London: Oxford University Press.

Calhoun, Craig J. 1971. Chaos or constancy: Time and the Concept of Order. Unpublished manuscript.

——. 1972. The Function of Experiences of Altered Perception for Social Organization. Unpublished manuscript.

Campbell, Joseph. 1962. The Masks of God: Oriental Mythology. New York: Viking Press.

——. 1965. The Hero with a Thousand Faces. New York: Bollingen. (First published 1949.)

Castaneda, Carlos. 1971. A Separate Reality: Further Conversations with Don Juan. New York: Simon & Schuster.

Coe, Michael D. 1964. Mexico. New York: Praeger.

Corey, Douglas Q., and Jeannette P. Maas. 1971. Existential Bible. Unpublished manuscript.

Diquet, Léon. 1911. Idiome Huichol: Contribution à l'étude de langues mexicaines. Journal de la Société des Americanistes de Paris 8 (n.s.): 23–54.

Douglas, Mary. 1966. Purity and Danger: An Analysis of Concepts of Pollution and Taboo. London: Penguin.

——. 1970. Natural Symbols: Explorations in Cosmology. New York: Pantheon.

Durkheim, Emile. 1954. Elementary Forms of Religious Life. Trans. J. W. Swain. London: Allen and Unwin. (First published 1915 as Les Formes élémentaires de la vie religieuse.)

Durkheim, Emile, and Marcel Mauss. 1963. Primitive classification. *In* Primitive Classification. Rodney Needham, trans. Chicago: University of Chicago Press. (First published 1903.)

Eliade, Mircea. 1954. The Myth of the Eternal Return. New York: Bollingen. (First published 1949.)

——. 1960. The yearning for paradise in primitive tradition. *In* Myth and Mythmaking. H. A. Murray, ed. New York: Braziller. Pp. 61–75.

——. 1961. Images and Symbols: Studies in Religious Symbolism. New York: Sheed and Ward.

——. 1962. The Two and the One. New York: Harper Torchbooks.

——. 1964. Shamanism: Archaic Techniques of Ecstasy. W. R. Trask, trans. Bollingen Series LXXVI. New York: Pantheon.

Evans-Pritchard, E. E. 1937. Witchcraft, Oracles, and Magic among the Azande. Oxford: Clarendon Press.

——. 1965. Theories of Primitive Religion. Oxford: Oxford University Press.

Fabila, Alfonso. 1959. Los Huicholes de Jalisco. Mexico: Instituto Indigenista Nacional.

Fairbairn, W. R. D. 1963. Synopsis of an object-relations theory of the personality. International Journal of Psychoanalysis 44: 224–225.

Findeisen, Hans. 1960. Das Schamanentum als spiritische Religion. Ethnos 25: 192–213.

Fortes, Meyer. 1962. Ritual and office in tribal society. *In* Essays on the Ritual of Social Relations. M. Gluckman, ed. Manchester: Manchester University Press. Pp. 53–88.

Furst, Peter T. 1965. West Mexican tomb sculpture as evidence for shamanism in pre-Hispanic Meso-America. Anthropologica 15: 29–60.

——. 1967. Huichol conceptions of the soul. Folklore Americas 27: 39–106.

——. 1968. The parching of the maize: An essay on the survival of Huichol ritual. Acta Ethnologica et Linguistica No. 14. Vienna.

——. 1969. Ethnographic film: To find our life: The peyote hunt of the Huichols of Mexico. 16mm, color and sound, 65 min. Distributed by Latin American Center, University of California at Los Angeles.

——. 1971. *Ariocarpus retusus*, the "false peyote" of Huichol tradition. Economic Botany 25 (1): 182–187.

——. 1972a. Some problems in the interpretation of west Mexican tomb art. *In* The Archaeology of Western Mexico. Betty Bell, ed. Guadalajara: Instituto Jalisciense de Antropología y Historia and Sociedad de Estudios Avanzadios del Occidente de México.

——. 1972b. To find our life: Peyote among the Huichol Indians of Mexico. *In* Flesh of the Gods: The Ritual Uses of Hallucinogens. P. T. Furst, ed. New York: Praeger. Pp. 136–184.

Furst, Peter T., and Barbara G. Myerhoff. 1966. Myth as history: The Jimson weed cycle of the Huichols of Mexico. Anthropologica 17: 3–39.

——. 1971. El mito como historia: Ciclo del peyote y del datura entre los Huicholes de México. *In* Coras, Huicholes y Tepehuanos. Estudios Etnográficos, Colección de Antropología Social del Institutio Nacional Indigenista. Mexico. Secretaría de Education Publica.

Geertz, Clifford. 1957–1958. Ethos, world-view and the analysis of sacred symbols. Antioch Review 17: 421–437.

——. 1960. The Religion of Java. Glencoe: The Free Press.

——. 1964. Ideology as a cultural system. *In* Ideology and Discontent. D. E. Apter, ed. New York: The Free Press.

——. 1965. Religion as a cultural system. *In* Anthropological Approaches in the Study of Religion. M. Banton, ed. New York: Praeger. Pp. 1–46.

Gluckman, Max. 1962. Les rites de passage. *In* Essays on the Ritual of Social Relations. M. Gluckman, ed. Manchester: Manchester University Press. Pp. 1–52.

——. 1964. The frailty of authority. *In* Custom and Conflict in Africa. M. Gluckman, ed. New York: Barnes and Noble. Pp. 27–53.

——. 1965. Mystical disturbance and ritual adjustment. *In* Politics, Law and Ritual in Tribal Society. M. Gluckman, ed. Chicago: Aldine. Pp. 216–267.

Goody, Jack. 1961. Religion and ritual: The definitional problems. British Journal of Sociology 12: 143–164.

Graves, Robert, and Raphael Patai. 1966. Hebrew Myths: The Book of Genesis. New York: McGraw-Hill.

Grimes, Joseph E. 1959. Huichol tone and intonation. International Journal of American Linguistics 25: 221–232.

——. 1964. Huichol Syntax. The Hague: Mouton.

Grimes, Joseph E., and Thomas B. Hinton. 1961. Huichol and Cora. *In* Handbook of Middle American Indians. E. Z. Vogt and R. Wauchope, eds. Vol. 8, part 2; Ethnology. Austin: University of Texas Press, 1969. Pp. 792–813.

Grimes, Joseph E., and Barbara F. Grimes. 1962. Semantic distinctions in Huichol (Uto-Aztecan) kinship. American Anthropologist 64: 104–112.

Guillaumont, A., *et al.*, trans. 1959. The Gospel According to Thomas. New York: Harper.

Guntrip, Harry. 1968. Schizoid Phenomena, Object Relations and the Self. New York: International Universities Press.

Helm, June, ed. 1968. Essays on the Problem of Tribe. Proceedings of the 1967 annual spring meeting of American Ethnological Society. Seattle: University of Washington Press.

Henderson, Joseph L., and Maud Oakes. 1963. The Wisdom of the Serpent: The Myths of Death, Rebirth, and Resurrection. New York: Braziller.

Hertz, Robert. 1960. Death and the Right Hand. London: Cohen and West. (First published in 1909.)

Jiménez Moreno, Wigberto. 1943. El Norte de México y el sur de Estados Unidos. Mexico: Sociedad Mexicana de Antropología, tercera reunion de mesa redonda. Pp. 41–44 and 128–130.

Jung, Carl G. 1946. Collected Works. New York: Bollingen.

——. 1949. Psychological Types. London: Routledge & Kegan Paul.

Klein, Melanie. 1932. The Psycho-analysis of Children. London: Hogarth.

——. 1960. A note on depression in the schizophrenic. International Journal of Psycho-analysis 41: 509–511.

Klineberg, Otto. 1934. Notes on the Huichol. American Anthropologist 36: 446–460.

Kroeber, Alfred L. 1925. Handbook of the Indians of California. Washington: Bureau of American Ethnology. Bulletin 78.

La Barre, Weston. 1960. Twenty years of peyote studies. Current Anthropology 1 (Jan.): 45–60.

——. 1970. The Ghost Dance: The Origins of Religion. New York: Doubleday.

——. 1972. Hallucinogens and the shamanic origins of religion. *In* Flesh of the Gods: The Ritual Uses of Hallucinogens. P. T. Furst, ed. New York: Praeger.

Langer, Susanne K. 1960. Philosophy in a New Key. Cambridge: Harvard University Press. (First published 1942.)

Leach, Edmund R. 1967. Introduction. *In* The Structural Study of Myth and Totemism. E. Leach, ed. London: Tavistock. Pp. vii–xix.

Lévi-Strauss, Claude. 1963a. Structural Anthropology. Claire Jacobson and Brooke Grundfest Schoepf, trans. New York: Basic

Books. (First published 1958 as Anthropologie structurale. Paris: Plon.)

——. 1963b. Totemism. Trans. Rodney Needham. Boston: Beacon Press. (First published 1962 as Le Totémisme aujourd' hui. Paris: Plon.)

——. 1966. The Savage Mind. Chicago: University of Chicago Press. (First published 1962 as La Pensée sauvage. Paris: Plon.)

——. 1967. The Story of Asdiwal. *In* The Structural Study of Myth. E. Leach, ed. Nicolas Mann, trans. London: Tavistock. Pp. 1–47. (First published as La Geste d'Asdiwal. École Pratique des Hautes Études, Section de Sciences Religieuses. Extr. Annuaire 1958–1959. Paris. Pp. 3–43.)

——. 1969. The Raw and the Cooked. Introduction to a Science of Mythology: I. John and Doreen Weightman, trans. New York: Harper Torchbooks. (First published 1964 as Le Cru et le cuit. Paris: Plon.)

Lommel, Andreas. 1967. Shamanism, the Beginnings of Art. New York: McGraw-Hill.

Lumholtz, Carl. 1900. Symbolism of the Huichol Indians. Memoirs of the American Museum of Natural History, vol. III, pt. 1, pp. 1–223.

——. 1902. Unknown Mexico. Vol. II. New York: Scribner.

——. 1904. Decorative art of the Huichol Indians. Memoirs of the American Museum of Natural History, vol. III, pt. 3, pp. 279–327.

McIntosh, John B. 1945. Huichol phonemes. International Journal of Linguistics 11: 31–35.

McLeary, James A., Paul S. Sypherd, and David L. Walkington. 1960. Antibiotic activity of an extract of peyote *Lophophora williamsii* (Lemaire) Coulter. Economic Botany 14: 247–249.

Madsen, William. 1955. Shamanism in Mexico. Southwest Journal of Anthropology 2 (1): 48–57.

Malinowski, Bronislaw. 1948. Magic, Science and Religion, and Other Essays. New York: Doubleday Anchor. (First published 1923.)

——. 1961. Introduction: Subject, method, and scope. *In* Argonauts of the Western Pacific. New York: Dutton Paperback. Pp. 1–25. (First published 1922.)

Myerhoff, Barbara G. 1966. The doctor as culture hero: The shaman of Rincon. Anthropological Quarterly 39 (2): 60–72.

——. 1970. The deer-maize-peyote symbol complex among the Huichol Indians of Mexico. Anthropological Quarterly 43: 64–78.

——. 1971. Organization and Ecstasy: The Dialectic of Structure and *Communitas*. Unpublished manuscript.

——. 1972. The revolution as a trip: Symbol and paradox. *In* The New Pilgrims. P.G. Altbach and R. S. Laufer, eds. New York: McKay. Pp. 251–266.

Nachtigall, H. 1952. Die kulturhistorische Wurzel der Schamanenskelettierung. Zeitschrift für Ethnologie 77: 188–197.

Nadel, S. F. 1954. Nupe Religion. London: Routledge & Kegan Paul.

Nash, Manning. 1966. Primitive and Present Economic Systems. San Francisco: Chandler.

Needham, Rodney. 1961. The left hand of the Mugwe: An analytical note on the structure of Meru symbolism. Africa 31: 28–33.

Neumann, Erich. 1954. The Origins and History of Consciousness. New York: Bollingen.

Ortega, José P. 1887. Historia del Nayarít. Mexico. (First published 1754 as Apostólicos Afanes de la Compañía de Jesús, en la América Septentrional, Barcelona.)

Paulson, Ivar. 1963. Zur Aufbewahrung der Tierknochen im Jagdritual der nordeurasıschen Völker. Vilmos Dioszegi, ed. Glaubenswelt und Folklore der sibirischen Völker. Budapest: Akadémiac Kiadó. Pp. 483–490.

Pérez de Ribas, Andrés. 1944. Historia de los Triumfos de N. S. Fe entre Gentes Mas Barbaras y Fieras del Nuevo Urbe. Mexico: Editorial Layac. (First published 1645.)

Plan, Lerma. 1966. Operación Huicot. Comision Lerma: Chapala, Santiago. Guadalajara.

Prell-Foldes, Riv-Ellen. 1971. The Holy and the Holy: Unification of Opposites in the Passover Ritual. Unpublished manuscript.

Preuss, Konrad Theodor. 1908. Die religiösen Gesänge und Mythen einiger Stämme der Mexikanischen Sierra Madre. Archiv für Religions-Wissenschaft 11: 359–398.

——. 1912. Die Nayarit-Expedition. Text-aufnahmen und Beobachtungen unter Mexikanischen Indianern. *In* Die Religion der Cora-Indianer. Leipzig: B. G. Teubner.

——. 1934. Der Charakter der von mir aufgenommenen Mythen und Gesänge der Huichol-Indianern. Proceedings of the International Congress of Americanists. Hamburg. Pp. 217–218.

Propp, Vladimir. 1958. Morphology of the folktale. International Journal of American Linguistics 24: 4.

Radcliffe-Brown, A. R. 1950. Introduction. *In* African Systems of Kinship and Marriage. A. R. Radcliffe-Brown and Daryll Forde, eds. London: Oxford University Press. Pp. 1–85.

——. 1952. The sociological theory of totemism. *In* Structure and Function in Primitive Society. London: Oxford University Press. Pp. 117–132.

Radin, Paul. 1914. A sketch of the peyote cult of the Winnebago: Study in borrowing. Journal of Religious Psychology 7: 1–22.

——. 1957. Primitive Man as a Philosopher. New York: Appelton. (First published 1927.)

Redfield, Robert. 1955. The Little Community. Chicago: University of Chicago Press.

Romney, A. K., and Roy C. D'Andrade. 1964. Transcultural Studies in Cognition. American Anthropologist Special Publication 66.

Ruiz de Alarcón, Hernando. 1892. Tratado de las supersticiones y costumbres gentílicas que oy viuen entre los Indios naturales desta Nueva España. (First published 1629.) In Anales del Museo Nacional de Mexico. Francisco del Paso y Troncoso, ed. Vol. VI. Mexico. Pp. 123–223.

Safford, William E. 1920. Daturas of the Old World and New: An account of their narcotic properties and their use in oracular and initiatory ceremonies. Annual Report of the Board of Regents of the Smithsonian Institution. Washington, D. C. Pp. 537–567.

Sahagún, Fr. Bernadino de. 1950–1963. The Florentine Codex: General History of the Things of New Spain. Arthur J. D. Anderson and Charles E. Dibble, trans. Santa Fe, N.M.: The School of American Research and the University of Utah. (First published 1831 as Historia universal de las cosas de Nueva España, Antiquities of Mexico. Lord Kingsborough, ed. London. 9 vols.)

Santoscoy, Alberto. 1899. Nayarít, Colección de documentos ineditos, históricos y etnongráficos, Acerca de la Sierra de Ese Nombre. Guadalajara.

Sapir, Edward. 1934. Symbolism. Encyclopedia of the Social Sciences. Vol. XIV. New York: Macmillan.

Sauer, Carl. 1934. The distribution of aboriginal tribes and languages in north-western Mexico. Ibero-Americana: 5. Berkeley: University of California Press.

Schachtel, Ernest G. 1949. On memory and childhood amnesia. *In* A Study of Interpersonal Relations, New Contributions to Psychiatry. P. Mullahy, ed. New York: Grove and Evergreen Press. Pp. 3–49.

Schröder, Dominik. 1955. Zur Struktur des Schamanismus. Anthropos 90: 848–881.

Schultes, Richard Evans. 1970. The botanical and chemical distribution of hallucinogens. Annual Review of Plant Physiology. Palo Alto, Calif. Pp. 571–598.

——. 1972. An overview of hallucinogens in the Western Hemisphere. *In* Flesh of the Gods: The Ritual Uses of Hallucinogens. P. T. Furst, ed. New York: Praeger. Pp. 3–54.

Silverman, Julian. 1968. Shamans and acute schizophrenia. American Anthropologist 69: 21–31.

Spiro, Melford E. 1951. Culture and personality: The natural history of a false dichotomy. Psychiatry 14: 19–46.

Thomas, Elizabeth Marshall. 1959. The Harmless People. New York: Knopf.

Turner, Victor. 1962. Three symbols of passage in Ndembu circumcision ritual: An interpretation. *In* Essays on the Ritual of Social Relations. M. Gluckman, ed. Manchester: Manchester University Press. Pp. 124–173.

——. 1967. The Forest of Symbols: Aspects of Ndembu Ritual. Ithaca: Cornell University Press.

——. 1968. The Drums of Affliction: A Study of Religious Processes among the Ndembu of Zambia. Oxford: Clarendon and the International African Institute.

——. 1969a. Forms of symbolic action: Introduction. *In* Proceedings of the 1969 Annual Spring Ethnological Society Meetings. Seattle: University of Washington Press.

——. 1969b. The Ritual Process: Structure and Anti-Structure. Chicago: Aldine.

——. 1971. Passages, margins, and poverty: Religious symbols of *communitas*. *In* Dramas, Fields, and Metaphors: Symbolic Action in Human Society. Ithaca: Cornell University Press, 1974.

Underhill, Ruth M. 1946. Papago Indian Religion. New York: Columbia University Press.

Van Gennep, Arnold. 1960. The Rites of Passage. M. B. Vizedom and G. L. Caffee, trans. London: Routledge & Kegan Paul. (First published 1909.)

Vogt, Evon E. 1955. Some aspects of Cora-Huichol acculturation. America Indigena 15 (4): 249–263.

Watts, Alan W. 1970. The Two Hands of God: The Myth of Polarity. New York: Collier Books. (First published 1963.)

Wax, R. H., and M. L. Wax. 1962. The magical world view. Journal of the Scientific Study of Religion 1: 179–188.

Weigand, Phil C. 1970. Co-operative Labor Groups in Subsistence Activities among the Huichol Indians of San Sebastián Teponahaustlán, Municipio of Mezquitic, Jalisco, Mexico. Doctoral dissertation, Department of Anthropology, Southern Illinois University.

Wheelwright, Phillip E. 1971. Heraclitus. New York: Atheneum. (First published 1959.)

Wilson, Monica. 1957. Rituals of Kinship among the Nyakyusa. London: Oxford University Press.

Winnicott, D. W. 1965. The capacity to be alone. *In* The Maturational Processes and the Facilitating Environment. London: Hogarth.

Zerries, Otto. 1961. Die Religionen der Naturvölker Sudamerikas und West Indians. *In* Die Religionen des Alten Amerikas: Religionen der Menschkeit. Vol. VII. Stuttgart: Kohlhammer. Pp. 271–384.

Zingg, Robert M. 1938. The Huichols: Primitive Artists. New York: Stechert.

Index